LOOKING AT THE
Dance

Edwin Denby

LOOKING AT THE

DANCE

Introduction by
B. H. HAGGIN

HORIZON PRESS   NEW YORK

AUTHOR'S NOTE

The articles brought together in this volume first appeared in the New York *Herald Tribune, Modern Music, The Kenyon Review, Dance Index, Mademoiselle, Town and Country, Dance News* and *Dance Magazine,* under the dates indicated. "The Critic" is part of a piece on the subject written for the *Dance Encyclopedia* (Anatole Chujoy, editor). For convenience' sake the material has been arranged under general headings, on occasion somewhat arbitrarily.

Contents

7. BALLET IN BOOKS, PRINTS, PHOTOGRAPHS AND FILMS

8. MODERN DANCERS

11. ADDENDA

INTRODUCTION BY B. H. HAGGIN

THE reviews and articles assembled in this book—like the theater reviews in Stark Young's *Immortal Shadows* and the reviews of musical happenings in Bernard Shaw's *Music in London*—are unique in their field. No one has written anything like them; and that is, first of all, because no one has operated with perception like Denby's. Perception isn't what criticism ends with; but it is what it must begin with: before the critic can evaluate what he has experienced he has to have seen or heard it accurately. This would seem to be easy enough; but evidently it is more difficult than it seems; for the poor quality of most criticism begins with its mere inaccuracy about what may be considered the objectively perceptible facts of what was presented to the critic's ear and eye. And on the other hand, the unique excellence of Shaw's, Young's and Denby's criticism begins with the illuminating accuracy of their reports of what they were enabled to hear and see by their extraordinary endowment of the perception that is the critic's special equipment for his operation. We have had no one with Young's eye and ear for what was happening in a performance of a play; and no one who has looked at a dancer or a ballet with as perceptive eyes as Denby's.

This made it possible for him to perform what—at the forum on dance criticism he describes on pages 296-8—he accepted as the critic's essential function, that of "animating the reader's own perceptions." The critic was the professional spectator with powers of perception which the non-professional didn't have, who saw what this non-professional didn't notice, and who described it to him in a way that enabled him to see it. "When you watch ballet dancers dancing," is the way Denby begins the first piece in this book; and as we read on we are enabled to see, after the first impact of a dancer's charm, that "she is showing you a dance . . . showing how the steps are related and make some sense . . . in relation to the music or in relation to the story, and now and then . . . also as dance phrases simply"; and to see further the "variety of visual emphasis" that produces "variety of expression."

This is part of a long discussion of meaning in ballet, in which Denby at one point establishes the nature of this meaning and the manner of its apprehension: to those who doubt that dancing can have the expressive power they concede to performance of music or a play, he remarks that "to recognize poetic suggestion through dancing one must be susceptible to poetic values and susceptible to dance values as well"—which, for all its apparent casualness, is in reality a formulation of the theme of the book. There are people, he says, who have this susceptibility, and to whom "several dancers, for example Miss Danilova and Miss Markova, are quite often able to give . . . the sense of an amplitude in meaning which is the token of emotion in art." And throughout the book he is concerned with the dance values which in this way communicate poetic values.

This appears in his illuminating comments on particular dancers. "In all the severity of exact classicism Danilova's dancing rhythm fills the time quantities of the music to the full; it does not, like the rhythm of lesser dancers, jab at a stress and then drag for a moment till the music catches up. Stress and release in all their variety are equally vivid, equally expressive to watch. And in watching her you feel, in the sustained flow of Danilova's rhythm, the alert vivacity of her personal dance imagination, the bite and grace of her feminine temperament, and a human sincerity that makes an artist both unpretentious and great." Or "It is the quiet which [Markova] moves in, an instinct for the melody of movement as it deploys and subsides in the silence of time, that is the most refined of rhythmic delights. The sense of serenity in animation she creates is as touching as that of a Mozart melody." Or, on the other hand, in a performance of *Giselle,* "Miss Toumanova with her large, handsome and deadly face, her swordlike toe-steps, her firm positions, her vigorous and record-high leg gestures—and with her bold and large style of dancing—by nature makes a very different figure from delicate Miss Markova," causing Denby to miss "the sustained otherworldly floating quality and calm completion of each pose and phrase that were Markova's specialty, and that helped make this ballet in particular extraordinarily thrilling." With these comments Denby provides vividly exact images of the operation of famous dancers we no longer see, which establish criteria of good and bad in dancing that we can apply to the operation of the dancers we do see. And in one instance he writes about a dancer in whose performances today we can see confirmation of the statement in 1944 that the happy discovery of Ballet International's season had been the great gifts of Francisco Moncion, and that "Moncion, well trained as a classic dancer, strong and manly, is like a modern dancer in the freedom with which he can use torso, arms and neck. But his exceptional gift is his intense imaginative sincerity. He creates a character completely, and he has power, musicality and humor."

So with the comments on ballets. Many are concerned with works that are no longer to be seen; and though Denby doesn't present the exact images of the choreography of Balanchine's *Danses Concertantes, Poker Game* (later known as *Card Game*) and *Le Baiser de la Fée* that he does of the dancing of Danilova and Markova, his discussion of *Poker Game* becomes a description of Balanchine's operation as a choreographer, which—like another piece called *A Note on Balanchine's Present Style*—will illuminate for the reader the Balanchine choreographies he sees performed by the New York City Ballet today. Moreover, four of these, *Apollo, Serenade, Ballet Imperial* and *Concerto Barocco, are* commented on in the book; and Denby does present exact images of two great moments in the Adagio of *Concerto Barocco* in a passage that will make the reality on the stage more powerfully effective when the reader sees it:

> At the climax, . . . against a background of chorus that suggests the look of trees in the wind before a storm breaks, the ballerina, with limbs powerfully outspread, is lifted by her male partner, lifted repeatedly in narrowing arcs higher and higher. Then at the culminating phrase, from her greatest height he very slowly lowers her. You watch her body slowly descend, her foot and leg pointing stiffly downward, till her toe reaches the floor and she rests her full weight at last on this single sharp point and pauses. It has the effect at that moment of a deliberate and powerful plunge into a wound, and the emotion of it answers strangely to the musical stress. And . . . the final adagio figure before the coda, the ballerina being slid upstage in two or three swoops that dip down and rise a moment into an extension in second—like a receding cry—creates an-

other image that corresponds vividly to the weight of the
musical passage.

Perception is the first, basic essential equipment of the
critic; but it isn't all: discipline also is essential; and the lack
of it is another cause of the poor quality of most criticism. The
critic must be able not only to hear and see, but to hold his
pen strictly to what he has heard and seen—which is to say,
to keep himself from producing the interesting writing that
can be done about imagined happenings, or the writing that
will impress readers with the critic's knowledge, cleverness
and charm (when a critic's eye is partly on the effect he wants
to make on the reader, it is by that much less on the thing he
is writing about). This discipline Denby had, in addition to
his perception; and it was a major factor in the excellence of
his criticism. "When you watch ballet dancers dancing," he
begins; and what we see, as he continues, is those dancers
dancing, not a performance by Denby.

And discipline, finally—of a man practiced in the poet's
disciplined operation with language—is evident in the writing
which formulates Denby's perceptions—in its limpid, luminous
clarity, its precision and subtlety, its occasional understated
power or wit. Consider what is concentrated in the apparently
casual statement "To recognize poetic suggestion through
dancing one must be susceptible to poetic values and susceptible to dance values as well"; how the reader's eye is directed, in the passage on Danilova, by the statement "Stress
and release in all their variety are equally vivid, equally expressive to watch"; the effect, in the passage on Toumanova,
of "deadly," and—after "her large, handsome and deadly face,
her swordlike toesteps, her firm positions, her vigorous and

record-high leg gestures"—of "makes a very different figure from delicate Miss Markova."

But an occasion like Balanchine's *Apollo* impels Denby to a poet's eloquence:

> *Apollo* is about poetry, poetry in the sense of a brilliant, sensuous, daring and powerful activity of our nature. . . . Balanchine has told [the] metaphysical story in the concrete terms of classic dancing, in a series of episodes of rising power and brilliance. Extraordinary is the richness with which he can, with only four dancers, create a sustained and more and more satisfying impression of the grandness of man's creative genius, depicting it concretely in its grace, its sweet wit, its force and boldness, and with the constant warmth of its sensuous complicity with physical beauty. . . . What you see on stage is strangely simple and clear. It begins modestly with effects derived from pantomime, a hint of birth pangs, a crying baby, a man dancing with a lute, and it becomes progressively a more and more directly classic dance ballet, the melodious lines and lyric or forceful climaxes of which are effects of dance continuity, dance rhythm and dance architecture. And it leaves at the end, despite its innumerable incidental inventions, a sense of bold, open, effortless and limpid grandeur. . . . You feel happily the nobility that the human spirit is capable of by nature.

LOOKING AT THE

Dance

1

Meaning in Ballet

HOW TO JUDGE A DANCER

WHEN you watch ballet dancers dancing you are observing a young woman or a young man in fancy dress, and you like it if they look attractive, if they are well built and have what seems to be an open face. You notice the youthful spring in starting, the grace of carriage, the strength in stopping. You like it if they know what to do and where to go, if they can throw in a surprising trick or two, if they seem to be enjoying their part and are pleasantly sociable as performers. All this is proper juvenile charm, and it often gives a very sharp pleasure in watching dancers.

But you are ready too for other qualities besides charm. The audience soon notices if the dancer has unusual control over her movements, if what she is doing is unusually clear to the eye, if there are differences of emphasis and differences of urgency in her motion. Within single slow movements or within a sequence you enjoy seeing the continuity of an impulse and the culmination of a phrase. Now you are not only watching a charming dancer, she is also showing you a dance.

When she shows you a dance, she is showing how the steps are related, that they are coherent and make some sense. You

3

can see that they make some sense in relation to the music or in relation to the story; and now and then the dancer shows you they make sense also as dance phrases purely and simply. You may notice that a dance phrase holds together by its rhythm in time (a rhythm related to that of music), as a sequence of long and short motions set off by a few accents. Again in other passages you may be most interested by the arrangements in space, motions that make up a rhythm of large and small, up and down, right and left, backward and forward. You watch dance figures that combine several directions, done by single dancers or by groups, in place or while covering distance. Such dance phrases are plastically interesting. But at still other moments you notice especially the changes in the dancer's energy, the dynamics of a sequence, which contrasts motion as taut or easy, active or passive, pressing or delaying, beginning or ending. Dynamics, space and time—the dancer may call one or the other to your attention, but actually she keeps these three strands of interest going all the time, for they are all simultaneously present in even the simplest dancing. But a dancer who can make the various factors clear at the proper passage so as to keep you interested in the progress of the dance is especially attractive because she is dancing intelligently. She makes even a complicated choreography distinct to see.

Intelligent dancing—which might as well be called correct dancing—has a certain dryness that appeals more to an experienced dance lover than to an inexperienced one. In any case, everyone in the audience becomes more attentive when he recognizes a personal impetus in an intelligent dancer's movement, when she has a way of looking not merely like a good dancer, but also different from others and like her own self.

Her motions look spontaneous, as if they suited her particular body, her personal impulses, as if they were being invented that very moment. This is originality in dancing—and quite different from originality in choreography. The original dancer vivifies the dance—plain or complicated, novel or otherwise— that the choreographer has set. She shows a gift like that of an actor who speaks his lines as if they were being uttered for the first time that very moment, though they have been in print a hundred years or though he has spoken them a hundred nights running.

Such vitality in dancing is not the same thing as that punch in projection sometimes called a "dynamic stage personality." A lively dancer does not push herself on the audience, except, of course, during curtain calls. Projection in serious dancing is a mild and steady force, the dancer who goes out to the audience with a bang cuts herself off from the rest of the stage action. Galvanic projection is a trick appropriate to revue, where there is no drama to interrupt. But in serious dancing the audience must be kept constantly aware of the complete action within the stage area, because the changes—and, therefore, the drama—of dancing are appreciated clearly in relation to that fixed three-dimensional frame. So the best dancers are careful to remain within what one may call the dance illusion, as an actor remains within the illusion of a dramatic action— when you cannot help imagining he is a young man speaking privately to a girl in a garden, though you see perfectly well he is middle aged, that he is talking blank verse for you to hear and standing on a wooden floor.

And just as you become really absorbed at a play when Romeo is not only distinct and spontaneous, but also makes you recognize the emotion of love, which has nothing to do with the actor personally or with acting in itself or with words in themselves, so the dancer becomes absorbing to watch when she makes you aware of emotions that are not make-believe at all. Some of my friends doubt that it is possible to give so much expressive power to dancing, though they grant it is possible to performers of music or of plays. To recognize poetic suggestion through dancing one has to be susceptible to poetic values and susceptible to dance values as well. But I find that a number of people are and that several dancers, for example Miss Danilova and Miss Markova, are quite often able to give them the sense of an amplitude in meaning which is the token of emotion in art. I myself go to dancing looking for this pleasure, which is the pleasure of the grand style, and find a moment or two of satisfaction in the work of a dozen dancers or more. In these remarkable flights the choreographer may be admired even more than the dancer, but here I am describing the merits of dancing only.

What I have said applies to any dance technique, and now that the ballet season is opening, it is a simple matter for any-one to go to the Metropolitan and check for himself the ac-curacy of it or the mistakes—*October* 10, 1943.

TUDOR AND PANTOMIME

MANY people who are disappointed to find little mean-ing in ballet dancing are struck by how much meaning the ballet figures in Tudor's *Pillar of Fire* and *Lilac Garden* convey to them. In *Lilac Garden,* for example, an about-to-be-abandoned mistress sees her lover standing alone, facing her at a distance. Desperately she rushes at top speed across the stage; she seems to leap straight on his shoulder. He holds her tightly by the waist, she crouches there above his head, tensely arching her neck. He does not look up. The action is as sudden as the leap of a desperate cat on moving day. But the pose also brings up the sudden sense of a private physical intimacy. It has that meaning.

Again, in *Pillar of Fire,* a chaste and frenzied young woman sees a vigorous young man. He looks at her suggestively. She leaps at him through the air in grand jete. He catches her in mid-leap in a split and she hangs against his chest as if her leap continued forever, her legs completely rigid, her body completely still. How is it one notices the momentary pose so distinctly?

It is partly because the stopped leap has a startling effect—like a fast tennis ball that goes dead. And the shock of the stop is heightened by the contrast to an onward full surge of the music. The timing, the placing of the pose; its contrast to the direction, the speed, the stopping and starting of the dance figures that went before; in brief, all the resources of what the cinema calls visual rhythm have been used to direct the eye to this special instance of bodily contact. The attention is focused on the parts of the body, their relation to one another, the physical force involved in the leap and the lift, almost as if by a motion-picture close-up. And the moment so distinctly presented registers all the more, because it registers as a climax in the story, as a pantomime of a psychological shock.

One "reads" the climactic moments in these ballets in a pantomime sense because from the outset Tudor has emphasized the pantomime aspect of the dance. He begins with

easily recognizable movements, gestures of greeting, of pushing back a strand of hair, of fiddling with clothes, of averting
the glance, of walking or standing not as in a ballet but as in
daily life. One's attention is caught by these gestures because
they at once specify the characters of a story, the situation, the
psychological tension. They are expertly stylized to fit the
music and to form sequences of motion that please the eye.
They combine smoothly with dance steps, and we unconsciously expect from the more complex dance figures that follow the same sort of narrative meaning, the pantomime exposition of story we have begun to look for. The two dance
figures described above show how completely Tudor succeeds
as a storyteller, using ballet images.

In fact, in these two ballets Tudor gives to the whole classic
ballet system of movement a pantomime bias. He uses ballet
technique to portray a particular attitude, an upper-class code
of behavior. In *Lilac Garden* he purposely exaggerates the
constraint of ballet carriage, the dancers dance rigidly, hastily,
with dead arms—as beginners might. But the ballet constraint
they show portrays the mental constraint of the characters in
the story, who rigidly follow an upper-class convention of behavior. Artificial upper-class constraint is the theme and the
pathos of *Lilac Garden*.

In *Pillar of Fire* Tudor goes further. He shows two different
ballet styles: an improperly strained one that characterizes the
anguished heroine, and a smooth, proper style for the nice
untroubled neighboring boys and girls. In addition, both kinds
of ballet are set against the non-ballet dancing of the exciting
low-life crowd—they dance and whirl in a sort of wild rumba
style, swivel-hipped, explosive and frenzied; while the calm
hero, in contrast to everyone, comes on not as any kind of

dancer, but walking across the stage as modestly as a Fuller-brush man. Tudor fuses these heterogeneous elements brilliantly, but the dance device I wish to call attention to is the use of ballet technique to describe a special kind of person, to represent a special habit of mind.

Tudor's meaning is admirably clear and his dramatic effects are intense. It is interesting, on the other hand, that the traditional ballet (whether of 1890 or 1940) tries for a radically different kind of meaning than that of pantomime description; it appeals to a different manner of seeing dancing and requires a different technical approach in the dancer—*July* 11, 1943.

ON MEANING IN DANCE

ANY serious dance work has an element of pantomime and an element of straight dance, with one or the other predominant. When you think about it, it is curious in how different a way the two elements appeal to the intelligence, how differently they communicate a meaning.

Tudor's *Pillar of Fire* is a brilliant example of contemporary pantomime ballet. It is as absorbing to us as Fokine's *Scheherazade* was to our parents in its 1910 version thirty years ago. The difference between the two is striking: *Scheherazade* was bright and luscious, *Pillar of Fire* is gloomy and hot; Fokine hacked at his subject with a cleaver, Tudor dissects his with a scalpel. But—apart from the big orgy they each work up to—the two ballets both hold the attention by a continuous, clear story. Both belong to the tradition of the stylized drama, and not (as *Coppelia* and *Ballet Imperial* do) to the tradition of the dance entertainment. The pantomime ballet focuses the attention on stylized movement; the dance ballet, on a suite of dances.

What is a "stylized movement"? It is a movement that looks a little like dancing but more like non-dancing. It is a movement derived from what people do when they are not dancing. It is a gesture from life deformed to suit music (music heard or imagined). The pleasure of watching it lies in guessing the action it was derived from, in guessing what it originally looked like; and then in savoring the "good taste" of the deformation.

Stylized movement has always been a perfectly legitimate pleasure in the theater. Sometimes it's merely a little quiz game thrown in for variety. In general, though, a stylized passage adds a pretty color to any dance. And stylization is one of the best recipes for a comic effect.

But in the pantomime ballet stylized movement is the main aspect of expression. It is what one looks at particularly, because it keeps making a serious dramatic point. Gesture by gesture, as if idea by idea, the drama is built up. The audience watches for each allusion in turn, it follows point by point. The interest becomes like that of a detective story. The audience peers eagerly, delighted to have caught on, anxious not to miss a cue. It solves harder and harder riddles. The story-telling gathers momentum; as in driving a car, it's the speed that's thrilling, not the incidental scenery. One is, so to speak, hypnotized by the future destination. One merely wants to know what happened, as in watching a motion picture.

On the other hand, a dance ballet (*Coppelia*, for example)

has a very different kind of appeal. True, it also has a story and it has pantomime portions. But you don't take them seriously. The parts that show you the heart of the subject, that are the most expressive, are in the form of dance numbers, of dance suites. They are like arias in an opera. In a dance ballet the story is not a pressing one, and it can be delayed awhile for a lyric comment on the momentary situation. The audience has come to enjoy the dancing; it is in no hurry to get the heroine married or murdered and be sent out of the theater again.

In a dance ballet there is a difference in the way the audience watches the movement. It does not identify the gestures with reference to real life, it does not search in each pose for a distinct descriptive allusion. It watches the movements in sequence as a dance. There is a sort of suspension in judgment, a wait and a wonder till the dance is completed, till the dancer has come to rest. When the dance is over one understands it as a whole; one understands the quality of the dancer's activity, the quality of her rest, and in the play between the two lies the meaning of the dance aria, the comment it has made on the theme of the ballet. One has understood the dance as one does a melody—as a continuity that began and ended. It is a nonverbal meaning, like the meaning of music.

The dancer in pantomime emphasizes what each of the gestures looks like, he appeals pictorially to intellectual concepts. The dancer in a dance number emphasizes the kinetic transformation, his dance is a continuity which moves away from one equilibrium and returns to another. Repose is as important to the meaning of a dance ballet as activity. But in pantomime a stop must be made to look active and pressing, it must keep the urgency of the history. This difference leads the dancer to a different emphasis in technique—*July* 18, 1943.

BALLET TECHNIQUE

WHEN they watch a ballet in the theater some people can take ballet technique for granted as easily as school kids take the technique of basketball for granted while they watch a lively game in a gym. These ballet lovers see the dance impulses perfectly clear.

Other people, however, are bothered by the technique. They watch the gestures without feeling the continuity of the dance; the technique seems to keep getting in the way of it. Ballet looks to them chiefly like a mannerism in holding the arms and legs, and in keeping the back stiff as a ramrod. They can see it must be difficult to move about in that way, but why try in the first place? Annoyed at the enthusiasm of their neighbors in the theater, they come to the conclusion that ballet technique is a snobbish fad, the perverse invention of some dead and forgotten foreign esthetic dictator who insisted on making dancing as unnatural as possible.

But ballet technique isn't as unreasonable as that. Just as a dazzling technique in pitching, for instance, is an intelligent refinement of throwing a ball for fun (which everybody does somehow), so ballet technique is a refinement of social dancing and folk dancing, a simple enough thing that everybody has tried doing for fun in his own neighborhood. You know the main technical problem of dancing the first time you try; it's to move boldly without falling flat on the dance floor. You have to get the knack of shifting your weight in a peculiar way. Next you try to keep in rhythm, and then you try to give the conventional steps that extra personal dash which makes the dance come off. It's a question, of course, of doing all this jointly with others, sometimes in groups, sometimes in couples —when a little sex pantomime may be added, by common consent all over the world. And incidental acrobatic feats are welcome if they don't break up the dancers' happy sense of a collective rhythm.

Exhibition dance technique is a way of doing the same things for the pleasure of the neighbors who gather to watch. You see the simple elements of common dance technique re-fined and specialized, with a particular emphasis placed on one element or another. In recent generations we have seen our own normal folk and social dances evolve into professional tap dancing, into exhibition ballroom, and most recently into exhibition Lindy.

Like these recent dance techniques, ballet, too, is the result of practical experiments by a number of exhibition dancers— a long line of professionals which, in the case of ballet, began in the seventeenth century and has not yet ended. The ballet dancers seem to have taken as their point of emphasis not the small specialty tricks but the first great problem everybody has in dancing—the trouble of keeping in balance. The problem might be described as that of a variable force (the dance im-pulses) applied to a constant weight (the body). The ballet technicians wanted to find as many ways as possible of chang-ing the impetus of the movement without losing control of the momentum of the body. When a dancer is not sure of his momentum he is like a driver who has no rhythm in driving, who jolts you, who either spurts or dawdles and makes you nervous. Watching a dancer whose momentum is under control, you appreciate the change in impetus as an expression. You follow the dance with pleasure, because the dancer has your confidence.

The foot, leg, arm and trunk positions of ballet, the way it distributes the energy in the body (holding back most of it in the waist and diminishing it from there as from a center)— this is a method of keeping the urgency of the movement in relation to a center of gravity in the body. The peculiar look of ballet movement is not the perverse invention of some dead esthetic dictator. It is a reasonable method which is still being elaborated by experiment. On the basis of a common technical experience—that of equilibrium in motion—this method tries to make the changes of impulse in movement as distinctly intelligible as possible. There have always been great dancers who danced in other techniques than that of ballet. But there have always been great dancers, too, who found in ballet technique an extraordinary range of clear expression—*July* 25, 1943.

ABOUT TOE DANCING

TO a number of people ballet means toe dancing, that is what they come to see, and they suspect that a dancer only gets down off her "pointes" to give her poor feet a rest. But toesteps are not what ballet is about. They are just one of the devices of choreography, as the sharp hoots of a soprano are one of the devices of opera. Toesteps were invented, the historians say, "toward 1826" or "toward 1830." And the historians also explain that ballet during the century and more before the introduction of toesteps was quite as interesting to its audience as performances at the Metropolitan are nowadays to us. It was fully two hundred years ago that the audience enjoyed the difference between Mlle Camargo, that light, joyous, brilliant creature, and Mlle Sallé, the lovely expressive dramatic dancer. In 1740, too, the public was applauding with enthusiasm the plastic harmony of M. Dupré, "who danced more distinctly (*qui se dessinait mieux*) than anyone in the world." There was evidently plenty to watch before there were any toesteps. Still without toesteps choreography became so expressive that first Garrick and later Stendhal compared dance scenes they saw to scenes of Shakespeare. And long before toesteps Noverre's *Letters on Dancing* discussed the esthetics of ballet so clearly that ever since ballet has been judged by the general standards of art, or has not been judged at all. You can see that toesteps are not the secret of ballet.

I do not mean that the feature of toe dancing is foreign to ballet, quite the contrary. As a matter of fact the principles of ballet technique—its gymnastic as well as its plastic principles—were accurately defined shortly before toesteps were invented, and their addition did not require any revision of the fundamental exercises or postures. Toesteps are an application of an older ballet device, the rigid stretch of knee, ankle and instep to form a single straight line. During the eighteenth century this special expression of the leg was emphasized more and more, though used only when the leg was in the air. Finally a girl discovered she could put her whole weight on two legs and feet so stretched (as in an 1821 ballet print), and even support it on one; that became our modern toestep.

Perhaps toe technique was due to the exceptionally severe exercises to which the dancer Paul Taglioni subjected his brilliant daughter, Marie; certainly it was her expressive genius that made the trick a phenomenal one. But she was a great dancer before she did toesteps, and she had at least six and perhaps ten years of success behind her when the new fashion began. The uncertainty of history over the exact date suggests that these initial toesteps were far less precise than ours. In any case, in the 1830's other dancers beside Marie Taglioni learned them; though done as they then were in a soft slipper darned across the toe every evening, they were often uncertain and dangerous. Now of course any student learns them painlessly and with no heartbreak at all.

But to do them expressively, as Taglioni, Grisi and Elssler did, is still not common. Gautier, the poet-critic of a hundred years ago, described expressive "pointes" as "steel arrows plunging elastically against a marble floor." Unfortunately we have all seen dispirited performances of *Sylphides* where they have been merely a bumpy hobbling. Toesteps inherently have a secret that is not easy for either the dancer or the public: It is the extraordinary tautness of the completely straight leg-and-foot line which seems to alter the usual proportions of the body, not only the proportion of trunk and leg, but also the relation of hard and soft. Dancing on and off the toes may be described in this sense as an expressive play of changing proportions.

But "pointes" have a psychological aspect, too. There is a sense of discomfort, even of cruelty in watching them, a value that often shocks sensitive persons when they fail to find in the emotion of the dance a vividness that would make this savage detail interesting. Well, from a psychological point of view, toesteps have here and there a curious link to the theme of a ballet. In *Giselle* they seem consistent with the shocking fascination of death that is the core of the drama, in *Swan Lake* they are a part of the cruel remoteness of the beloved, in *Noces* they hammer out a savage intoxication. Elsewhere, in scenes of intelligent irony, they can look petulant or particular, absurd or fashionable.

But it would be a complete mistake to tag toesteps in general with a "literary" meaning. Their justification is the shift in the dance, the contrast between taut and pliant motion, between unexpected and expected repose, between a poignantly prolonged line and a normal one. Toesteps also increase the speed and change the rhythm of some figures. On paper these formal aspects sound less dramatic than psychological ones; but they are what one actually sees on the stage, and out of them, seeing them distinctly, the better part of the dance emotion is made—*October* 3, 1943.

A NOTE ON DANCE INTELLIGENCE

EXPRESSION in dancing is what really interests everybody and everybody recognizes it as a sign of intelligence in the dancer. But dancing is physical motion, it doesn't involve words at all. And so it is an error to suppose that dance intelligence is the same as other sorts of intelligence which involve, on the contrary, words only and no physical movement whatever. What is expressive in a dance is not the dancer's opinions, psychological, political, or moral. It isn't even what she thinks about episodes in her private life. What is expressive in dancing is the way she moves about the stage, the way she exhibits her body in motion. A dancer's intelligence isn't shown by what intellectual allusions she can make in costume or pantomime, or if she is a choreographer, in her subject matter. It is shown by how interesting to look at she can make her body the whole time she is on the stage.

In the coming ballet season you may be able to compare Alexandra Danilova, Nana Gollner and Alicia Markova, each as the Swan Queen in *Swan Lake* and each one celebrated in that particular part. Each will be interesting to look at the whole time she will be on the stage, but the effect they make will be different. Watching the three in turn you may see what differences in their physical movement parallel their difference of expression and see how the dance intelligence of each leads her to a slightly different visual emphasis in identical steps and gymnastic feats.

For apart from questions of choreography it is variety of visual emphasis that we see when we feel variety of expression. And there are many resources for visual emphasis in dancing. There are the shifts in the pacing of a sequence, the points where the dancer hurries or delays. An identical step or arm gesture can be attacked sharply or mildly, it can subside or be stopped short. These differences draw the eye to one phase of motion rather than another, to one line of the body rather than another, or to the dancer's partner, or else to her momentary position on the stage, or even to a moment in the music which sharpens our sense of her movement.

But the most interesting resource for visual emphasis is the heightened perception of the dancer's body not in a line or silhouette, but in its mass, in its all-aroundness. A dancer can emphasize a passage in the dance by emphasizing the shape her body takes in the air. When she does this she does not call attention merely to the limb that moves, she defines her presence all around in every direction. At such moments she looks large, important, like a figure of imagination, like an ideal human being moving through the air at will. The great dancers seem to do this throughout a dance, but they vary it in intensity.

These are some of the physical characteristics of dance expression, and the brilliant use of them to arouse our interest, to thrill and to satisfy us, is proof of an artist's exceptional dance intelligence. She may have several other sorts of intelligence besides, but it is of no consequence to the public if she has not. It is the boldness and tenderness of her dance intelligence that the public loves her for—*March* 26, 1944.

A TECHNICAL WEAKNESS OF OUR
MALE BALLET DANCERS

IN CONVERSATION with Roger Pryor Dodge—a man who is an authority both on jazz music and on ballet dancing—the subject of ballet rhythm naturally came up. He told me how some years ago when he was watching a ballet class here in town conducted by the great dancer, Pierre Vladimi-

roff (who succeeded to Nijinsky's roles in St. Petersburg in
1913), Mr. Vladimiroff was giving combinations of leaps—
jetes, entrechats and sissonnes—to his pupils, among whom
were some of the best young male dancers in the country. Mr.
Dodge noticed that the young dancers executed the steps and
leaps in a sort of one-two-one-two military rhythm, closing
the sequence a moment after the end of the music. Their action was rapid, vigorous and fairly neat, but the effect was
colorless and undistinguished. But when Vladimiroff himself
performed the same sequence, Mr. Dodge could see very
clearly a variety of emphasis in the movement.

At one moment, for instance, the action of separating the
legs was stressed, and though it was just a fraction of a second,
the eye could distinguish it sharply. At another point in the
sequence there was a passing stress on the action of holding
the legs joined in the air, or else on the start upward of a leap;
and the feet had closed the phrase and were firm in repose
when the music stopped. In short, Mr. Vladimiroff had a free
rhythm in his leg action, which gave color and form to the
succession of steps, varying the stress of them and relating
them to one another, much as the small differences in speed
and in stress join together the words that form a well-spoken
sentence (an art of phrasing one can admire, for instance, in
President Roosevelt's or in Miss Hayes's elocution).

The young dancers in the class, however, by giving each
leap an equal stress and an even metronomic regularity of
time length gave the effect of a singsong recitation of *Hia-
watha;* or the effect of a pianist who pounds the beat under
the illusion that he can thereby make the music move forward
in lively fashion.

Mr. Dodge and I agreed that Miss Danilova and Miss

Markova are both brilliant examples of dancers who can vary the time values of steps—or, more exactly, of the component phases of a step—so as to create in a sequence the sense of a homogeneous dance phrase with a rise, a climax and a finish. Their sense of the time values in a sequence of motions is also a sense of the visual values that every sequence contains. The quickening or retarding of motion allows some moments in the movement to be seen more sharply than others, and these stressed moments become the central images around which the observer's mind groups the rest of the motion. And the sort of movement these central images stress—whether it is a spreading or joining, a movement toward the partner or away, a strong countermovement of one part of the body against another, or a pose in relation to the stage space—these central images by their momentary plastic and architectural tension afford the eye a point of reference in virtue of which a lengthy passage makes emotional sense; a little as a stressed musical motive gives the ear a point of reference in a lengthy passage of music.

The dance phrase is formed by variation in speed and variation in stress. Its total length is determined by the length of the musical phrase; its total dynamic range by the nature of the steps and leaps that are used, by the amplitude that is given them in this particular musical setting. And from these different elements the visual reality of dance phrase emerges; and in the course of a piece, the special dramatic characterization of a dance role.

But these variations of speed and stress which make the dance interesting or dramatic to look at are possible only with a highly developed leg and thigh and waist and back technique. It is possible our young male dancers who do not give us the sense of a live rhythm in dancing either lack a sense of rhythm in time or that they lack a sense of rhythm in three-dimensional stressing of movement. But it is just as likely that their thigh and waist training is insufficient. They cannot give variety enough to their steps and leaps because their technique has been directed to going through the motions of these steps and leaps as if they could be done only one way, in one sort of timing and with one kind of stress to the component parts of them. Their technique has not been directed to variety—human variety—within these traditional muscular sequences known as ballet steps and ballet leaps. That is what makes their dancing look monotonous. They should be able to make correct and similar jetes, that if photographed by Mr. Mili with his stroboscopic camera would produce radically different patterns on the print.

Our young dancers, for all their admirable feats of athletics, are all too often engaged in repeating their poems in ballet by rote, they do not give them rhythm. They aren't able to give them rhythm in the sense that Harlem ballroom dancers, for instance, give rhythm to the traditional steps of the Lindy. Of course the Lindy isn't nearly as hard as the *Bluebird;* but it's not the difficulty of a dance that makes the audience happy, it's rhythm—*December,* 1943.

FLIGHT OF THE DANCER

IF YOU travel all over the world and see every brilliant and flying dance that human beings do, you will maybe be surprised that it is only in our traditional classic ballet dancing that the dancer can leap through the air slowly. In other kinds of dancing there are leaps that thrill you by their impetuousness or accuracy; there are brilliant little ones, savage long ones and powerful bouncing ones. But among all dance techniques only classic ballet has perfected leaps with that special slow-motion grace, that soaring rise and floating descent which looks weightless. It isn't that every ballet leap looks that way. Some are a tough thrust off the ground, some travel like a cat's, some quiver like a fish's, some scintillate like jig steps; but these ways of jumping you can find in other dancing too. The particular expression ballet technique has added to leaping is that of the dancer poised in mid-flight, as easy in the air as if she were suspended on wires. Describing the effect, people say one dancer took flight like a bird, another was not subject to the laws of gravity and a third paused quietly in mid-air. And that is how it does look, when it happens.

To be honest, it doesn't happen very often. It is a way of leaping only a few rare dancers ever quite achieve. But it can be achieved. You can see it in the dancing of Alicia Markova, the English-born star of our present Ballet Theater company; though no one else in this country—perhaps no one else in the world—can "fly" quite as perfectly as she does. No one else is so serenely calm with nothing underneath her. In *Pas de*

23

Quatre she sits collectedly in the air, as if she were at a gen-
teel tea-party, a tea-party where everyone naturally sat down
on the air. There is something comic about it. That is because
Miss Markova, who in the part of Giselle is a delicate tragic
dancer, also has a keen sense of parody. *Pas de Quatre*, a
parody ballet, represents the competition in virtuosity of four
very great ballerinas at a command performance before Her
Majesty Queen Victoria. (It actually happened in 1845.) In
the ballet, Miss Markova takes the part of the greatest of the
four, Marie Taglioni—Marie *pleine de grâces*, as she was
called—who was a sallow little lady full of wrinkles, celebrated
not only for her serene flight through the empty air, but also for
the "decent voluptuousness" of her expression. Watching Miss
Markova's performance one feels that not even the eminently
respectable British queen could have found any fault with
the female modesty of such a look as hers. And that "refined"
look is Miss Markova's joke on Victorian propriety, and a
little too on the vanity of exhibiting technique just for its
own sake.

Her expression is parody, but the leap itself is no parody
of a leap. It is the real, incredibly difficult thing. Taglioni's
leap couldn't have been any better. A leap is a whole story
with a beginning, a middle and an end. If you want to try it,
here are some of the simplest directions for this kind of soaring flight. It begins with a knee bend, knees turned out, feet
turned out and heels pressed down, to get a surer grip and a
smoother flow in the leg action. The bend goes down softly
("as if the body were being sucked to the floor") with a slight
accelerando. The thrust upward, the stretch of the legs, is
faster than the bend was.

The speed of the action must accelerate in a continuous

gradation from the beginning of the bend into the final spring upward, so there will be no break in motion when the body leaves the ground. The leap may be jumped from two feet, hopped from one, or hopped from one with an extra swing in the other leg. But in any case the propulsive strain of the leap must be taken up by the muscles around the waist, the back must be straight and perpendicular, as if it had no part in the effort. Actually, the back muscles have to be kept under the strictest tension to keep the spine erect—the difficulty is to move the pelvis against the spine, instead of the other way around; and as the spine has no material support in the air, you can see that it's like pulling yourself up by your own bootstraps.

But that isn't all. The shoulders have to be held rigidly down by main force, so they won't bob upward in the jump. The arms and neck, the hands and the head, have to look as comfortable and relaxed as if nothing were happening down below. Really there's as much going on down there as though the arms and head were picnicking on a volcano. Once in the air the legs may do all sorts of things, embellishments sometimes quite unconnected with what they did to spring up, or what they will have to do to land. And if there are such extra embellishments during the leap, there should be a definite pause in the air before they begin and after they are finished. No matter how little time there is for them, the ornaments must never be done precipitately.

But the most obvious test for the dancer comes in the descent from the air, in the recovery from the leap. She has to catch herself in a knee bend that begins with the speed she falls at, and progressively diminishes so evenly that you don't notice the transition from the air to the ground. This knee bend slows down as it deepens to what feels like a final rest, though it is only a fraction of a second long, so short a movie camera will miss it. This is the "divine moment" that makes her look as if she alighted like a feather. It doesn't happen when she lands, you see, it happens later. After that, straightening up from the bend must have the feeling of a new start; it is no part of the jump, it is a new breath, a preparation for the next thing she means to do.

In other words, the action of a leap increases in speed till the dancer leaves the ground. Then it diminishes till it reaches the leap's highest point up in the air. From then on it increases again till the feet hit the ground, when it must be slowed down by the knee bend to a rest; and all these changes must be continuously flowing. But most important of all is the highest point reached in the air. Here, if the dancer is to give the feeling of soaring, she must be completely still. She must express the calm of that still moment. Some dancers hold their breath. Nijinsky used to say he just stopped at that point. But however he does it, the dancer must project that hairsbreadth moment as a climax of repose. The dancer must not be thinking either of how she got up or how she is going to get down. She must find time just then to meditate.

When Nijinsky entered through the window in the *Spectre de la Rose* thirty years ago it was the greatest leap of the century. He seemed to the audience to float slowly down like a happy spirit. He seemed to radiate a power of mysterious assurance as calmly as the bloom of a summer rose does. Such enthusiastic comments sound like complete nonsense nowadays, when you go to the ballet and see a young man thumping about the stage self-consciously. But the comments were made by sensible people, and they are still convinced they

were right. You begin to see what they mean when you realize that for Nijinsky in this ballet the leaps and the dance
were all one single flowing line of movement, faster or slower,
heavier or lighter, a way of moving that could rise up off the
ground as easily as not, with no break and no effort. It isn't
a question of how high he jumped one jump, but how
smoothly he danced the whole ballet. You can see the same
quality of technique today in Miss Markova's dancing.

In one respect, though, Nijinsky's way of leaping differed
from hers: in his style the knee bend that starts the leap up
and the other one that catches it coming down were often
almost unnoticeable. This is a difference of appearance, of
expression, but not really of technique. Nijinsky could make
the transitions in speed I spoke of above with an exceptionally
slight bending of the knees—a very unusual accomplishment
indeed. When a dancer can do this it gives an expression of
greater spontaneity to the leap; but several modern ballet
dancers who try to do it aren't able really to land "light as a
sylph or a snowflake," as Nijinsky could. The slight jolt when
they land breaks the smooth flow and attracts more attention
than the stillness of the climax in the air. And so the leap
fails to concentrate on a soaring expression. The "correct"
soaring leap is a technical trick any ballet dancer can learn
in ten or fifteen years if he or she happens to be a genius.
The point of learning it is that it enables the dancer to make
a particular emotional effect, which enlarges the range of expression in dancing. The effect as we watch Markova's pure
flight can only be described as supernatural, as a strangely
beneficent magic. It is an approach to those mysterious hints
of gentleness that occasionally absorb the human mind. It is
a spiritual emotion; so Nijinsky's contemporaries described it,

when he danced that way, and so did the Parisian poet Théophile Gautier when he saw first Taglioni and then Grisi take flight a hundred years ago.

It was a hundred years ago, most likely, that the trick was first perfected, together with that other trick so related to it in expression, the moment of airy repose on one toe. (Toe dancing, like leaping, has many kinds of expression, but the suggestion of weightless, poised near-flight is one of its most striking.) Toe dancing, like the technique of aerial flight, took a long series of dance geniuses to develop. The great Mlle Camargo two centuries ago, in Paris and in London, was already "dancing like a bird." But it seems likely that she fluttered enchantingly, rather than soared calm and slow; certainly Camargo's costumes didn't allow some technical resources that are related to our technique of flight; they allowed no horizontal lift of the leg, no deep knee bends, no spring and stretch of foot in a heelless slipper.

In her century, soaring of a different kind was being perfected. They literally hung the dancer on wires, and hoisted him or her through the air. Theaters had machinery called "flight paths," one of them fifty-nine feet long—quite a fine swoop it must have made. Maybe these mechanical effects gradually gave dancers the idea of trying to do the same thing without machinery. In an 1830 ballet, girls dressed as woodland spirits bent down the lower boughs of trees and let themselves be carried upward into the air on the rebound, which sounds like some wire effect. And in 1841 the great dancer Carlotta Grisi—Taglioni's young rival—opened in the ballet *Giselle,* in the second act of which there was one passage at least where her leaps were "amplified" by wiring. (She was supposed to be a ghost in it, and it was meant to look spooky.)

In the little engraving of her in this part she certainly floats over her grave in a way no ballet star ever could; but probably the pose is only an imaginary invention by the artist. The same *Giselle* is still being danced today both in America and Europe, and according to report, in Paris, in London and in Leningrad at least, this particular hundred-year-old wire trick is still being pulled—*October, 1943.*

AGAINST MEANING IN BALLET

SOME of my friends who go to ballet and like the entertainment it gives are sorry to have it classed among the fine arts and discussed, as the other fine arts are, intellectually. Though I do not agree with them I have a great deal of sympathy for their anti-intellectual point of view. The dazzle of a ballet performance is quite reason enough to go; you see handsome young people—girls and boys with a bounding or delicate animal grace—dancing among the sensual luxuries of orchestral music and shining stage decoration and in the glamor of an audience's delight. To watch their lightness and harmonious ease, their clarity and boldness of motion, is a pleasure. And ballet dancers' specialties are their elastic tautness, their openness of gesture, their gaiety of leaping, beating and whirling, their slow soaring flights. Your senses enjoy directly how they come forward and closer to you, or recede upstage, turning smaller and more fragile; how the boys and girls approach one another or draw apart, how they

pass close without touching or entwine their bodies in stars
of legs and arms—all the many ways they have of dancing
together. You see a single dancer alone showing her figure
from all sides deployed in many positions, or you see a troop
of them dancing in happy unison. They are graceful, well-
mannered, and they preserve at best a personal dignity, a
civilized modesty of deportment that keeps the sensual stimulus from being foolishly cute or commercially sexy. The
beauty of young women's and young men's bodies, in motion
or in momentary repose is exhibited in an extraordinarily
friendly manner.

When you enjoy ballet this way—and it is one of the ways
everybody does enjoy it who likes to go—you don't find any
prodigious difference between one piece and another, except
that one will have enough dancing to satisfy and another not
enough, one will show the dancers to their best advantage
and another will tend to make them look a little more awkward and unfree. Such a happy ballet lover is puzzled by the
severities of critics. He wonders why they seem to find immense differences between one piece and another, or between
one short number and another, or between the proficiency of
two striking dancers. The reasons the critics give, the relation
of the steps to the music, the sequence of the effects, the
sharply differentiated intellectual meaning they ascribe to
dances, all this he will find either fanciful or plainly absurd.

Has ballet an intellectual content? The ballet lover with the
point of view I am describing will concede that occasionally
a soloist gives the sense of characterizing a part, that a few
ballets even suggest a story with a psychological interest, a
dramatic suspense, or a reference to real life. In such a case,
he grants, ballet may be said to have an intellectual content.

But these ballets generally turn out to be less satisfying to watch because the dancers do less ballet dancing in them; so, he concludes, one may as well affirm broadly that ballet does not properly offer a "serious" comment on life and that it is foolish to look for one.

I do not share these conclusions, and I find my interest in the kind of meaning a ballet has leads me to an interest in choreography and dance technique. But I have a great deal of sympathy for the general attitude I have described. It is the general attitude that underlies the brilliant reviews of Théophile Gautier, the French poet of a hundred years ago, who is by common consent the greatest of ballet critics. He said of himself that he was a man who believed in the visible world. And his reviews are the image of what an intelligent man of the world saw happening on the stage. They are perfectly open; there is no private malignity in them; he is neither pontifical nor "popular"; there is no jargon and no ulterior motive. He watches not as a specialist in ballet, but as a responsive Parisian. The easy flow of his sentences is as much a tribute to the social occasion as it is to the accurate and elegant ease of ballet dancers in action. His warmth of response to personal varieties of grace and to the charming limits of a gift, his amusement at the pretensions of a libretto or the pretensions of a star, his sensual interest in the line of a shoulder and bosom, in the elasticity of an ankle, in the cut of a dress, place the ballet he watches in a perspective of civilized good sense.

Ballet for him is an entertainment—a particularly agreeable way of spending an evening in town; and ballet is an art, it is a sensual refinement that delights the spirit. Art for him is not a temple of humanity one enters with a reverent exaltation. Art is a familiar pleasure and Gautier assumes that one strolls through the world of art as familiarly as one strolls through Paris, looking about in good weather or bad, meeting congenial friends or remarkable strangers, and one's enemies, too. Whether in art or in Paris, a civilized person appreciates seeing a gift and is refreshed by a graceful impulse; there is a general agreement about what constitutes good workmanship; and one takes one's neighbors' opinions less seriously than their behavior. Gautier differentiates keenly between good and bad ballet; but he differentiates as a matter of personal taste. He illustrates the advantages the sensual approach to ballet can have for an intelligence of exceptional sensual susceptibility and for a man of large sensual complacency.

Gautier assumes that all that people need do to enjoy art is to look and listen with ready attention and trust their own sensual impressions. He is right. But when they hear that ballet is an elaborate art with a complicated technique and tradition, many modest people are intimidated and are afraid to trust their own spontaneous impressions. They may have been to a few performances, they may have liked it when they saw it, but now they wonder if maybe they liked the wrong things and missed the right ones. Before going again, they want it explained, they want to know what to watch for and exactly what to feel. If it is really real art and fine great art, it must be studied before it is enjoyed; that is what they remember from school. In school the art of poetry is approached by a strictly rational method, which teaches you what to enjoy and how to discriminate. You are taught to analyze the technique and the relation of form to content; you are taught to identify and "evaluate" stylistic, biographical, economic and anthropological influences, and told what is great and what is minor so you can prepare yourself for a great reaction or for a minor one. The effect of these conscientious labors on the pupils is distressing. For the rest of their lives they can't face a page of verse without experiencing a complete mental blackout. They don't enjoy, they don't discriminate, they don't even take the printed words at face value. For the rest of their lives they go prying for hidden motives back of literature, for psychological, economic or stylistic explanations, and it never occurs to them to read the words and respond to them as they do to the nonsense of current songs or the nonsense of billboards by the roadside. Poetry is the same thing, it's words, only more interesting, more directly and richly sensual.

The first taste of art is spontaneously sensual, it is the discovery of an absorbing entertainment, an absorbing pleasure. If you ask anyone who enjoys ballet or any other art how he started, he will tell you that he enjoyed it long before he knew what it meant or how it worked. I remember the intense pleasure reading Shelley's *Adonais* gave me as a boy—long before I followed accurately the sense of the words; and once, twenty years later, I had two kittens who would purr in unison and watch me bright-eyed when I read them Shakespeare's *Sonnets*, clearly pleased by the compliment and by the sounds they heard. Would they have enjoyed them better if they had understood them? The answer is, they enjoyed them very much. Many a college graduate might have envied them.

I don't mean that so orderly and respectable an entertainment as that of art is made for the susceptibilities of kittens or children. But consider how the enormous orderly and respectable symphonic public enjoys its listening, enjoys it without recognizing themes, harmonies or timbres, without evaluating the style historically or even knowing if the piece is being played as the composer intended. What do they hear when they hear a symphony? Why, they hear the music, the interesting noises it makes. They follow the form and the character of it by following their direct acoustic impressions.

Susceptibility to ballet is a way of being susceptible to animal grace of movement. Many people are highly susceptible to the pleasure of seeing grace of movement who have never thought of going to ballet to look for it. They find it instead in watching graceful animals, animals of many species at play, flying, swimming, racing and leaping and making gestures of affection toward one another, or watchful in harmonious repose. And they find it too in seeing graceful young people on the street or in a game or at the beach or in a dance hall, boys and girls in exuberant health who are doing pretty much what the charming animals do, and are as unconscious of their grace as they. Unconscious grace of movement is a natural and impermanent gift like grace of features or of voice or of character, a lucky accident you keep meeting with all your life wherever you are. To be watching grace puts people into a particularly amiable frame of mind. It is an especially attractive form of feeling social consciousness.

But if ballet is a way of entertaining the audience by showing them animal grace, why is its way of moving so very un-animal-like and artificial? For the same reason that music has evolved so very artificial a way of organizing its pleasing noises. Art takes what in life is an accidental pleasure and tries to repeat and prolong it. It organizes, diversifies, characterizes, through an artifice that men evolve by trial and error. Ballet nowadays is as different from an accidental product as a symphony at Carnegie Hall is different from the noises Junior makes on his trumpet upstairs or Mary Ann with comb and tissue paper, sitting on the roof, the little monkey.

You don't have to know about ballet to enjoy it, all you have to do is look at it. If you are susceptible to it, and a good many people evidently are, you will like spontaneously some things you see and dislike others, and quite violently too. You may be so dazzled at first by a star or by the general atmosphere you don't really know what happened; you may on the other hand find the performance absurdly stiff and affected except for a few unreasonable moments of intense pleasure; but, if you are susceptible you will find you want to go again. When you go repeatedly, you begin to recognize what it is you like, and watch for it the next time. That way you get to know about ballet, you know a device of ballet because you have responded to it, you know that much at least about it. Even if nobody agrees with you, you still know it for yourself.

That the composite effect of ballet is a complex one is clear enough. Its devices make a long list, wherever you start. These devices are useful to give a particular moment of a dance a particular expression. The dancers in action give it at that moment a direct sensual reality. But if you watch often and watch attentively, the expressive power of some ballets and dancers will fascinate, perturb and delight far more than that of others; and will keep alive in your imagination much more intensely long after you have left the theater. It is this after effect that dancers and ballets are judged by by their audience.

To some of my friends the images ballet leaves in the imagination suggest, as poetry does, an aspect of the drama of human behavior. For others such ballet images keep their sensual mysteriousness, "abstract," unrationalized and magical. Anyone who cannot bear to contemplate human behavior except from a rationalistic point of view had better not try to "understand" the exhilarating excitement of ballet; its finest images of our fate are no easier to face than those of poetry itself, though they are no less beautiful.

BALLET—THE AMERICAN POSITION

BALLET is the one form of theater where nobody speaks a foolish word all evening—nobody on the stage at least. That's why it becomes so popular in any civilized country during a war. Its success here during the recent one surprised many people who didn't realize how civilized the country is. I have been asked to guess what will happen to it in the next few years. Anyone's guess is as good as mine. My guess is that its civilized qualities will continue to be remarkably attractive for some time; the difficulty will be for ballet to keep them, rather than for the public to appreciate them.

Ballet is absurd by nature. But its absurdities are civilized ones. It is as absurd as a symphony concert. A symphony is seventy-five men on a stage who make noises together very earnestly for a couple of hours; and music lovers beam at some of the noises and lose their tempers over others. Ballet is a lot of young people hopping about to music in a peculiarly exhilarating way. Sometimes they're being sad and sometimes funny, but they're always in the pink of condition, charmingly built, graceful, well-mannered and serious. Like an orchestra of musicians or a cast of actors they are busy building up the illusion of some sort of event; but they don't waste so much time about it as actors and they are pleasanter to watch at work than musicians. Dancers appear briefly in all the glamor of orchestral sonorities and surprising fancy dress, and you find intelligent people who long afterward remember with affection some brief illusion that dancers created. Ballet is in the habit of using the fantasy gifts of serious composers and painters without depreciating them. It is by nature a form of poetic theater and it is the form that is liveliest at the moment in this country. Theater lovers sometimes hope its popularity may even lead to a more imaginative spoken drama.

The fine moments of ballet frighten but they do it gently; and for that it needs accurate dancers. They have to be trained from early youth to precision in rhythm, to a clear, bold, large articulation (even in light or soft passages), to variety and virtuosity and personal modesty and ensemble work. Their way of building up a dramatic effect is to project its rhythmic beat or pulse and its individual rhythmic continuity. The quality of motion they show—now heavy, now light, rapid or still, gliding and stabbing, soaring or darting, successively solo, duet or in chorus—gives the situation on stage its special imaginative meaning. You sense it in the clear shapes their bodies make, in their contact with each other in dance figures and in the cumulative transformations of choreographic architecture.

A ballet usually tells a story too and so it uses pantomime;

but people don't go for the pantomime, they go for the dancing. Ballet dancing is not an imitation of anything else. It is an invention to convey imaginative meaning—an invention something like that of occidental concert music, which isn't a very much older one historically but is one that has been far more widely practiced and elaborately developed. Concert music and ballet are each ways of communicating an interesting fantasy without the use of words or verbal logic. They each invented a nonverbal semantic system which audiences for the last few centuries have found agreeable and even internationally intelligible. Ballet now and then almost makes literal sense as pantomime; but a moment later it obviously doesn't and then it is often more absorbing than ever as fantasy because then the beat and sweep of the dance become more powerful and its shapes seem to enlarge.

As everyone knows, ballet's international semantic system is based on a standard dance technique. The problem of theater dancing is how to keep a number of performers going with a steady liveliness that can weave a spontaneous spell. Ballet technique simplifies the problem for the choreographer in the way, say, a piano simplifies the problem of the composer who wants to arrange noises so they will be interesting to listen to in sequence. It limits but it is more workable. It is workable under theater conditions because that's how it was invented; and that's why its conventions are inseparable from the hard facts of theater music and stage architecture. Ballet technique was evolved by generations of theater dancers who were proud of their best effects and tried to pass them on to youngsters. It is a time-saving device for dancers as well as for choreographers. After only six or eight years of practicing it, dancers achieve a high standard of liveliness, clarity and coherence in a wide range of effects. They can readily be used in companies, they can learn new dances quickly, they can do brilliant things reliably and easily. To achieve this, ballet technique limited itself to certain kinds of movement. But it discovered so sound and so flexible a language that new dance rhythms or dance images and new expressive qualities in dancing are constantly appearing in new ballets. It provides only one of the possible techniques of theater dancing; Javanese dancing has, for instance, a different and a very lovely one. The modern dance aims to provide a third, but so far its simplest units of posture, of movement and of rhythm have either been too complex to be handy in the theater or else, with Jooss, too wooden. Modern-dance technique missed the simple bounce of growing up on stage with dance tunes around and children howling, the way ballet first did. For the present, ballet's technique is the most manageable, the most sociable and goodnatured.

This is why ballet is a civilized kind of theater entertainment. It is by nature an exact and flexible language to communicate formal fantasy; and it is a medium of communication wonderfully fresh and sensuous, since it exists only while young people are dancing it conscientiously and happily to serious music and in imaginative fancy dress.

All this has been what ballet dancing is like by nature and what it intends as theater entertainment. Though difficult and expensive to produce, its graceful and civilized sense in nonsense makes it for many people a particularly exhilarating show, and in recent years audiences all over the country who were unfamiliar with it before have taken to its peculiarities without trouble. Ballet has now become acclimated because nobody thinks of it as foreign any more. And it has become homegrown because almost everyone on stage nowadays was born and trained in America, and it is for their kind of dance gift and their American look that the new productions are intended. Their collective innocently American flavor in action is a novelty in big-time ballet but it looks natural to the audience that sees it here, and pleasing.

The charming figures, the long legs of American girls, are a part of that new American flavor. In any kind of dancing a bunch of young Americans do together, they are likely to show a steadier and keener sense of beat and a clearer carriage of the body than Europeans would, and they are apt to wear a more sober and noncommittal look than European Latins or Slavs. In our ballet these national traits show up too and often turn out very handsomely. Large, clear, accurate and un-affected, our ballet style looks—and particularly among the slender young girls remarkable for speed, toes and prowess; its phrasing is not very personal; and George Balanchine has mentioned a kind of angelic unconcern toward emotion as being perhaps a special charm of American dancers.

We could see our traits more sharply if we could see for con-trast the current foreign companies. Till they come over, the only style we can compare ours with is the pre-war Ballets Russes one of the thirties. Compared to ours its atmosphere was more hot and bothered, its rhythm in dance scenes made more sweeping climaxes, its techniques looked more casual and undefined and its temperament was more exotically fiery. None of our companies since then has been as striking as that at its best. But if Ballet Theater, the Monte Carlo and Ballet Society were to pool their stars, soloists and repertory and add the ex-Ballet Theater contingent now with the Original (and two first-rate conductors) they would form a company of about the same size as the best pre-war Ballet Russe and one of even finer dance quality.

How the present European dancers compare to ours I only know from deceptive photographs and conflicting reports by travelers. The general impression seems to be that our ballet is better in straight dancing and in dance invention than any of Western Europe. It is apparently less good in effects of imaginative impersonation, of imaginative atmosphere or stage presence—qualities which the Paris Champs-Elysées Ballet seems to project with especial brilliance and wit. As for the Soviet ballet, the magnificent abundance of energy and force of Moscow's enormous company would no doubt thrill anybody; but that innocent and unintentional subtlety of human response between fantasy characters which is the heart of our idea of style—how that looks over there no one has clearly told us; all I have seen of it was an action shot of a supported leap in the *Aurora* pas de deux, in which both stars showed a radiant glow of good nature all over, wonderfully simple in its amazing largeness of scale.

Till the contrast of foreign ensembles gives us a sharper view of our style, one senses its nature best in the clearness of our young ballerinas—Alonso, Boris, Hightower, Kaye, Moylan and Tallchief, to list them alphabetically—but it shows too in thirty or forty good soloists. Ballet Theater crystallized its version of our style with *Pillar of Fire* and the Monte Carlo with *Danses Concertantes*. Our dancing would of course never have become so strong without a great deal of stimulus from abroad and from ex-Ballets Russes artists in particular. It is obvious that without Balanchine and Tudor as choreographers, without as stars Danilova, Markova, Toumanova, or

Eglevsky, Franklin, Laing and Youskevitch, our stage would lose its current luster. And it would be silly to underestimate their decisive importance to our ballet in the years ahead. But one notices too that foreign-trained artists who stay in our companies acclimate themselves to the local dance atmosphere or else get fidgety and lose their power. When they stay they enrich our style by the example they give; but working here leads them to an unconscious shift of emphasis in their own manner. Eglevsky's present style—much more exact than five years ago—is an example. Danilova's new tautness in rhythm that a few years back gave a fresh power to her wonderful grace is another. A third is the change in emphasis Tudor has given the 1946 production of *Lilac Garden* compared to the one we saw five years earlier—the dancing now is far lighter and more flowing in arm motions, has far more impetus and three-dimensional clarity in phrasing. The stimulus that Tudor's work here has given our native choreographers and dancers is obvious; perhaps the increasing ease in his phrasing (which *Undertow* sometimes suggested too) is due to a reciprocal influence.

But the artist from abroad who has responded most to our special dance gifts and climate has been Balanchine. And he is also the man who more than any other individual created and founded our American ballet. The fact that we have not wasted time trying to imitate the Ballets Russes style; the local freshness and the high standards of technique in dancing and in choreography we take for granted—these are due above all to his quiet persistence and his pervasive influence since he came here fourteen years ago. He has developed the physical qualities and the zest of our dancers as elements of style. He has made our dancers look natural in classicism. His pieces carry on stage when they dance them classically clear and large, without nervousness or self-conscious glamor; he has shown how fascinating their buoyant rhythm can be in all sorts of variations of forthright impetus. That way they learn to dance correct ballet as straightforwardly and simply as one speaks the language one is born to, and learn from their experience in his contemporary classicism to dance the nineteenth-century classics as unaffectedly. Finding out how to dance these as real dancing is a big step in a young dancer's deprovincialization. They are dances created as far away from us in time and space as ballet reaches, and an American who finds herself bringing them to life feels her power as a dancer. Their undistorted gesture, their clear rhythm invite no faking; they are void of malice or acedia; but the theater effect of their good manners and large poetry is often more obvious to the audience than to our performers.

Balanchine too has shown us in his own choreography the kind of theater effect classic ballet can have. His pieces are not assertive smash numbers; they are pleasant the first time, and the more you see them the more you can find in them. They present themselves politely as ballet entertainment in which the dancers can look brilliant. Not the story, but the dance rhythm, the surprising dance figures, the witty solutions, the clarity and above all the musicality of the action seem to carry the piece. It all looks like brilliant dance fun. And something else happens too. In your excitement as you watch the quick dancing, it will often evoke in passing an intensely poignant fantasy image of human relations. Such moments are not self-consciously underlined; they seem to happen of their own accord in the dancing and so they remain suspended in the world of fantasy. Their dramatic meaning or emotional relevance is no burden on anyone's conscience, least of all on the dancers'. Some people respond to these dramatic meanings sharply, some dimly and some not at all; but it is fantasy of the highest imaginative honesty. The American ballet audience responds to his pieces with pleasure just as they do to *Giselle* or *Swan Lake* and they like the peaceful excitement of them better and better the more they see it.

I have stressed Balanchine's classicism of dance "meaning" and the American flavor he develops in classic dancing because these are novel and unique qualities which just now we are contributing to international ballet and because they are based on qualities natural to ballet and to our dancers. They are important because they are novel dance qualities; but because they are dance qualities (not literary ones) they are hard to talk about. It is easier to talk about the novelty of our gay local-color Americanism in ballet or about the gloom-steeped psychological aspects of Tudor's gripping large-scale dramas of frustration. These pieces make a good deal of their appeal through their literary content, and from a literary point of view the value of them in nationalizing our ballet or in modernizing it has been properly stressed by many reporters. I myself do not think the literary ideas I see in Tudor or in the American folk ballet are very novel ideas as ideas go in contemporary literature—the local color generally strikes me as too cute and the sex psychology too weepy. But the action of these pieces on stage has many very brilliant passages. The qualities of novel dance invention and of dramatic confrontation, of observation and timing and punch shown in Tudor's work as well as in Agnes de Mille's and Jerome Robbins' are qualities of which American ballet—and the American theater in general—can well be proud. And it is. Of Robbins' choreographic genius, after his new *Facsimile* there can be no doubt. Our public loves the zest, the jokes, the local steps and vitality of the American-scene pieces and admires the intensity of Tudor's. Our intelligent public recognizes too that Martha Graham's modern-school choreography is an even more extraordinary achievement and that her personal stage presence as a dancer is a theater event of the highest class.

Ballet in America has developed a standard of technique internationally valid and a style founded on characteristics by nature our own. Though it is too early to be dogmatic about what is or is not American in ballet, people are aware that our ballet is not an imitation of the pre-war Ballet Russe manner but a new manner entirely. It compares favorably in enough respects with the post-war ballet style abroad to make one hope it will continue a development so soundly started.

It strikes me that theoretically speaking what our ballet needs more and more to continue its development is lessons in serious impersonation, in transforming the dancer on the stage into a character of fantasy. Even a Petipa Prince Charming is a real fantasy character, not a glamor boy. Very few of our dancers dare transform themselves—they are afraid of losing that audience-contact through charm which they are used to. They indicate a character but they want to keep in every case a simple juvenile sex appeal. When our dancers act a character they are likely to show what they mean; but they seem to be explaining him to you instead of turning into someone else. Impersonation in dancing comes less from explaining the "psychology" of the character than from sensing who he is from the dance rhythm of the part. For only the effects of dance rhythm can touch the heart in ballet. They are the only ones that look unself-conscious and innocent and therefore really serious. In that sense good models for a ballerina are our great vaudeville comedians with their innocent air of not caring whether they are noticed or not.

The theatrical effect of the pre-war Paris-Russian style lay in a gift for impersonation through dance rhythm. Even before the war however the gift was already disintegrating into a mania for rhythmic and gymnastic distortion. Our own musical instinct allows only a very slight latitude of phrasing against a firm beat, and when our dancers learn impersonation through rhythm it will be the simpler and the larger in its effect. Our current story ballets are good for giving them practice in dance impersonation but they stress oddity of pantomime rather than expression through undistorted rhythm. So far there are not more than four or five Americans who achieve the necessary air of complete unself-consciousness in critical situations. Most of the others seem to confuse the issue by indicating a moral approval or disapproval of the character they are acting.

"Storyless" ballets on the other hand can treat almost any situation without impropriety or moralizing, and people can enjoy the excitement of watching as innocently as they can listening to music. For the audience to take in an exciting action without quite knowing what is going on can be an advantage over following a story self-consciously step by step. A story so easily becomes censorable at its most interesting moments, one watches it nervously. Nervousness isn't fun, it's excitement that is.

My point so far has been that choreographers, dancers and dance public have established a new kind of ballet in this country which is inherently American and internationally valid. Our wartime eagerness for ballet, wartime isolation and easy money brought it into flower. It sounds like a Horatio Alger success story. Unfortunately the weather prophets don't see the immediate future as rosy. But the difficulties ahead are organizational rather than artistic. Ballet normally runs at a loss, just as a symphony orchestra does, and the loss under current general conditions has already jumped. Our two American-style companies, Ballet Theater and the Monte Carlo, strike the weathermen as growing timid artistically in proportion. Lack of artistic enterprise by the management quickly demoralizes the company's dancers.

Economy has also reduced the size of both companies to half strength. Both companies are now so small that the dancers must be perpetually overworked. It is a miracle our dancers survive the strain added to the brutal beating that the months of touring bring. They have no time for technique classes; in performance they can't trust the orchestra; since they are overworked they dance negligently for half the evening and grow used to run-down productions. They dance wrong in parts they have to fill in a hurry, and aren't corrected. Tired as they are it isn't doing a part right, but getting as much notice as possible that they must aim for. They come to count how often they appear in good parts, not how well, and they come to wow a part, an effect on their individual "stage glamor." All these dishonesties in dancing are hard to resist in exhaustion. It is enormously to the credit of our dancers when despite such conditions they succeed in developing as artists. But the survival of a few individuals does not make such conditions rational. No baseball manager would expect his team to shine, worked as our dancers are worked.

The only remedy is to double the size of a company and halve the burden on the dancers. If our two companies could combine to one of double strength the dancers could take classes, rehearse and prepare their parts. They would appear less but appear in brilliant form—and it is only in their best form that dancers really develop. With a combined repertory, the run-down pieces could be dropped and the rest kept well rehearsed. With a stronger repertory and more rehearsal time a bolder and more long range risk could be taken with novelties. A good ballet often takes a while to grow in performance and an original one may well take a year or more for the general audience or even the critics to come around to.

The necessary step of organizing an American company twice the present size would cost probably two or three hundred thousand a year in deficit. It would require above all a director of rare artistic integrity and courage. But by the end of last fall's New York season many people were troubled about the future of our companies. Ballet is no fun when it looks routine.

But the low point of last fall, its most discouraging and dismal experience, was not due to our local companies but to an imported one, the Original Ballet Russe. In pre-war days the company of this name had been a brilliant one. Last fall, obviously a run-down company, shoddy in dance technique and in atmosphere, it presented in New York a decayed version of the pre-war style. It was saved from collapse only by its astute impresario, S. Hurok, who added a contingent of local stars and local productions that had nothing in common with the atmosphere of the importation.

But in this sad picture the weather prophets agree that a
new subscription organization in New York, Ballet Society,
is a cheerful spot. Ballet Society is a deficit venture. It offers
four programs a year of ballet and ballet opera besides an
evening or two of lectures or dance films. (Ballet opera means
an opera sung in the pit and danced on stage by dancers.) By
January two programs had been presented which included
three novelties; two ballet operas never staged in New York;
some lovely Javanese dancing by Ratna Mohini and the two
young Javanese gentlemen, Soekaro and Pamoedjo; some modern dance solos; a new orchestra piece by Colin McPhee.
Together these two evenings had more novelties of interest
than the whole fall season of three big ballet companies.
There had been décor by interesting easel painters too. One
of the operas, Stravinsky's *Renard* had brilliant animal costumes and a fine drop by Esteban Francés. Another painter
presented was Kurt Seligmann who did the décor for a ballet,
The Four Temperaments.

A tenet of Ballet Society is to present novelties by local
choreographers, the first of which was *Pastorela*, which Lew
Christensen had set to a score by Paul Bowles. But the dance
events of the winter were Balanchine's two new ballets, *The
Four Temperaments* and *Divertimento*, the latter to a score
by Alexei Haieff, the former to one by Paul Hindemith.
Divertimento is quick and sharp. It has a hint of juvenile
romance, a curiously tender, very novel pas de deux, a virtuoso girl's solo that looks all simple and dewy, and a wonderful ending. *The Four Temperaments* on the other hand is a
large long piece packed close with intricate but boldly powerful dance invention. It appears to have the dispassionate
ferocity of a vital process; its subject is the "four tempera-

ments" (or humors) of medieval endocrinology and it suggests the grandiose impersonal drama of organic energies. It is an impersonal drama that appears to be witty, cruel, desperate and unconsoling, like that of our time. Yet all that actually happens on stage is rapid exact ballet dancing in classic sequences that are like none you could ever imagine. In fact the technical procedure of both ballets is that novel aspects of classic ballet technique—aspects apparently contrary to those one is accustomed to—are emphasized without ever breaking the classic look of the dance continuity.

The originator and manager of Ballet Society is Lincoln Kirstein, who in '33 invited Balanchine to this country and who has worked with him ever since, running a ballet school, managing successive local ballet companies, producing repertories, commissioning untried choreographers, composers and painters, inventing scenarios, writing books and editing a magazine. The dance company of Ballet Society is composed of dancers connected with Kirstein's American Ballet School and is an excellent one; Mary Ellen Moylan is its bold young ballerina. I have here reported the Society's lucky beginning at quite disproportionate length partly because it is a new, much talked of enterprise, partly because it may well, after several years of trial and error, turn out to have been the origin and foundation of the sensibly organized, exciting American ballet company we need now so badly.

Sensibly organized to produce dancing as an art, which is a ballet company's proper function. Kirstein and Balanchine together have—as *Time* pointed out in reviewing Ballet Society —worked since 1933 to de-Russianize our ballet as art. Now they have begun the necessary organizational work to decommercialize it as a branch of our theater. At the moment it is the most effective way of keeping it civilized though the method is obviously a lot of trouble. But unless it stays civilized, ballet is no fun. Staying civilized is always everybody's trouble, so why not ballet's?—*April,* 1947.

2

Ballets in Recent Repertory

VICTORIAN PASTICHE

DOLIN'S ballet, *Romantic Age*, the world premiere of which the Ballet Theater presented last night at the Metropolitan Opera House, is cute as candy. And before it is over, it turns out to be a pretty big lump of confectionery to swallow. But the dancing of Alicia Markova in the lead is quite another thing. Wit and good nature, incredibly perfect technique and a fantastic grace quite of her own turned her part in the piece into one of those little jewels for ballet lovers.

Essentially *Romantic Age* is an expanded and beribboned sequel to Dolin's *Pas de Quatre*. It is another but much more elaborate Victorian pastiche; parody of ballet at its dullest. The story is of a nymph, who alone among her sister nymphs is awkward. She can't dance ballet. Amor shoots her with his golden arrow and she becomes the best dancer of them all. A handsome Faun seems to please her for a while, but really a polite youth turns out to be the better partner. The Faun's anger is appeased and that leads to a grand finale.

The various dances themselves are in Dolin's usual choreographic style, grateful for the dancer, in good taste, perfectly clear and not very interesting. Dolin himself danced the

Youth, and exhibited as always perfect manners and clean style. Everybody on the stage did well and the audience was willing, but without Markova the whole thing wouldn't have come through as a joke. When this most exquisite of technicians pretends she can't dance, she is a miracle of grace and a perfect showman.

The Bellini music deserves a better fate than to be used for a decorative parody; it has a real passion. The score was arranged by Antal Dorati—*October* 24, 1942.

POETIC REALISM

THE ending of the new Tudor-Delius-Berman *Romeo and Juliet*, omitted at the first performance, was given Saturday night at the Metropolitan Opera House. It completed the story and added two more extraordinary scenic effects to a ballet which for scenic beauty is unparalleled in our time.

At a second view, the quality of the ballet itself is clearer. It is made up of exquisite pantomime fragments ranging in style from quattrocento poses to a reference to Judo. It is full of nuances in timing and placing, like an Eisenstein film. And it does not sweep through the story. It is, so to speak, a meditation on the play. But it is strangely moving. Its strength is that of an intensely and consistently poetic attitude. And so *Romeo and Juliet* turns out to be big news for dance lovers, because this attitude is the real point in dancing and it is not often shown.

In all this, of course, the marvelous Markova excels. And technically, no matter how odd the timing of her interrupted phrases may be, she gives them a rhythmic clarity and coherence which turns everything into dancing. But above all it is Juliet, who dances.

The poetic realism of *Romeo and Juliet* is everywhere heightened by Berman's scenery and costumes. One can admire their elegance—the hats are better than John-Frederics'. Or their architectural learning; or their sense of the human figure. But it is their sincere homage to the glory of the Italian Renaissance, like a meditation on the beauty of the human spirit, that makes them look like living poetry—*April* 12, 1943.

FRESH, DIRECT, VIGOROUS

FAIR AT SOROCHINSK, a ballet on a Ukrainian folk theme by David Lichine, was given its world premiere last night by Ballet Theater at the Metropolitan Opera House, and it was an event worthy of a great ballet company. Again and again in the course of the ballet there are choreographic inventions that reveal an originality of the first class. Lichine's gift as a choreographer is vigorous, and it is different in quality from any other choreographer's in the country.

The plot of *Fair at Sorochinsk* is not that of the Moussorgsky opera, though some of the characters are the same, since the ballet too is based on Gogol's stories about his own birthplace. In the ballet, a witch who is intimate with Red Coat, the Devil of the Ukraine, tries to thwart the true love of her beautiful stepdaughter and a handsome village boy. The Devil and the witch succeed in luring the boy and girl as well as many other villagers to a Witches' Sabbath; but the innocence of the lovers preserves them at least from harm.

The ballet opens with a half-pantomime, half-dance scene at the witches' inn, moves to a scene at the fair where after some Russian-fair pantomime there are two big folk-dance scenes; then comes the *Night on Bald Mountain* scene, with dances of witches and bedeviled villagers; and last is a quiet ending with almost no movement at all.

The general dance style of the piece is in Ukrainian or Cossack folk steps, heightened and varied for the stage. The group figures, however, the massing or thinning out of movement, the dead pauses and sudden rushes, are where the choreographer's instinct for dance form shows itself brilliantly. These folk dances are not hackneyed ballet reproductions; they have an impact and a decision in their contrasts that is altogether Lichine's. It is the same instinct for vigorous dance dynamics that Lichine has shown in his own dancing.

There are also original details in the dancing. Dolin's Cossack toesteps and toe-pirouettes (Dolin takes the part of the Devil and dances it with the greatest brilliance) are a happy invention and suit the part perfectly. Lichine has always shown a gift for direct characterization in dancing, and all his characters are defined not by mugging, but by dancing.

The performance by the entire company was brilliant. André Eglevsky was remarkable, Miss Banks, Miss Chase excellent—*October* 15, 1943.

A COMEDY BALLET

THE indulgent public applauds Massine's new ballet, *Mademoiselle Angot,* and this reviewer, though he does not care for the piece, is glad that the production promises to be no financial loss to the company. It is a pity, however, that so much effort and expense ($35,000 according to rumor) should have given no more positive result than one more piece that gets by. The materials out of which it is made are good ones. The music of Lecocq, though dry, is animated, of excellent workmanship, and easy to listen to. The décor by Doboujinsky is perhaps clumsy, but it has nevertheless more presence than many sets in current ballet repertory. The dancers are first class and do whatever they do with enthusiasm. The trouble with *Mademoiselle Angot* is simply that for all its constant commotion it seems endless and pointless, the successive dances seem to flounder around without either a steady subject or any consecutive form.

The dancing might have expressed the plot of the operetta the ballet is based on, *La Fille de Madame Angot.* The latter has a solid plot—solid because it shows the character development of its heroine, as she comes in contact with a foolish but loving workman, a fascinating but unreliable intellectual, a self-important plutocrat, and a brilliant temperamental demimondaine. The heroine begins as a bright slum girl educated in a good convent, she falls in love with the intellectual, goes to jail for him, is released by her rival, the influential demimondaine, is disillusioned about her first love and ends by good-humoredly making fun of everyone and staying friends with everybody.

During the rehearsals of the original operetta the people around the theater had no faith in the piece at all. A seasoned pit musician said to Lecocq, "It's a good job, but there's not a laugh in it." On the first night the manager (who had skimped on the sets) was dumbfounded by the tremendous success. No one had realized during the rehearsals that the serious logic of the libretto gave warmth and humor and pathos to the comedy situations.

Massine, however, in adapting the piece has passed over the human drama of the characterizations. He has turned the people of the story into dance marionettes, and the plot becomes merely a peg to hang dances on. No character is ever surprised at the action, and none of them cares at all about anyone else on the stage. His heroine is as knowing at the beginning as at the end, and so you feel that in the end nothing has happened to her at all.

When the choreographer fails to individualize his dancing characters he gives up his chance for narrative interest and humor of situation. But in place of a story-ballet, he can still make an amusing dance suite. Massine has made successful suites of this kind in *Capriccio Espagnol* and *Gaîté Parisienne*. This time, in *Mademoiselle Angot*, too many of the dance jokes—particularly the gags in Massine's own role—are in the most foolish ballet-boy-acting-cute manner, and the dance sequences give no sense of plan or climax. The line of movement is so blurred and cluttered with conflicting simultaneous dance figures that you don't know which place to look and your eye can't follow anything longer than a few seconds. What you see is a jerking, leaping, twisting, arm-waving, run-

ning in and out, and if it stops, it stops in a pose that is point-
lessly difficult and that sums up nothing.

Massine's reputation does not rest on the success or failure
of one more novelty. It is merely a matter of regret that this
year he has given us neither a good comedy nor an effective
dance suite, two styles he has often been highly successful
with before and no doubt will often be equally successful
with in the future—*October* 17, 1943.

SLIGHT STREAM OF CONSCIOUSNESS

BALLET THEATER presented at the Metropolitan last
night the world premiere of *Dim Luster,* a ballet by
Antony Tudor, the brilliantly original choreographer of six
other ballets in the company's repertory. *Dim Luster* is weaker
than any of the others, both in the inventiveness of the dance
detail and in the general over-all dramatic effect. It seems to
me that the one real distinction it has is Tudor's name on the
program; and the incidental presence of Tudor, Nora Kaye,
Rosella Hightower and Hugh Laing on the stage.

The story of the piece, a "psychological episode," is that of
a gentleman and a lady at a ball. As they dance among the
other couples, a chance gesture, a perfume, a kiss reminds
one or the other of what once happened—a shadow of memory that dims the real present for a few moments. It is the
stream of consciousness technique in storytelling. In *Dim
Luster* each time the memory sets in the lights go out; when

they come on again the hero or heroine is brought back to reality.

It struck me that there was little difference in rhythm or dance style between the world of reality and that of imagination. There was a slight change in the mood, two of the memories were a trifle tender, two were a trifle frustrated; but I didn't see that the characters had much to choose between dreams and facts. And at the end, though they seemed disconcerted for a moment by their memories, hero and heroine ended by dancing like everyone else at the party. This slight touch of bitterness, of accepting an unsatisfactory reality since it is expected of you, is, I imagine, the real theme of the ballet. For *Dim Luster* Tudor has chosen as dance style something closer to exhibition ballroom dancing than to ballet. The dancing does not keep stopping in a pose as it does in other ballets of his; it is a continuous movement, reminiscent of *Lilac Garden*. Arm movements are of little interest. The dancing has an agitated rather than a sweeping effect; it looks heavy too.

The agitation is heightened by the empty loquacity of the score (R. Strauss's *Burleske,* an early piano concerto written previous to his conversion to Wagnerism). It is heightened, too, by the flat cartoon quality of the overloaded backdrop.

The dancers, however, especially the principals, dance as handsomely as one expects of them; Miss Kaye looks particularly lovely, and both Laing and Tudor are highly interesting as usual—*October 21, 1943.*

BACK TO THE FAIR AGAIN

DURING the intermission of Ballet Theater's matinee yesterday, the five golden tiers of the Metropolitan buzzed with children's conversations, and a little girl in the aisle downstairs, after gazing into the orchestra pit, couldn't quite keep her feet from trying a dance step.

The program began with Prokofieff's *Peter and the Wolf*, staged some years ago by Bolm. This reviewer finds that the steps that characterize the animals and people of the story are too often coy and conventional where one expects them to be fresh and true; to be sure Disney has set an extremely high standard for dancing animal impersonations. I also miss in this ballet a dance climax; the various characterizing phrases remain fragmentary, instead of developing into a coherent lively dance form. The young audience, however, does not realize what it is missing, and enjoys what it gets. The performance itself was a very pleasant one. Rex Cooper, who as the Wolf has the best part, dances it expressively, and he did, among other things, a very neat backward roll. Miss Alonso was a charming Bird.

The matinee also brought the second performance of Lichine's new ballet, *Fair at Sorochinsk*. A second view of it confirmed this reporter's impression that Lichine's gift as a choreographer is a highly notable one. It is shown clearest in the Russian folk-dance scene (At the Fair), which has a dance impetus that is straightforward and sure fire. Its effect is derived from the sharp shifts of the movement back and forth

60

from soloists to ensemble, and from the shift of attention between slower choral arm movement and rapid solo leg-and-
foot steps. But these shifts, large though they are, are so well
placed for the eye that the continuity is kept and the climactic
effect is inevitable.

Lichine's gift as shown in *The Fair at Sorochinsk* is a gift
for broad and rousing dance effects. There is clearly no great
seriousness in his treatment of diabolic forces—they are not
frightening. Clearly, too, the choreography is without the
complex overtones we are accustomed to in our best choreographers. There is no psychological strain, there is no poignant
tension in the conception of dance form. Lichine is not a poet-
choreographer as Balanchine so pre-eminently is.

But the firm control of frank vigor which Lichine has—and
he alone, it seems—is a quality to be highly admired. His good
scenes are straight and impulsive dancing, with no apologies
to what is fashionable. And the quiet lyric section at the end
of the Fair scene strikes me as being sincere and from the
heart—*October* 17, 1943.

FALL BALLET SEASON DISAPPOINTS

IN THE recent Ballet Theater season the new choreographies were—except for the Fair scene in Lichine's *Fair at
Sorochinsk*—disappointing. I am not referring to the disappointing roughness of execution of the opening nights, but
speaking of the ballets as they look at their best. At its best, a

little of Massine's *Mademoiselle Angot* was amusing in a sort
of over cute, opera bouffe style; and all of Tudor's *Dim Luster*
was a competent dance version of a modern English drawing-
room play. They both had less conviction than manner, and
both tried too anxiously to play safe; they were meant to look
elegant, but the effect they made was only a trivial one.
Luckily we know Massine and Tudor well enough as choreographers so that we needn't judge them merely by what dis-
appoints us.

Lichine, however, has not yet established a choreographic
reputation. He has shown several ballets, and beside four inconclusive ones, I remember with sincere pleasure the comedy
Graduation Ball, done by the de Basil company. *Helen of
Troy* in its present state is an excellent farce, and he is officially responsible; but after its many changes and after the
persistent rumors of large-scale collaboration, one hesitates to
judge him by it. The qualities in the Fair scene of *Sorochinsk*,
however, are distinctive and add a new style to our ballet
repertory. In this scene Lichine too plays safe (as do Massine
and Tudor), but he does it in more innocent a fashion. For
there is obviously never anything oblique about it, in intellectual or choreographic manner. The sentiment is straight,
the dancing vigorous or plain, and the sequence of it is determined by dance contrasts. The points it makes are simple
but they are not stupid: in the moonlight dance, the way the
girls sail easily across the stage when the boys have bowed to
them, the moment of hesitation (against the music) before
the boys grab the girls, the moment of delay (also against the
music) when they all face toward the moon and lift their arms
—these plain effects ring true after the multiple exuberance
of the folk dances before. It is no use looking for an intellec-

tual intentness or refinement in these dances; but it is a pleasure to find that whatever there is is aboveboard: the dancing carries as dancing, the sentiment carries as sentiment.

I am not speaking here of the foolish (Witches' Sabbath) scene in Lichine's ballet, but only of the Fair scene. The good scene is so long and complete that the bad one in the same ballet doesn't change my high opinion of Lichine's capability; but the bad one does, I am sorry to say, add to the other choreographic disappointments of this particular season. Incidentally, the Moussorgsky music for the Fair scene is magnificent to dance to; the *Bald Mountain* music of the Witches' scene isn't as good for dancing, and unless the dancers keep clear of the music's rhythm and beat they look dwarfed by its force—*November* 14, 1943.

BILLY THE KID AND ITS DANCE FAULTS

THE ballet *Billy the Kid* is a peculiar piece. Any sensible person can point out its absurdities, yet sensible people like it. It bobs up year after year in one company or another, always in inadequate performance, but it keeps on the boards. It is not satisfactory while you look at it, it is obscure and pieced out awkwardly; but something of it stays with you, something original that it alone has. I find its flavor very different from that of *Rodeo*, our other serious American ballet. *Rodeo* is about the West as it is lived in; *Billy* is about the

West as it is dreamed of, as it is imagined by boys playing in empty lots in the suburbs of our cities. And for this reason *Billy* is unreal in its local description, but real in its tragic play. An anthropologist would recognize it as an urban puberty ritual; I like it because there is somewhere in its folderol of stylization the sense that tragedy is natural, and this is, after all, the most interesting emotion that the theater can present.

Because *Billy* as a theater piece has a sense of the tragic, because the music is of the finest quality, and because *Billy* was frankly conceived as a serious artistic collaboration, I admire it sincerely. All the more because it was made around the corner and talks about things I know. Of course, if our big ballet companies could afford it, we should have, after all these years, more than merely two American ballets that are meant as a serious and touching image of the spirit. But till we get more such pieces we should at least pay attention to the two we have, watch and criticize and generally participate in their existence. Both ballets have naive faults of choppy, gesture by gesture pantomime; just the same both of them, in their main over-all expression, appeal to the imagination and get across a suggestion of reality to the audience. They are truer, in this respect, than many more adroit and more celebrated ballets.

Looking at the pantomime movements that Loring invented for *Billy*, I find them more interesting when they tend to be literal than when they tend to be symbolic. The storytelling gestures—those of the cowboys riding or strolling, the gun play, the sneaking up on the victim, Billy's turning away from his sweetheart or lying down, all this has more life as dancing than the gestures meant as "modern dance." The latter pound a beat, but often they don't add up to a dance rhythm.

The eye gets snagged on them, one at a time, as by sign

language. In the "March" for instance the energetic horizontal arm thrusts with open palms look as if our ballet dancers were mimicking "pushing back the frontier." The "Come-on-out-West" gestures back to the electricians off stage, the praying, digging, running, housekeeping, ever westward, ever westward is meant as a frieze of history; but it is history like that shown us in the slick-paper ads.

The technical fault is that the gesture does not lead out into space and relate to the full dimensions of the stage; it only leads back into the dancer's figure. It makes the stage close in on the dancer, instead of showing him boldly taking possession. Only the double turns in the air at the end of the "March" give an effect of real vigor.

On the other hand, the "Street Scene" that follows is most interesting. The wandering individual floor patterns by not emphasizing a fixed place on the stage and the gestures by not emphasizing a climax in rhythm give the sense of unfenced spaces and of all the time in the world. Nothing could be more characteristically American or more original as a dance conception.

But it is the lack of emphatic grouping, of a compact center of attention which makes the "Macabre Dance" a foolish letdown—much later on in the ballet. The center-stage ladder-like floor pattern of the "Gun Battle" just before has been so insistent that it would refresh the eye (and indicate a new scene) if there were a sudden focus on a new, completely different grouping off center. Instead, there is just a wavering line-up. (I wish, too, that the scene were danced straight as a naive celebration; the "macabre" element is mere la-dee-da. The steps themselves are all right.)

The half-hearted placing at this point blurs also the wander-

ing scenes that follow. Then, just in time, the climax is saved
by the interpolated waltz adagio, which is especially effective
if the girl seems to spin out the distances of her dance from
Billy's fixed position down stage right. Billy's death itself is
excellent as a scene and very much in character, particularly
if there is no nervousness in his movements, only wariness.

The character of Billy derives its interest not from his murders, but from his attempts at human contact, contact with his
mother, with his friend Garret, the Sheriff, and with his
sweetheart. His feeling for them is reciprocated. When this is
clear then the story of his solitary fate becomes tragic; really
tragic because he never appeals to us for sympathy or considers
himself wronged. He accepts his isolation and lives the life he
has. Billy's real enemy is the plain crowd of frontiersmen, who
being a crowd can ignore him and whom he ignores by an act of
pride. Billy's friend, Garret, is at ease in the crowd, but different from it; Billy and he are both individualists, but of opposite social types. I regret that the crucial dispute between
the two—over a card game at night on the prairie—no longer
expresses either their natural interest in one another or their
profound difference. And I regret that in the crowd scene
(Billy's first murder) Garret does not—now that Lew Christensen no longer dances the role—remain distinct enough from
the crowd either in the sustained smoothness of his movement
or in his stage presence.

Often Loring's contrasts between relaxed American movement and jerky, accentuated, Massine-style gesture are effective, often they seem accidental. But there is no doubt that
Loring was the first to bring this different quality in movement into a ballet. It is this that gives *Billy* its core of dance
sincerity, its fascination. And its further tragic implications,

though obscure and hesitant, are perfectly real if you look closely, and they make the ballet a very remarkable American theater piece. I haven't mentioned in this the role the Copland score plays, but it is a masterpiece, at every point a decisive help to realizing the poetic meaning of *Billy—October* 31, 1943.

EIGHTEENTH-CENTURY JIVE

AGNES DE MILLE'S new *Tally-Ho,* which had its local premiere last night on Ballet Theater's program at the Metropolitan, was not quite a hit, but it was certainly not a flop. And it is not an imitation of her previous ballets. She has created a new and touching character—the loving, intelligent, temptable wife, the woman of thirty. She has also found a different dance material for her wit to play with—the refined social dances of the French eighteenth century. She makes them over into something as lively, as sexy and as American as Broadway dancing. The farce-comedy numbers are brilliant. But there isn't enough serious dancing for contrast, and so the piece seems too much of one thing and long.

The story of *Tally-Ho* is a charming one. In the Louis XVI park of a French château, on a long, lovely summer day the lively young people of the court amuse themselves; they aren't prudish, they have a good time. Among the guests is a serious young man, "a genius" (Hugh Laing) and his wife (Miss de Mille). He loves his wife and he loves to read. The atmosphere doesn't trouble him, but it does trouble her. The Prince, a very grand young man indeed (Anton Dolin) sees her, follows her, finally meets her alone. She returns to her husband, and the charm goes out of the long afternoon. He slaps her, gently but clearly. Finally an innocent girl who just came to court that day (Lucia Chase) reconciles them, and the Prince grandly bows out.

The production by Ballet Theater is excellent. The choreography gives the principals (Maria Karnilova is also one) and the minor figures each a chance, and they all dance with distinction and wit. The decor is summery and out-of-doors (by Motley), the lighting excellent. The score—an arrangement of Gluck pieces by Paul Nordoff—has no musical distinction, but it is all of a piece and it makes the Gluck tunes sound a little like a hit parade of a few years back; it makes them serve for farce-comedy dancing.

Miss de Mille herself is wonderfully real on the stage, she is a great actress-dancer. Her own part is the quietest and the most graceful she has ever had. Her brilliant pantomime inventions, her shifts of rhythm and timing, her use of ballet for jokes at the expense of sex, and her group arrangements, these are full of variety. But the serious parts of the story that should support the jokes, these parts are too much in pantomime, so that they don't get a lift that they would have if they, too, were dances. She is poetic, and so is Mr. Laing in her presence on the stage; if her passages with him had been more "abstractly" dance passages, her comedy would have been a marvel. As it is, it is pleasant, but it relies on shock value, and that doesn't last all through.

The cast of the piece is admirable. Miss Karnilova, Miss Bentley and Miss Golden as the "bad" ladies are wonderfully witty and Lucia Chase as the dumpy little innocent succeeds completely in one of her most subtle roles—*April* 12, 1944.

PLEASURES OF FAMILIARITY

AT THE City Center last night the Ballet Russe de Monte Carlo opened its program with the oddly beautiful *Chopin Concerto,* a familiar ballet by Mme Nijinska set to the *E Minor Concerto.* It is an oddly beautiful one because it is clear and classic to the eye but tense and romantic in its emotion.

The structure of the piece—like that of much of Mme Nijinska's work—is based on a formal contrast: in the background rigid impersonal groups or clusters of dancers, that seem to have the weight of statues. In the foreground, rapid arrowy flights performed by individual soloists. One appreciates their flashes of lightness and freedom because of the weight they seem to rise over, as if the constraint of the group were the springboard for the soloist's release.

Sometimes Mme Nijinska—not unlike our own modern-school choreographers—may seem obsessed by her own neatness, by her own horror of leaving any loose ends of anatomy trailing around. But at her best—and *Chopin Concerto* is one of her best ballets—her stylization is strangely poignant. The contrast she achieves between the rigid poses and the tense brief freedom of ballet virtuosity has a romantic emotion very

true to the brilliance and poignancy of the Chopin music—
April 13, 1944.

BALANCHINE'S CLASSICISM

BALANCHINE'S *Serenade* was beautifully danced last night by the Monte Carlo at the City Center, and it is a completely beautiful ballet.

George Balanchine is the greatest choreographer of our time. He is Petipa's heir. His style is classical: grand without being impressive, clear without being strict. It is humane because it is based on the patterns the human body makes when it dances; it is not—like romantic choreography—based on patterns the human body cannot quite force itself into. His dance evolutions and figures are luminous in their spacing, and of a miraculous musicality in their impetus. Sentiment, fancy and wit give them warmth and immediacy. But as the audience actually watches, it all looks so playful and light, so unemphatic and delicate, it doesn't seem to call for noisy applause. Ten years later, when noisier successes have faded, one finds with surprise that his have kept intact their first freshness and their natural bloom.

Serenade is a kind of graduation exercise: The dancers seem to perform all the feats they have learned, both passages of dancing and passages of mime (or plastique). There is no story, though there seems to be a girl who meets a boy; he comes on with another girl and for a while all three are together; then at the end, the first girl is left alone and given a sort of tragic little apotheosis.

I was delighted to hear some giggling in the audience at the parts where all three were together—it showed how well the point got across; the audience at plays giggles too when the sentiment becomes intimate, it is our national way of reacting to that emotion. After giggling last night they gasped a little at some particularly beautiful lifts and then began applauding them—*April* 15, 1944.

HOW THE CHILDREN LIKE IT

A T THE City Center, at the Saturday matinee, the Monte Carlo gave their three-scene version of *The Nutcracker,* and the children in the audience were impressed when little Clara—no older than they—came on in the third scene and all the dancers bowed to her and she to them. But at the jumping Chinaman they crowed and burbled with pleasure all over the house. Later, they approved the rodeo scene in *Rodeo* as audibly, especially when the heroine fell off her imaginary horse and rolled over on the floor. A few of them, I imagine, will remember many years from now the gently wonderful radiance of Danilova and Youskevitch in *The Nutcracker* duets, and will be in doubt if dancing could really have been as beautiful as that. But it was.

In *Rodeo,* Vida Brown took Miss Etheridge's part as the cowgirl heroine. Miss Brown's version of the part is more open, more assertive, more horsey. She looks healthy and attractive, she puts the pantomime points across clearly and she has no trouble filling a star role. On the other hand she does not give—as Miss Etheridge so brilliantly does—the sense of a girl who only gradually discovers what it means to be a girl. It is this gradual, painful and at the end happy discovery that is the dramatic heart of the piece. And you realize that Miss Etheridge's cowgirl is really in love with the honest and open-hearted champion roper whom she gets; while Miss Brown's seems to take him good-naturedly as a second choice in place of the dark and fascinating chief wrangler—*April 16, 1944.*

PSEUDO-NAIVE

ANCIENT RUSSIA a new ballet by Bronislava Nijinska, for the Monte Carlo, had its second performance last night at the City Center. It is a slight piece, adroitly danced, and mounted very prettily in the bright sets Natalie Gontcharova made six years ago for Massine's uninventive *Bogatyri*.

Ancient Russia is better than *Bogatyri* because it is shorter and doesn't try so hard. But the Russian dark ages haven't had any adequate expression in ballet since Mme Nijinska's magnificent *Noces,* twenty years ago.

Ancient Russia tells a little legend in a sort of expensive Russian candy-box style. The story is of Russian women held prisoners by the bad Tartars, liberated by the good Russians, and it ends with a wedding for the stars. Action and dances have been squeezed to fit to Tchaikovsky's B *flat minor Piano Concerto*. They have no expressive relation to the music, and they don't have much invention. As dances they are small and pseudo-naive. The ensembles, except for a short moment of buffoonery, are nothing; Alexandra Danilova and Frederic Franklin have nothing of interest to do, but they remain agreeable and serious; Igor Youskevitch as the hero does two remarkably elegant brief numbers, extremely rapidly and whirling barely above the ground. His instant return to his quiet role right after the dancing is a prodigy of change of pace.

Saturday night the Monte Carlo had given its "new version" of Fokine's famous Polovtzian Dances from *Prince Igor*. The reason for a new version seems to be that the company is too small to dance the old one. The changes, at any rate, are all bad ones. Once again a few of the dancers, exuberant Frederic Franklin and the Polovtzian girls headed by Anna Scarpova, saved the day for the general public at least. The amazing costumes, as far as they are new, would serve better for a barbaric number Miss de Mille might compose to this music under the title of *Prince Igor on Second Avenue*.

Mme Nijinska's *Snow Maiden*, which I also saw over the week end at the City Center, flirts with greeting-card effects and sentiments. But the groupings and the dance phrases often develop very interestingly and by preserving just enough independence of rhythm in relation to the sugary Glazounoff score they keep a certain acid edge. The total result, if not a thrilling work, is yet a very elegant one. I find that only Igor Youskevitch has the right note of elegantly indicating the idyllic sentiments and of making the peasant dances take on a worldly halo of suavity—*April 17, 1944.*

SUPERB SUPER-VAUDEVILLE

JEROME ROBBINS' *Fancy Free,* the world premiere given by Ballet Theater last night at the Metropolitan, was so big a hit that the young participants all looked a little dazed as they took their bows. But beside being a smash hit, *Fancy Free* is a very remarkable comedy piece. Its sentiment of how people live in this country is completely intelligent and completely realistic. Its pantomime and its dances are witty, exuberant, and at every moment they feel natural. It is a direct, manly piece: there isn't any of that coy showing off of "folk" material that dancers are doing so much nowadays. The whole number is as sound as a superb vaudeville turn; in ballet terminology it is perfect American character ballet.

Straight character dancing has to do with low-life characters. *Fancy Free* deals with three sailors on shore leave who come into a bar. They pick up one girl who happens by, then a second girl. That makes two girls for three sailors. The three sailors first show off, and then they fight: result, they lose both girls. Now, too late, a third girl shows up. They decide it isn't worth getting into another fight about her. And then comes a tag-line, so to speak, and a blackout.

If you want to be technical you can find in the steps all sorts of references to our normal dance-hall steps, as they are done from Roseland to the Savoy; trucking, the boogie, knee-drops, even a round-the-back done in slow motion. But the details aren't called to your attention. Or when each of the sailors to show off does a specialty number you may take John

74

Kriza's turn (the second) as a Tudor parody and Jerome Robbins' rumba as a dig at Massine mannerisms. But they are just as effective without an extra implication. Most effective of them was the first dance of the three, Harold Lang's brilliant acrobatic turn, with splits like those of the Berry Brothers. It was in this number that the house took fire, and from there on the ballet was a smash.

Leonard Bernstein, the young composer of *Jeremiah,* wrote the score for *Fancy Free* and conducted it brilliantly. It has complex nervous rhythms and violent contrasts of thin and thick orchestral texture. I thought it a little overcomplicated, and not quite charming enough; but it was a hit, too, and the musicians I spoke to commented on the brilliance of its orchestration. I liked best the rumba for Robbins' solo. Oliver Smith's set is in the style of vaudeville sets, it is a perfect space for the seven characters of the piece to dance in, but it is less interesting to look at than his previous sets. It, too, was applauded. Kermit Love's costumes for the three girls were perfect. So were the girls—*April* 19, 1944.

(A Second View)

Fancy Free, the new Robbins-Bernstein-Smith triumph of Ballet Theater at the Metropolitan holds your interest as consistently the second time you see it as the first. The pacing of the ballet is very fine, and the sober moment at the close is real and appealing without being in the least pathetic. The game the sailors play with the first girl's purse, the recognition scene between the girls and the pauses before each of the sailor's solos—the passages all have a wit that is sound because it is not so affable as you expect. The piece is not conceived as a charm number.

The dancers don't play it as a charm number either. They dance it with a direct vitality and a sense of real life that are even more remarkable than their dance brilliance. The three sailors, of course, (Robbins, Kriza and Lang) have the best roles. But Janet Reed's transition from the stiffness she first gives her hard-boiled part to the later natural abandon is superb. Equally astonishing is how Muriel Bentley and Shirley Eckl instantly convey the particular character of their roles; you know all about these girls, and you remember even the one you only see for a moment distinctly.

I noticed the second time how forcefully the score seconds the dramatic effects and builds big climaxes where they are needed and where the small cast couldn't quite create them alone. The orchestra under Mr. Bernstein plays magnificently. As for the set, when the curtain went up the house broke into real applause, and a gentleman back of me said, "Solid!" under his breath—*April 24, 1944.*

BALLET THEATER'S PARSIFAL

TUDOR'S *Dark Elegies,* on yesterday's program at the Metropolitan, is Ballet Theater's *Parsifal.* A sort of Weihefestspiel given only once or twice a season, it is said to be Tudor's favorite among his works, and Miss Kaye and Mr. Laing, the stars who interpret his work so brilliantly, are said to consider it his masterpiece. The reviewer feels respect for these opinions, but he does not share them.

Dark Elegies is set to Mahler's *Kindertotenlieder*, a luxurious, slightly overstuffed symphonic setting of the touchingly intimate song cycle by Rueckert on the death of a child in the family. In the orchestra a man sings the words. On the stage seven young women and four young men, dressed in the Youth Movement fashions of Republican Germany, dance a stylized version of Nordic folk dances. The dance figures have the flavor of a vestigial ritual and the solemn expression of the dancers is ritualistic also. They look a little like modern dancers of some years back doing a symbolic number.

The actual dance detail of *Dark Elegies* is willfully spare, but it is also of a remarkable elegance in its arrangement. The timing of the accents, the placing of the dancers, the correspondences of dance phrases to musical ones, the variety of invention—all this is completely interesting. The look of helplessness in the men's arm movements, in the women's toe-steps and in the remarkable lifts has a distinct pathos. The running circles at the climax are very effective. But the fact that this helpless and impoverished tone is continued so long, and continued even during the consolatory last section, leaves me with the feeling that at the end there has been no dramatic progress, that the stage characters have exhibited their suffering and have gone off content with that. It gives the ballet a faintly stuffy, holier-than-thou expression—*April* 26, 1944.

BRIGHT PLUMAGE

THE Monte Carlo opened the new dance season last night at City Center with a new ballet as beautiful and elusive as the play of bright birds in a garden, birds fluttering, stalking, twittering and teasing one another; joyous birds that we watch in a summer of wartime.

The program and the costumes did not explain anything. The above is the reviewer's account of the new *Danses Concertantes,* choreography by George Balanchine, music by Igor Stravinsky, costumes and backdrops by Eugene Berman. It is a sumptuous and yet a delicate production, and it is all of a piece. It was greeted with cheers last night, as a work so rich in sensuous delight and one so perfect in workmanship deserved. But even after the loud applause, the new piece keeps a strangeness in its joyous flutter that is fascinatingly elusive.

Danses Concertantes is a ballet without a plot, a suite of dances. One can distinguish a sort of flirtation between the two stars—a flirtation that they know beforehand will come out happily, but that they do for fun. Twelve other dancers, divided in groups each with two girls and one boy, form the chorus; and each group has a special little number of its own. The effervescence and the grace of the dance invention all through is extraordinary; here and there are little jokes, jokes of style like the jazz steps, or like the entwining figures that dancers make holding hands; but nothing is emphatic, it is all lightly done, and already they are doing something else.

Astonishing is the ease with which Balanchine understands the flow of the unsymmetrical periods of the music and gives them a visual grace and a logic that illuminates the musician's musical intentions. The music is delicious instrumentally, but it is very firm in its melodic and rhythmic logic, and the absence of any rhetoric gives it a gentle serenity that is strangely bewitching. It is that rarity, a modest masterpiece.

The costumes and backdrops by Berman are so striking that they stopped the show. They are also of an originality in elegance that we all too rarely see on the New York stage. A ballet that is choreographically, musically and scenically first class is a big event in the dance world at any time and anywhere; the Monte Carlo is to be thanked for giving us once more that great pleasure, a real ballet production. That the work makes no effort to impress by scale makes it, if one may say so, all the more touching—*September* 11, 1944.

VINTAGE OF CHU-CHIN-CHOW

SEEN on a current ballet program, *Scheherazade*, which was on the Monte Carlo bill last night, is an illustrious warhorse foundering in dishonor. Not that there isn't some kind of life left in the old girl. The bundling and the clinches are still fine for laughs and whistles and cries of "Take it off"; the piece would still be a wow on the G.I. circuit. One sees a great many people register sex all over the stage with an earnestness that is disarming rather than embarrassing. But one wonders what *Scheherazade* could have looked like when it scandalized our parents or when Parisians swooned at the lushness of it in 1910.

In the 1910 photographs the slave girls look soft and abandoned. Nijinsky bounded about them like a panther in thrilling spasms that grew to a paroxysm of death at the climax. Bakst, the great decorator—the Berman of his day—dazzled the public by the sensual shock of his brilliant décor. And the "Slavic harmonies" of Rimsky's score dunked the orgy on stage in a bath of gold.

Nowadays the small orchestra, the clumsily executed décor, the earnest but overworked dancers can't create any sense of abandon. The trouble is that there is no dance form, nothing for them to do as dancers. There is only miming and hubbub, and that doesn't keep for thirty years. A dance ballet can keep fresh because of its form, because arms and legs stay arms and legs; but when the dancers have to pretend to be something they aren't, a ballet gradually disintegrates into a charade.

A pleasant charade when, as last night, the exquisite Danilova sits and stalks with an imperious delicacy and dies with an oriental sincerity. It is at the end that Fokine's timing still makes good theater—*September* 14, 1944.

BALANCHINE'S DANSES CONCERTANTES

THE Monte Carlo's new *Danses Concertantes* is a glittering little piece, brilliantly animated and brilliantly civilized. As a production it combines the talents of Stravinsky, Balanchine and Berman—a ballet composer, a choreographer and a ballet decorator so eminent that each in his field can be called the best in the world. A new piece involving any one of them is something to look forward to; a piece that involves all three at once and allows each to do his sincere best, is that rare luxury, a ballet production in the grand style—in the grand style Diaghileff insisted upon and thanks to which ballet acquired its peculiar artistic prestige. *Danses Concertantes,* with fourteen dancers on stage for twenty minutes, is a ballet quite small in scale. But as a new ballet by three great artists it is a big event, an event of interest to London, Paris and Moscow, an event the American ballet world can take pride in.

The first thrill of *Danses Concertantes* is that of Berman's costumes and drops. Before an inner curtain the dancers cross over quickly by twos and threes, bowing to the audience, looking as brilliant as scarabs, if scarabs came in several colors. Then the inner curtain rises. Now the dancers stand assembled, glittering sharply against a black drop, but it is a drop that is as atmospheric as the open sky of night. You peer into nocturnal distance. And in this lofty blackness every motion of the dancers coruscates. Berman has emphasized their limbs and molded their bodies with black ornaments and with rhinestones so that each motion is distinct in itself.

The dancing is a suite of brief numbers, classically correct in steps but in surprising sequences that contrast sharply and have a quick effervescent invention. The changes from staccato movements to continuous ones, from rapid leaps and displacements to standing still, from one dancer solo to several all at once follow hard on one another. The rhythm is unexpected. But the shift of the figures and the order of the steps is miraculously logical and light, and so even fitful changes have a grace and a spontaneous impetus. What had first seemed separate spurts, stops and clipped stalkings turn out to be a single long phrase or impulse that has risen and subsided in a group of dancers simultaneously. The line of the large phrase is seen in their relations to one another, and each dancer independently remains open and free in bearing, the arms natural and elegant.

One notices how each dancer in all this coruscating complexity remains a charming and a natural person. They are like characters in a garden, individuals who communicate, respond, who modify and return without losing their distinctness. The dance is like a conversation in Henry James, as surprising, as sensitive, as forbearing, as full of slyness and fancy. The joyousness of it is the pleasure of being civilized, of being what we really are, born into a millennial urban civilization. This is where we are and this is what the mind makes beautiful. *Danses Concertantes* makes it beautiful by presenting a sumptuous little garden pastoral, a highly artificial, a very exact and a delicately adjusted entertainment.

The dancers performed the piece to perfection. Even those of them just out of school danced like soloists, with a light and civilized deportment. And Danilova and Franklin, the stars whose happy flirtation is the central theme of the piece—and a birdlike duet it is—characterized their parts charmingly and lightly—he with the fatuousness of a happy male, she with the willfulness of a tender woman—*September* 17, 1944.

SCALLIONS TO THE MANAGEMENT

LE BOURGEOIS GENTILHOMME, the new ballet the Monte Carlo presented at the City Center Saturday, could have been a delightfully elegant trifle. But despite the magnificence of its decoration, it opened lamentably. The piece failed because the management showed it half-baked. The public came for a premiere and was shown a disheveled dress rehearsal. The ballet was ruined, the public imposed upon. This has happened before at ballet premieres, and it is a malpractice.

Your reporter, however, does not want to throw out the baby with the bath. *Le Bourgeois Gentilhomme*, even in its present puling state, reveals too much originality to be blamed for the debacle. It is—or some day will be—a dance entertainment by George Balanchine, mounted by Eugene Berman and set to Richard Strauss's incidental music to the play of Molière. The action of the ballet covers the love interest and Turkish ceremony of the play and serves as a framework for a series of dances, for a ballet vaudeville of several joking pantomimes, two character pieces, a classic number and one very touchingly playful love duet. What survived of these dances Saturday night was never commonplace in detail, and their originality of tone lies in their relaxed unseriousness; *Bourgeois* is much more relaxed than *Danses Concertantes*.

Le Bourgeois has no intention other than to be a feast for the eyes, a dance dessert, fantastic and light, of a splendor evoking the after-dinner ballet amusements of Louis XIV and of the munificent Fouquet. The pomp of *Le Bourgeois* is a

83

triumph for Berman. To see such novel invention and dazzling taste in splendor is an intense delight; it was on Saturday even though the costumes were pinned on and sometimes tore, even though the stage was abominably lit.

In the dancing Miss Moylan and especially Miss Maria Tallchief sparkled, and brave Miss Krassovska looked very pretty. The company was valiant, inaccurate and frightened. The Strauss score is so amorphous that it would take several orchestra rehearsals for the dancers to catch their cues and the instrumentalists to mark the rhythm. It is a cumbersomely Teutonic score, but having accepted it the management was bound to rehearse it.

But the management's most shocking error was to open *Le Bourgeois* without a real star to pull it together, to be a focus of attention. After Franklin's accident two weeks ago Magallanes took over his part. Magallanes is an honest but far from a sparkling young dancer. In addition he had turned his ankle two nights before the opening. After doing leads all evening before *Le Bourgeois*—and, according to the program, at the Saturday matinee also—it was no wonder that by 11:30, when the crucial love duet got going, he could barely hobble through it—*September 25, 1944.*

COPPELIA TELLS THE FACTS OF LIFE

THE Monte Carlo *Coppelia* might well be more celebrated than it is. With radiant Miss Danilova and either Franklin or Youskevitch in the leads, and given in its entirety—as it

wasn't this fall—it is a very happy version of a delightful
classic. The score Delibes made for it so carefully has lost
none of its charms. And in the Monte Carlo production the
choreography and the decoration are—like the music—distinguished, gracious and light. *Coppelia* is a modest little
comedy, but it has a peculiar grace, an 1870 secret, a bouquet
as fresh as a summer morning in the country. The Monte
Carlo dancers dance it clearly, they do it gaily and they do it
straight. And, thanks to their lack of affectation, I noticed
with some surprise that if you follow the action quite literally
it isn't a silly story, as people claim it is. A part of *Coppelia's*
secret is the serious good sense with which it treats a serious
subject—the basis for a good marriage.

This is the action you watch: Two very lively and very real
young persons love each other and are about to marry. But the
boy is struck by the sight of a mysterious stranger, the beautiful Coppelia, who sits on a balcony. Naturally, his first girl is
vexed and hurt. That night the mysterious Coppelia turns out
to be only a mechanical doll. The flesh-and-blood girl breaks
the doll, she harries the old dollmaker, she even rescues the
boy whom the dollmaker has drugged with a sinister intent.
The boy acknowledges his fault, and the next day there is a
celebration at which the local duke pays for everything, the
boys and girls all get married and get money, and everybody
watches dancing and dances happily, too.

Critics have claimed that the celebration scene added nothing and could as well be omitted. It cannot, because you
haven't until then seen the boy and girl dance together and
exhibit all their virtuosity, their combined dance power at its
highest pitch. When you see their motions and physical proportions beautifully balanced, when you see them harmoni-

ously overcoming impossible difficulties, you have seen a convincing image of what would make two young lovers happy in marriage.

And the divertissement that clusters round this grand duet bears logically on the same subject. The dances are entitled "Dawn" (a solo), "Prayer," "Work" and "Follies" (several of them); and taken together the series represents rather well the nonsexual basis for a happy domestic life. On the other hand, the pitfalls that prevent marriage are told in the earlier action, when the boy is infatuated by a beautifully mechanical ideal: he wants a real girl and he wants an ideal one in addition. In this psychological dilemma, like a man, he goes to sleep. But the girl, like a Shavian heroine, solves the dilemma by her independent courage. And then the boy proves his real worth by his strength and his gentle control in the nuptial dance duet. All these ideas of marriage are reasonable ones; though the lightness, the wit and tenderness they have in dancing is lost in retelling.

As you watch the dance you notice how the more perturbing the emotion becomes, the purer becomes the movement of dancing and the more open and free the dancer's bearing. You see the magic of the heart's sincerity, its most urgent necessity, transform a village girl into a grand and gracious ballerina. And what a solace the transformation is! But *Coppelia* has only two such really serious episodes; it shifts easily to a pantomime scene, to a folk dance, to a sparkling parody. Its theme is domestic and it ends with a modest circle of dancers inclosing the stars in a running ring. I only wish the young Monte Carlo would take some lessons in classic pantomime; it is a charming game when dancers play it right. And I wish I had space to tell you about Danilova, who is the most wonderful *Coppelia* heroine in the world—*September 24, 1944.*

DANCING FOR FUN

FOR the third time this fall George Balanchine has given us a dance ballet of the best quality and for the third time the opening performance has not been a good one. Last night Ballet Theater gave the local premiere of his *Waltz Academy* at the Metropolitan. One had to watch the sweet and open little ballet closely to see its remarkable virtues. The lambent grace, the joyous lightness in invention, and the gently rising climax of keen delight in dancing—these happy qualities of structure did not shine as brightly as they might have. But they are the qualities of which Balanchine has built *Waltz Academy.*

Waltz Academy is a dance suite which takes its departure from morning ballet practice in the rehearsal room. Oliver Smith's set suggests a loft under a wonderful cupola, a hint of the rehearsal room at the Paris Opera and somehow a hint of the old Aquarium too. It is airy, modest and alive, and his most distinguished set to date. Into this room the dancers come, the girls in bright tarlatans, the boys in the practice uniform of the Maryinsky (costumes by Alvin Colt). They do a few of the traditional exercises, there is a little joke or two, and soon they are crowding into the center for the second part of practice. But, instead, they start to dance, and the rest of the ballet is a suite of pretty dances that show young dancers in all their airy brilliance and vivacity.

Last night it was Nora Kaye who was the truest and sweetest (and most brilliant) of the young dancers. But Janet Reed, Albia Kavan, John Kriza and Harold Lang (who held himself particularly well) were all of them excellent. The misfortune of the performance seemed to be trouble in the first pas de six, and a misplaced miming of glamor in the climactic pas de deux of Miss Gollner and Mr. Petroff, which did not look humorous and spoiled a beautiful dance. The score was played too slowly and that may well have troubled the company.

The score, a new one by Vittorio Rieti, is a melodious and witty and elegantly written one. It is excellent for dancing and agreeable to hear.

Waltz Academy is a great addition to the Ballet Theater repertory, which lacks contemporary dance ballets that are neither ironic nor topical. *Waltz Academy* is dancing for the pleasure of dancing; a ballet for dancers and dance lovers. It will be a pleasure to see repeatedly, and to see emerge into full brilliance—*October* 12, 1944.

AURORA AND PETIPA

WATCHING Ballet Theater's *Princess Aurora* last Tuesday in a routine performance—no super-stars around—I was struck by how sincerely the piece itself has come to interest the audience. They take to it as a piece, for its animation as dancing, its choreographic atmosphere. A few years ago this 1890 Petipa number used to interest the public very little and the company even less. Everyone waited around for the leaps in the "Bluebird" and then for the Rose adagio, as a kind of obstacle course. And when Ballet Theater first did its *Aurora* back in '41, as lively an effect as any was the one made by the king who entered with a grand fanfare and without his trousers on. But that was before the present response to classic dancing. Now the interest of the audience is, it seems to me, teaching the company, too, to take a livelier interest. On both sides of the footlights there is a growing realization that the Petipa style expects all the dancing by everyone on stage to contribute actively to a theater spell.

The public begins to recognize the classic spell and it wants all the dancers to help create it and to keep within it. They are expected to keep the same animated and spontaneous elegance in simple steps that the ballerina shows in her grand-prize feats. The fine hint of abandon or of heartbreak that her acrobatics can have in a Petipa ballet needs the foil of youthful spirits in the rest of the company. One enjoys her firm delicacy far more in a surrounding atmosphere of clear and buoyant grace, and only accurate classic ensemble dancing can create such an over-all spell.

Now that the public appreciates accurate ensemble dancing, we might also have longer versions of classic ballets. The climactic dance thrills make more sense theatrically in their context; the proper approach, the proper tempo for a climax is created by introductory numbers and by contrasting kinds of dances, and the big duets, coming where they were intended, look more touchingly noble, more natural, even. We might have a renovated *Aurora* as long as our present *Giselle*—and what a ballet for Eugene Berman to mount that would be! And to renovate *Aurora* handsomely, Ballet Theater might also ask the great dancer Pierre Vladimiroff to dance Prince Charming and show us for once what the Maryinsky grand manner in supporting a ballerina really looks like.

The present *Aurora* is merely a selection from the three-act *Sleeping Beauty* of Petipa. The lovely string of solos, for instance, that now comes in the middle, was originally intended as a string of dances by Good Fairies who are bringing gifts of beauty to the infant princess—the grace of pine woods, or that of humming birds, or that of song birds, or that of particular flowers. The light evocation of these graces of nature—in the dances and in the Tchaikovsky score—and the sense of blessing a child with them are a part of the full effect of these solos. Placed as they are in *Sleeping Beauty*, their story point does not change the steps and gestures but it colors the dancer's attack. And similarly the Rose adagio, too, has a story context which gives its formal bravura an amiable overtone.

It is a proof of Petipa's great power as a choreographer that even without their context those of his dances we see can create a wonderful spell. They are not show-off numbers; they all have some basis in human relationships. But they are not meant to be mimed, they are meant to be danced. Even without knowing what their story function may be, an attention to their rhythmic and plastic detail, a response to their impetus and current as dancing is enough to delight the audience and to make the dancer on stage look her very best. And by his choreographic virtue, Marius Petipa, who was born in France in 1822 and died in Russia in 1910, is now here in the United States—like a living man—enlivening dancers and audience, and actively animating an art he loved—*October 22, 1944.*

NEW YORK'S NEW BALLET

BALLET INTERNATIONAL, the ballet intended primarily as a New York company, opened its handsome home, the International Theater on Columbus Circle, last night, to a distinguished audience eager to be friendly. The occasion didn't quite come off. One had expected a clear sense of artistic unity, a sense of style, and that didn't show at this first performance. A sense of style in ballet is what we badly need just now.

This first program brought two world premieres in *Brahms Variations* and *Colloque Sentimental,* a revival of Fokine's *Sylphides* and one of Mme Nijinska's *Bolero.*

The *Brahms,* which Mme Nijinska has set to the Hadyn and Paganini *Variations,* is two ballets in one. It is endless, highly ingenious and pointless. Perhaps the décor by Vertés is its worst feature; in any case, it kills the dance. It makes the stage look like a perfume counter in a department store. One did see André Eglevsky dancing magnificently, better than he has ever danced, and looking extraordinarily handsome. All the other dancers were leaping about and forming uninteresting plastic groups. A good deal of soulful throwing back of heads didn't help. A disappointment generally.

Colloque Sentimental is a muted duet set by Eglevsky to a rich, elegantly gloomy and mellifluous score by Paul Bowles. It has a brilliantly novel gray backdrop by Dali that crowds the dancers forward. Everything is tangled up in long white streamers of veils and an enormous stage turtle with more veils and autumn leaves goes into action, crawling. The whole has a strange morbid calm. It has style and it is supposed to be about memory. Marie-Jeanne and Eglevsky were the principals and lovely they looked.

Sylphides, rehearsed by Mme Fokina, opened the program. It was interesting in a certain greater animation in the choreography that distinguished it from the usual versions, a clearer sense of climax. The corps de ballet was not of course as good as that of Ballet Theater, nor even of the Monte Carlo. Marie-Jeanne was delicate in the valse and pas de deux. William Dollar, who had the male role and did some rushing leaps, is an interesting dancer; he looks unsure but he also looks very alive.

One of the fine features of International is its excellent orchestra; it is a pleasure to have an accurate and also a sensitive orchestra, as it was under Alexander Smallens' direction. I am not sure he always helps the choreographic effects, but he certainly gives musical distinction to ballet, a place where it is badly needed.

Ballet International has a number of elements of distinction. They do not get their full value, because they are not given clear preponderance. The dancers themselves as an ensemble are not brilliant, but they are well rehearsed. Still, ballet companies are not created in a few months' rehearsal. It takes a good deal of dancing together in performance for everyone, including the management, to see what they are really after. But a resident ballet company, and one with excellent intentions in artistic directions, is something New York dance lovers can well be a little patient with, at its beginning—*October* 31, 1944.

FINE PETIPA

THE grand pas de deux from *Don Quixote*, which Tamara Toumanova and Anton Dolin performed last night for the first time, is the best dancing of the three classic duets they have done during this Ballet Theater season at the Metropolitan. It is the best because it is closest to true Petipa style. It shows you arms as well as legs, and it projects an atmosphere. Miss Toumanova's powerful impetus and assurance, for once strictly disciplined, was thoroughly impressive.

The duet, now staged by Mr. Oboukhoff, the great Petersburg dancer, is from a full-length 1869 ballet by Petipa, and it was last seen here in 1926 danced by Pavlova. It is striking how Petipa as choreographer does not repeat his big effects; how clear and grand the line of the dance is and the figures the two bodies form, and how the emotion rises in joyousness from the opening straight lifts to the final brilliant zigzag of leaps by the man and the dazzling whirling circle by the ballerina.

In the adagio Miss Toumanova's arms were clearly placed; and her feats, particularly a climactic arabesque, were bold and stunning; the following pizzicato variation was for its steely sharpness even more extraordinary. One regretted a trifle the unconvincing broad smile she had, and even more the trick of milking the applause whenever possible. This dance is a brief joyous number, and would have a much greater cumulative effect danced right into incidental applause—*October 26, 1944.*

POOR FOKINE

BALLET THEATER presented last night at the Metropolitan a revival of Fokine's *Carnaval*, said to have been taught the company by Fokine himself some years ago. They must have forgotten meanwhile what he taught them. The Monte Carlo *Carnaval*—dilapidated as that is—has more precision and more flavor than this one. Ballet Theater's looked amateurish, empty and pointless despite a cast of fine dancers.

Carnaval is a very famous piece and the enraptured reviews of thirty years ago are perfectly convincing reading. In my own experience Danilova and Youskevitch as Columbine and Harlequin have been wonderfully fascinating, but the piece as a whole has never made any sense at all. Its effervescence, subtle characterization, malicious wit, delicacy of sentiment, I only know from history books.

Last night Miss Chase mimed Columbine prettily but she didn't dance the part. Mr. Tudor strangely enough conveyed nothing of interest as Pierrot. Lovely Miss Karnilova gave her Chiarina a dim trace of warmth and lightness. Orloff's Pantaloon had some wit but was rowdy. Hugh Laing had trouble with his hat. Miss Hightower's impetuous Papillon and several very good passages of Harold Lang's Harlequin were the only dancing done. Mr. Lang has not yet the sharpness of beats, pirouettes and turns in the air, nor the lithe malice the part calls for. But he could learn; he has strength, naturalness and animation, he is by nature a fine dancer, and one always likes to see him.

94

Set and costumes for *Carnaval* were rudely executed after the Bakst sketches. Well—poor Fokine!—*October* 27, 1944.

MECHANIZED FARM

BRONISLAVA NIJINSKA'S *Pictures at an Exhibition,* the world premiere of which Ballet International offered last night at the International Theater, is an orderly group composition in stylized Soviet-Russian clothes, a sort of mechanized Russian farm celebration, without much dancing or very interesting ideas. The company as a whole gave a perfectly satisfactory performance.

The choreography is a stylization of Russian folk steps and village games. It has a good many chain-gang huddles and a number of rows standing face upward, looking fervently glad. Instead of looking like a monument, however, the piece looks like a poster. The community farmers look careful and clean but not—as the farmers in Nijinska's *Les Noces* did—anonymously passionate and powerful. The sports and jokes, the joys and sorrows that the piece is about have not in the dance a rhythm startling or jubilant enough to be emotionally convincing. *Pictures* is a serious, a remarkably ingenious, work, but it is not a bright one.

Pictures is based, the program states, on "the essentially Russian spirit of Moussorgsky's music" and set to most of his *Pictures at an Exhibition* (orchestrated by Ivan Boutnikoff). The score's descriptive side is very often ignored; its melodic line is ignored, too, and the rhythmic counterpoint that the dance offers is overheavy. The finale, which mimics pulling on ropes to ring bells, doesn't work in the dance and it doesn't work in the score either. Unfortunately all through the ballet the spirit of the music is much more amusing, cordial and nobly direct than what you see on stage, much more alive and easy.

Pictures gains immensely by a clean stage design by Boris Aronson. The production is supposed to resemble Soviet staging of the present; there is in the dance action a certain reminiscence of the "Blue Blouse" or Agitprop technique of twenty years ago but the photographs of present Moscow ballet staging are much more like International's *Sylphides*. Aronson has imitated pine boards, monk's cloth and such materials; they would have been prettier real than painted; nevertheless I very much enjoyed the clear space of the décor and the general coolness. Miss Geleznova danced the lead very charmingly—*November* 4, 1944.

BRIGHT AND PRETTY

M*UTE WIFE,* last night's novelty at the International on Columbus Circle, is a bright piece in perfect taste, a little dance comedy with intelligent choreography (Antonia Cobos), elegant mounting (Rico Le Brun) and excellent orchestration (Vittorio Rieti orchestrating Paganini). It is a trifle that is fun to watch and a first-rate production that puts you in fine humor.

The action follows the plot of Anatole France's play—a husband who has his pretty wife cured of muteness only to find her chatter unbearable and take refuge in deafness himself. Miss Cobos has left out France's Rabelaisian overtones and transposed the action to a politer eighteenth-century Spain; and her dance idiom is largely "classic" Spanish—an amusing novelty, too.

She herself acts and dances the lead with restraint and with an intelligence not unlike that of her fellow Californian, Miss de Mille. She is not a strong dancer, but she is an interesting one. She expresses her muteness rather as an elegant frustration. Her operation scene, with hints of bullfighting, is inventive. When, after that, Miss Cobos chatters with castanets and heeltaps, she rather draws out the effect too long, but the confusion of household is well timed in detail. It is a pity there is no general dance at least at the climax, but the smaller dance numbers are clear. Miss Cobos is a promising choreographer.

Mr. Moncion as the husband was excellent, and his miming of deafness at the end last night pulled the piece together just in time. In the smaller parts all the dancers were shown to their best advantage. They were inventively costumed, too, and Miss Cobos' own eighteenth-century "precautionary drawers" were charming. As a stage designer, Mr. Le Brun takes Eugene Berman for his model and does very well that way.

Rieti's orchestration is sour and sweet in happy juxtaposition, and though it seems sometimes a little too soft for the dancers to hear, it generally makes the orchestra sound rich and varied, and always musically elegant. George Schick conducted excellently—*November* 23, 1944.

THE NUTCRACKER 1890 MODEL
BALLET

THINKING of Christmas, I remembered the Christmas tree conspicuously on stage and the Christmas party in the first scene of *The Nutcracker,* the venerable fairy-tale ballet that Petipa's collaborator Ivanoff set long ago to Tchaikovsky's lovely score. Has the action anything to do with Christmas? What is its nonsense plot really about and how does *The Nutcracker* create its mild and beneficent spell? This serene old vehicle, complete with all the 1890 ballet conventions—pantomime scene, ballroom dance, grand pas de deux, divertissement and ballabile, all of them strung in a row on a story nobody pays attention to—still works as a theater piece. It does even in such a form as the Monte Carlo's three-scene version, which though cut, patched and mauled by years of hard wear, keeps the formal continuity of the original three acts. At the Monte Carlo most of the young dancers show no manners in the pantomime part and they may do their stint in the dance scenes as if they were reciting *Thanatopsis.* But the great Danilova as the Sugar Plum Fairy (especially with Youskevitch as partner) has a radiant and tender presence that lets you see the heart of the ballet and convinces you of its expressive power. Through her performance the choreographic intentions of the work emerge once more. If you are curious about choreography, you find that the dance logic of *The Nutcracker* is solid and that the nonsense plot—its idea content—has a rational structure too. The intentions of *The Nutcracker,* when you do catch on, are hu-

98

mane and sensible, and its 1890 formal method is highly intelligent.

What is the method? This is what happens on the stage. The long first scene is a clear pantomime story. The dance is plain, realistic, without embellishments, it does not lead to leaps; it is all *terre à terre*. The second and third scenes, in contrast to the first, tell hardly any story; instead they are dancing that clearly looks like dancing, with steps in patterns, leaps and lifts, dancing with "elevation." The two dance scenes are made up of successive dance numbers, each with a beginning and an ending, each a set piece, all of them together arranged in a suite ending with an ensemble finale.

The suite method in ballet, as in opera, does not have the urgency of the continuous, symphonic method. The suite ballet does not try so hard to get somewhere. The emotional tone is stable, it changes en bloc from number to number. The series of emotions that constitute the whole work are grouped in clear rubrics, the imagination dwells on one at a time and then proceeds satisfied to the next. The momentary detail is seen in relation to the number it appears in; when the number is finished one has a complete image, and the detail loses its insistency. There is a sense of repose in action, a control of the emotion that is both modest and noble. In short, the set-piece structure is not at all a foolish device.

The Nutcracker is not foolish in form, nor is it foolish either in its literal content. It is a fairy-tale ballet and certainly looks like nonsense. But nowadays with psychoanalysis practically a household remedy, grownups take the nonsense of fairy tales more seriously than children. We call them narratives in free association and solve them like crossword puzzles. *The Nutcracker* is an easy one—the title gives it away. The story begins on Christmas Eve in an upper-class home, the *locus classicus* of ambivalent anxiety. An elderly bachelor with one eye gives a pre-adolescent girl a male nutcracker (the symbols and inversion couldn't be more harrowing). Her young brother tears it away from her by force and breaks it. But she takes it up from the floor and nurses it; she loves it. She dreams that the nutcracker turns almost into a boy. Then she dreams of a deep forest in winter with restless girl-snowflakes and a handsome young man who keeps lifting up a young lady (and who is this lady but the little heroine's own dream image?). And after that she dreams she is watching a lot of dancing Chinamen and Russians and oddly dressed people—all of them somehow "sweets"; and at last the previous young man and the previous young lady turn up again, too. They furnish a brilliant climax, and that leads to a happy dazzle for everything and everybody everywhere at once.

You can see that the suite of dances presents an intelligible association series, operated with unconscious sexual symbols; that the piece makes sense enough as a subconscious reverie beginning with a cruel sexual symbol, the nutcracker, which is also its literal title; and in this sense the various subjects of its pantomime and dance scenes are intelligible, too. It is the kind of sense one expects of a fairy-tale plot, since it is how fairy tales are rationally understood. But what you see on the stage is a suite of well-mannered dances, graceful and clear. The clarity of the dance suite form controls the pressure of the unconscious theme and by easy stages brings on a pleasing change of emotion. Using the methods of 1890, *The Nutcracker* reaches an unconsciously satisfying final goal by a series of choreographic effects, and even in what appear to be merely formal evolutions, this old-fashioned dance entertainment follows a sincere emotional logic.

At the start of the piece, the effect of the pantomime scene—sadistic in content for all its upper-class Christmas party manners—is gloomy and oppressed; the dancers don't really get off the floor. What a relief when the dancing begins with leaps and airy lifts in the next snow scene. But the choreography here preserves a coolness and a remoteness that doesn't quite satisfy. The third, last scene, is friendlier, lighter, more open to the audience, more animated, more playful in detail, and in the end there is a happy sense that everyone on the stage has leaped about freely and sufficiently. So they can all stop and smile straight at you, looking pretty without the least embarrassment.

And there is another unconscious satisfaction in the sequence of the dances. For the strictness of bodily control inherent in dance virtuosity, a strictness that grows more exacting as the dance becomes more animated and complex, seems at the end a satisfactory sublimation for the savagely cruel impulses suggested in the disturbing pantomime opening of the piece. And so *The Nutcracker* is really a dream about Christmas, since it succeeds in turning envy and pain into lovely invention and social harmony.

Compare this conciliatory dream libretto with the dream libretto of the Dali-Massine *Bacchanale*. The latter proceeds from anxiety to disgust and hysteria and bogs down in a pile of umbrellas. If one took the *Bacchanale* seriously one would find it a very unsatisfactory story.

No doubt Ivanoff, the choreographer of *The Nutcracker*, didn't look for symbols in a fairy tale; he was interested in danc-

ing that one could see clearly and that would have a cumulative effect. He would find my account of his ballet absurd, and
so would the many thousands who like it and don't ask for a
reason. Thousands of people all over the world find *The Nutcracker* touching and comforting without knowing why. My
point is simply that if you look for a reason, if you are interested in what ballet means rationally, you can find a great deal
of meaning in *The Nutcracker* and excellent reasons for its peculiar effect.

It is not quite by chance either that they are to be found. *The
Nutcracker* was derived in one way or another from a long fairy
tale of E. T. A. Hoffman's *The Nutcracker and the King of
Mice*. The ballet has a little of the story and much of the tone
of Hoffman, his special note of hurt and tender assent. Hoffman was one of the brightest of men and master of the free
association device. The free association device was as familiar
to educated persons in 1820 as it is to us, and practiced by
them with more sense of humor. Their joke was: as long as the
association of images is free, why not make it come out pleasantly? Perhaps this is the secret connection between Hoffman's
conciliatory fairy tale and the emotional control of the set-piece
ballet form; and the connection, too, between the quality of the
score Tchaikovsky composed and that of the dancing and the
story. At any rate, story, score and choreographic style join very
beautifully in this academic ballet—*December* 10, 17, 1944.

MONTE CARLO TRANSFORMATION

IN *BALLET IMPERIAL,* the novelty that the Monte Carlo presented at its opening last night at the City Center, the company looked miraculously renewed. It danced with an animation, a lightness in neatness, that was far from the disheveled young valiance it showed only last September. The transformation that the dancing in Balanchine's *Danses Concertantes* then suggested is now in full view in his brilliant *Ballet Imperial.* And Mary Ellen Moylan, the leading ballerina of the piece, is a lovely jewel and a joy.

Ballet Imperial, which was first danced here by Private Kirstein's American Ballet a few years ago at the New Opera, is a vivacious, exacting, inexhaustibly inventive classic dance ballet, a ballet that evokes the imperial dazzle of the St. Petersburg style in all its freshness. It is no period parody. Everything is novel in its effect. But you recognize the abounding inner gaiety, the touch of tenderness, the visual clarity and elegance, the bold dance impulse that exist—often in only vestigial form —in the Petipa-school classics still in our repertory. Balanchine has recreated the spirit of the style which was its glory. And you look at *Ballet Imperial* with the same happy wonder that our grandparents may have felt in the '90s, when the present classics were novelties.

Ballet Imperial is a ballet without a plot, as luminously incomprehensible as the old classics were. It begins with a solemn, pompous, vaguely uneasy mood, groups and solos that turn into brilliant bravura; then comes a touching pantomime scene, with softer dances, a scene that suggests a meeting, a misunderstanding, a reconciliation, a loss; and then a third section succeeds, even more vertiginously brilliant than the first, in which everybody shines, individually, in clusters, the boys, the girls, the stars, and all in unison. The musicality of the choreography is as astonishing as its extraordinary ease in affording surprises and virtuoso passages.

Young Mary Ellen Moylan, dewy in diamonds, delicate, long, and with a lovely pose of the head and a beautiful freedom in her correctness, was the star. But Maria Tallchief, brilliant in speed and with a steely exactness; and Nicholas Magallanes, easy, sincere and animated, were real stars as well.

The handsome backdrop, by Doboujinsky, suggests the architectural glories of Petersburg. The score, Tchaikovsky's *Second Piano Concerto,* was brilliantly conducted by Mr. Balaban. Rachel Chapman was ideal for dancers in the piano part, and the orchestra, too, was exact and strong, as it was all evening —*February* 21, 1945.

SINGULAR MASTERPIECE

THE Monte Carlo company presented last night an impeccable performance of Balanchine's *Danses Concertantes* and an agreeable one of Nijinska's *Snow Maiden. Danses Concertantes,* which has become a success with the audience, remains the boldest ballet of the season, the most original and singular.

Danses Concertantes is a triumph of succinctness. In fifteen minutes it offers as many contrasting dance images as if it took an hour. The more you look, the more you see. The clusters of dancers toss the current of motion up, down, they soften it for a moment, then whirl it, stop it and flutter or stalk or run to a new departure. But though the single phrase looks very brief, it is bold and distinct; and the next phrase takes over its power, and in the end the force of the piece has been continuous and the effect is ample and grand.

But the magic of *Danses Concertantes* lies in its friendly and untragic atmosphere. It lies in the ease, the spontaneity and well-bred amusement which the individual gestures have, and in the young responsiveness to one another among the dancers which their composite dance figures so clearly show. The Monte Carlo company presents the piece with exact clarity and good manners, and further with a happy dancer's lightness and charm. And last night Danilova and Franklin danced the leads once more as the lightly natural comedians they can inimitably be.

Snow Maiden, on the other hand, is as prolix as *Danses Concertantes* is succinct. It is rather like a fairy tale told by a poetical maiden aunt, who doesn't care to be hurried. But she is a well educated and an intelligent lady, and she has a curious urban grace in her affectation of sweetness. In *Snow Maiden* the masculine assurance of the shepherd, the timidity of the Snow Maiden, the open simplicity of the peasants all come through and strike a clear balance. And a number of dance passages, especially the hero's, play lightly over the cumbersome saccharine music in a highly intelligent manner.

Miss Krassovska danced the heroine with charm and exactitude. Mr. Danielian was a pleasant hero, and his leaps were superb; his main variation, however, still could gain in fluency. Mr. Lindgren, who danced the chief peasant, was lively in the steps, though he added little warmth to them; he is excellent, however, as the Fencer in *Bourgeois*. Miss Horvath was rather stiff as Spring, but in this part only Danilova has succeeded in spreading the radiance of spring on the stage. The peasants were very good indeed, and the tone of the whole performance was fresh and clear—*February* 28, 1945.

FRANKIE AND JOHNNY, AN INDECENT BALLET?

FRANKIE AND JOHNNY, the 1938 Page-Stone charade which the Monte Carlo revived last week at the Center, is no bawdier than Nedick's orange drink. It tells the story of the ballad, but gives it the raciness of a daring sorority glee-club version. References to Frankie's and Nelly Bly's profession are strictly horsed, and when Frankie and Johnny get together what they do is a bit of high-school "necking." The low-life characters milling about the stage are gloomily hunched up at first, and you think you are in for a social-consciousness number—German-expressionism style—but it all ends up as a night-club joke, good, clean fun, and nobody meant anything they did. They were just acting out the words like a charade.

A pretense of innocence, even in the most unlikely situations, is, if you will, an American custom, but it is not a characteristic of the ballad called *Frankie and Johnny*. Its force and its humor in the best versions of the text—the Negro ones —come from its plainness. It describes the hero after being shot: "He fell down on his knees/ Looked up at her and said/ 'Oh, Frankie, please/ Don't shoot me no more, babe/ Don't shoot me no more.'" Or when the sheriff approaches, "Well," says Miss Frankie/ "I don't care if I die/ Take and hang me to a telegraph pole/ Hang me good and high/ He was my man but he done me wrong." And after her arrest, "Passing through the jailhouse/ Went by Frankie's cell/ Asked her how she was feeling/ She said, 'Go to hell.'" This is the Frankie that is poetic, and that is worth putting on the stage in a ballet or in any other form. The cute little Page-Stone Frankie isn't at all like her.

But besides missing the best point of its subject matter and the chance to present a plain American poem, *Frankie and Johnny* is muddled as a dance composition. The dancers step, jerk and posture repeatedly, but no dances emerge, no effect of rhythm or of mounting vitality; they just seem to go on milling. Not that the piece shows no talent; far from it. It has a number of bright ideas, in stage business rather than in dancing, which call for laughs. And one cannot be angry with a piece that brings some original jokes, that aims to please in a harmless way and that doesn't try for slickness; its talented amateurishness is perfectly aboveboard.

From this point of view, *Frankie and Johnny* has a perfect right to its good repute as a pioneer effort in amusing dance Americana, a repute it won in a 1938 Chicago W. P. A. production. But *Rodeo* and *Fancy Free* have since then so far raised the standards—in dance construction, in humor of character and situation and, best of all, in American savor—that *Frankie* can no longer compete.

The "unashamed" thing about this revival of *Frankie* is only that the management brought it to town. It should have been clear on the road, first, that it doesn't represent ballet Americana and, second, that the piece makes the Monte Carlo dancers look foolish, since it doesn't give them a chance to dance. By keeping it in repertoire notwithstanding, the management harms the dancers, and it seems to bank on our gullibility—or, say, our natural leniency with native local color in ballet—to put over an inferior product. One sniffs the same smell of "sucker bait" that hangs about the Monte Carlo's equally inept but not so innocent *Red Poppy*. But I don't see there's a chance of its being closed for immorality even by Mr. Moss—*March 4, 1945.*

SUNNY MASTERPIECE

MOZARTIANA, the new Balanchine ballet that the Monte Carlo presented last night at the Center, is in atmosphere light and subtle; it is as full of personal life as an ancient town on the Mediterranean on a holiday morning in the bright sun. In point of form, Balanchine recaptures the flavor of an old-style grand ballet like Petipa's *Don Quixote*, recaptures in novel terms its variety of playfulness, tenderness and virtuosity, and he does it with only four principals and a chorus of eight girls. *Mozartiana* is another of his unassuming pocket masterpieces which restore to ballet its classic clarity and joyousness.

Mozartiana is a straight dance suite without a plot set to Tchaikovsky's *Suite No. 4*, an orchestral arrangement of Mozart piano pieces. Against an airy backdrop that suggests a crossroad at the edge of an Italian town, you see a young man in an eighteenth-century abbé's costume, dancing full of vivacity by himself. Enter a chorus of girls that are classic ballet's version of villagers, whom he joins in a little game.

They are followed by a girl who appears to be very sad and comes in carried by two veiled figures, a bit comic in their emphatic mysteriousness. She dances a touching "Prayer." And after that comes a series of lively dances by the stars, by individuals from the chorus, by the first young man and the sad lady, now very gay in a tarantella costume. Then a poignant grand adagio by the stars, now crowned with gold leaves. And last comes a blithe little country-dance finale.

Full of novel sequences and novel bravura effects as all this is, it is striking how the variety of character in the principals becomes perfectly clear and how happily the chorus contrasts with them. Balanchine presents all the dancers at their best, and the Monte Carlo shines in *Mozartiana* once more. Danilova, both in her first pizzicato allegro and her second earnest and beautifully dramatic adagio is a very great ballerina. But Franklin's joyous lightness, Lazovsky's happy vivacity and Miss Etheridge's serious grace and clear quickness are all wonderfully effective. And the little chorus is a chorus of soloists in achievement. *Mozartiana* was first produced by the Ballets '33, 1933 in Paris; I thought I recognized some of the dances—they are all said to be the same—but the open, clear and sunny tone of it now seems very different, very new—*March 8, 1945.*

LOVELY INCIDENT

BALANCHINE'S new *Pas de Deux* which Danilova and Franklin introduced last night at the Center is a lovely incident in the grand manner but too brief a one. When you see these two stars dancing beautifully on the stage you want them to go on dancing; and though the piece isn't called a "grand" pas de deux, the audience none the less was hoping for solo variations and a coda to come when the curtain went down.

Not that the piece itself is fragmentary in feeling or in form. It is set to entre acte music from Tchaikovsky's *Sleeping Beauty*, music composed to carry a mood of suspense through an interval required for a scenic transformation, but omitted in the original production at the suggestion of Alexander III who thought it more amusing to speed up the machinists. Balanchine's duet too is a sort of transformation scene, an episode between conclusive actions. A prince appears with a lovely princess, he holds her gently and as she flutters and turns and bends, he lets her free, and she returns to him, and they exit together. Their intimacy is that of young people in love and engaged, and their dance figures express the dewiness, the sense of trepidation in the girl and the generous strength of the man.

Technical feats are an integral part of the delicately nervous rhythm, of the romantic suspense that the music, too, has. And at every point the plastic clarity of the two figures in their many relations is as surprising as it is unemphatic. The style for the ballerina—the piece is hers—is not the bold but the gentle grand manner, the manner that requires delicate toesteps, lovely arms,

110

a pliant back, and extensions that are not stressed. The marvelous Danilova, lovelier to look at than ever, is as perfect in this new field as if she had never danced in any other way. Franklin held and supported her perfectly, too, with his natural generosity of stage presence.

The bolder grand style they had both shown earlier that evening in the completely different and equally beautiful second pas de deux they have in *Mozartiana—March* 15, 1945.

PEACEFUL AND EXCITING

THE second all-Balanchine evening which the Monte Carlo presented last night at the Center was once again a happy triumph of George Balanchine's magic. *Bourgeois Gentilhomme*, *Mozartiana*, the new *Pas de Deux* and *Ballet Imperial* (all brilliantly danced), which composed the program, are in their striking variety of sentiment and form an indication of his inexhaustible classic invention; in their clarity and spontaneity, the dancing grace and wit, they prove his easy choreographic mastery. But the special secret of his magic is to make you forget the choreographer for the dancers you see before you, dancing in their lovely young freshness on stage.

Their freshness comes from the fact that they understand completely the classic dancing they are asked to do, understand it in dancers' terms. Classic dancing is what they chose as a vocation and carefully learned, what they are happy to do. For Balanchine they need not understand a dance by rationalizing psychologically, they need not put it over by emoting their role or glamorizing their personality. When they get the physical feel of a dance sequence, the bodily rhythm of the movement (and this is a profoundly personal and instinctively emotional recognition) they know they are right and that nothing will fail to carry. The audience will love them.

Nothing will fail to carry because Balanchine by accepting the classical system of body balance (foot positions) and the steps based on it has—for all his exciting invention—taken care of the flow of the dance phrase and the line of the deployed human figure. He has placed the gesture of the dancing figure in space so that you see it in positive relation to the visible stage center or the wings and to the figures of the other dancers. And you see it too in happy relation to the music you hear, to its formal as well as its emotional stress or ease. So the dancer dances lightly, distinctly, rhythmically, and is constantly the natural focus of attention and the source of a happy excitement.

If clarity in excitement is one of the classic tenets, the other is human naturalness of expression. Balanchine, by asking his dancers to do what they best can, by allowing each to be independently interesting, by combining the figures easily and following the emotional overtones of the rhythm and line of a human body in action, leaves the dancer his naturalness, his freshness, his dignity. The secrets of emotion he reveals are like those of Mozart, tender, joyous and true. He leaves the audience with a civilized happiness. His art is peaceful and exciting, as classic art has always been—*March* 23, 1945.

A NOTE ON BALANCHINE'S
PRESENT STYLE

SINCE 1940, it seems to me, Balanchine's choreographic style has more and more clarified the dancer's momentum in motion. That is what you follow as you watch the dance. You follow the variable momentum of the dancer's phrase and the dance impulse in it that animates her is clearly defined. The spring of the steps and the thrust of the gesture clarify and characterize the dancer's changing impetus. Easy and elusive she moves positively in coherent and unforeseen sequences. Her energy suits their emphasis, the figures of the dance suit her dancing figure. Free in following her impetus, light in responding to its surprising variations, her own human figure keeps its plastic unity. The unity it keeps for your eye makes the dancer a consistent character in your mind. You see her as an active, intelligent character on the stage whose variable play fascinates by its natural coherence. Because she creates her own momentum unimpeded and because you see her so clearly doing it, you watch her with pleasure as if she were doing what she spontaneously liked to. And because the rise and fall of the dancer's momentum is so clear and so expressive and the extended phrases appear to be the free dance impulse of an interesting human character, the dancer herself remains the force on stage you watch, the force that moves you. And since in performance there are many dancers to watch, stars and chorus, young men as well as girls, and since the impetus of each remains free and clear whether they dance solo or in harmony with others, the ballet on stage is full of variety, exhilarating and touching in its lively mutual responsiveness.

The novelty in this is the fact that Balanchine's style like the classic Petipa-Ivanoff style of the '90s moves you by the act of dancing and not, as the fashion was from 1910 to 1940, by opposing to that act obstacles of various kinds of mimicry—pictorial, psychological, musical or social. Choreography from Fokine on had made the most of such obstacles to dancing and of the intermittences in rhythm, the oddity and distortion of the human figure (the stylization) which resulted. Fanciful, startling, intelligent and stylish it often was, and Balanchine himself began by rather outdoing other choreographers in all these qualities. "Modernism" was the liveliest fashion of its day, and it made every new piece obviously very peculiar; but it tended to focus one's interest not on what the dancers were doing but on what they were supposed to do, what they had been told to. Dancers solidly trained in classic continuity of rhythm and balance projected an eloquent pathos by over-coming the choreographer's willful obstacle course; but dancers with little experience in a straight dance attack couldn't be effective in the oblique two-things-at-once impetus of stylization. Balanchine's shift from "modernism" may be due to the fact that he has worked for the last eleven years wholly in America, and generally for American dancers, whose incompletely trained dance impetus had to be stressed to make it carry in performance. But this new style may also be due to a spontaneous change in his point of view, to a new interest in classic coherence, limpidity and grace that contemporary poetry and music are also beginning to show. In any event his present style is not an oblique neo-classicism, it is a direct new classicism. It is the new choreographic style of the '40s, which is in emotion

unlike the preceding style, the style we know from *Sylphides,
The Faun, Tricorne, Noces,* and *Apollo*—each one a masterpiece, as everyone knows. Tudor's work too has been "modernistic," and I have no intention of suggesting that the style has
no life left in it; I am merely trying to analyze the novelty of
a newer one.

One can of course point out that back in Diaghileff's day
Balanchine was already recognized by the discerning as a classicist, and classicist he was in comparison to the modernistic
choreographers. But I have the impression that *Balustrade* in
the first and last part of it, in which the movement was simple
and open and made its effect directly by its dance rhythm
began definitely in the present direction; although it was the
wonderfully sensual acrobatics of the middle section that delighted one part of the audience and shocked another. Shocking,
Balanchine has not been since then, perhaps because shocking-
ness, especially in America, injects a non-dance excitement that
interrupts and diminishes the straight dance emotion. At any
rate, *Concerto Barocco, Ballet Imperial, Danses Concertantes,
Waltz Academy* and the present version of *Mozartiana* (and in
a simpler form the big number in the second act of *The Merry
Widow* and the one at the end of *Song of Norway*) are direct
dancing, limpid and exhilarating.

Despite the popular success our two ballet companies have
had with his new pieces this winter on tour many people feel
that so straight and ungloomy a style as this does not convey
emotion. They are distressed by the absence of a literary subject by which to get at the ballet. They feel that Balanchine's
Baiser de la Fée was, because of its story and pathos, a greater
work than his new ones. More grandiose in scale it was, and I
wish this grandly morbid piece were still in repertory. It is a

loss certainly that Balanchine has not had an opportunity to set a long and ample work. I should be happy, for instance, to see a 1945 classic hour-long version of a Tchaikovsky ballet, right next to the familiar 1890 classic versions in our repertory. But a plot and its attendant emotional situations are after all a device for continuity, an aid to attention; it is not the situation that achieves emotion but the impetus of the dance that creates it.

Balanchine, in these new animated, constantly shifting, plotless and unneurotic pieces, by stressing the dancer's impetus makes one follow a dance performance with consistent interest without drawing attention to familiar unhappiness. You don't watch the dance to see if the dancers come up to an emotion you expect beforehand, you watch to see what they do, and their variety in animation exhilarates; you are interested without knowing how to label the emotion. And so you are not tempted to excuse your pleasure, or rationalize it, or appreciate it mentally. I think that this direct enjoyment of dancing as an activity is the central aspect of ballet style that Balanchine has rediscovered. As in the new style the dancer is no longer divided between divergent impulses of motion, and as there is no longer a conflict for precedence between dancer and choreographer, so there is as you watch no painful split of emotion between your social consciousness and your dance pleasure. These classic and free pleasures of peace are as great as those of a tortured romantic disorder. They offer us a new emotion one is eager to enjoy—*February–March, 1945.*

GISELLE'S RIVAL

FOKINE'S *Prince Igor* dances, looking as pleasant as a newly weeded Victory garden in August, reappeared nicely cleaned up in the Monte Carlo's repertory at the Center, Thursday. The event of that evening, and an event of local dance history, was the *Coppelia* performance which preceded *Igor*. It was all through in spirit and in style the finest presentation of an old-style classic that this reviewer has seen. Had it been shown in the flattering frame of the Metropolitan instead of the impossible one at the Center, it would have been not only the success it was, but the unique triumph it deserved to be.

If *Giselle* is ballet's *Hamlet, Coppelia* is its *Twelfth Night*—its masterpiece of comedy. Less effective dramaturgically than *Giselle,* it has more variety and vivacity. *Giselle* is grandiose and morbid. *Coppelia* is captivating and unneurotic. It treats of love and marriage, and beginning with adolescent joys and troubles, it suggests in its radiant last grand pas de deux an adult happiness. The range of its leading role is equal to *Giselle's,* its incidental dances have far more fancy, and its score is far lovelier.

Last night's Monte Carlo performance was at nearly every point an extraordinary one. Alexandra Danilova, incomparably brilliant in coquetry, wit, warm feminine graces and warm intelligence, was last night miraculous in classic clarity, in subtlety of rhythm, in darting and soaring elevation, in the biting edge of her toesteps and the wide, strong line of her wonderful extensions. Her dancing of the "Ear of Wheat" and of the suc-

117

ceeding number with the village girls in the first act was both
in its lightness and its nobility the most glorious dancing in
the world; the elegance of her playfulness in this act and in
the second were that of a peerless ballerina. The third act had
here and there a trace of tiredness, but the grandeur and limpidity of the greatest ballet were there, and the last lift, for
instance, to Franklin's shoulders, was entrancing.

But the unique merit of the Monte Carlo performance was
the company's natural grace all through. Franklin, as the hero,
shone happily with the incomparable vitality he has and in classic passages he was clean in style, manly and imaginative. Quite
extraordinary in their beauty of style were the eight girls who
are the heroine's friends—the Misses Boris, Goddard, Chouteau,
Lanese, Etheridge, Riekman, Svobodina and Horvath, of whom
I noticed the first four in particular. Never has such a chorus
been seen here. But the rousing folk dances, the doll dances,
the mimed passages, the divertissements all delighted by the
sense of a happily inspired company. And on this occasion Miss
Chouteau celebrated her sixteenth birthday by dancing alone
a "Prayer" that was lovely in every way—*March* 10, 1945.

POLISH HARVEST

H ARVEST TIME presented by Ballet Theater as a world
premiere at the Metropolitan last night is as foolish as
the worst of the ballets Pavlova used to tour about in. Miss
Toumanova, for whom it was constructed, is no Pavlova, how-

ever. Nor does Ballet Theater look well when it is asked to super in vehicles for her. *Harvest Time* shows off Toumanova's record arabesque all right, but it is embarrassing as a world premiere by a great company.

Harvest Time—set by Mme Nijinska to a potpourri of Wieniawski pieces—is a series of show-off passages for a classic ballerina (with diamonds in her hair, of course) and for her partner. There are also evolutions and poses by six ballet girls (ballet peasants who carry a garland, of course) and by four peculiarly awkward men who crouch and stamp about in brown tights, indicating peasant "character." The piece might be explained as a pastoral scene—a Polish harvest—in the 1860 Petersburg style. But the trouble with *Harvest Time* is that it neither gets going as dancing, nor does it offer a gracefully urban view of country sentiment. It is a perversity in corn that one wishes were at least intended as parody; though it isn't choreographically interesting enough, even for that.

What can be said for it is that Nijinska at one point in a duet devised three or four poses in succession for Toumanova that are beautiful to see and that suit her peculiar personal style better than anything in the repertory. Their curiously static rhythm, their intensity of gymnastic prowess, their accent on powerful separation of the limbs rather than on a graceful deployment are strikingly effective. Three or four poses are very little really in a piece; but they serve to prove that what Toumanova needs is a choreographer to rescue her from her present too brutally acrobatic manner and restore to vivid expression her extraordinary capabilities—*April 6, 1945.*

BEETHOVEN IN A CHROMO

POOR Toumanova. Poor Ballet Theater. With a kind of numb dismay, your reporter watched them submitting to a new choreographic indignity when Massine's *Moonlight Sonata* was shown Saturday night for the first time at the Metropolitan. Slick the performance was; but "Russian ballet" can hardly sink any lower than it does in offering us this clammy hallway chromo. And to have the great Massine and our fine Ballet Theater responsible is ignominious for everyone.

Massine himself appeared as that stock chromo character, "The Poet." Against a chromo backdrop representing a lake in the moonlight—it looked like an inexpensive Swiss lake in the off season—he stuck out his chest, waved his arms importantly and kept having to go somewhere off stage. Miss Toumanova was that other stock chromo character, "The Young Girl." Unbecomingly dressed for her hip formation, she was still much the handsomest girl staying at the same deserted Swiss hotel as he. They seemed to realize stonily that there just wasn't anyone else to go around with—which is pretty much the expression of lovers on chromos.

Later, while Miss Toumanova was sitting in the moonlight alone upstage—and sitting very beautifully, really—two further characters came on, a Cupid and a Dark Lover. Cupid, in a ginger-ale colored spotlight, turned out to be Miss Kavan, who hastily acted like the Cupid in Dolin's parody, *Romantic Age.* The Dark Lover was less conventional. He turned out to be

Mr. Petroff without a toupee, dressed in an old-fashioned black bathing suit several sizes too small so that he could get it up over one shoulder only. For propriety's sake, he also was wearing long, black stockings. He looked as if he were employed at the local bathing establishment, though the program billed him as a figment of fancy. Fancy or no, he made persistent advances to Miss Toumanova and finally succeeded in lifting her so that she faced the audience in the air with—oddly enough—his backside on view just below her. Cupid came back and cleared up matters.

The orchestra all this while had been playing a fantastically brutal orchestration of Beethoven's so-called *Moonlight Sonata*, which, as everyone knows, has nothing to do with moonshine on Lake Lucerne or anywhere else. They had begun disemboweling it long before the curtain went up, clammy strings appropriating the left hand and loud brass the right. Beethoven expressed his views on orchestral transcription of his piano pieces the same year this sonata was published; you can imagine what they were—*April 9, 1945.*

TUDOR'S UNDERTOW

UNDERTOW, Tudor's new ballet which Ballet Theater is giving at the Metropolitan, is well worth seeing. Though not so effective theatrically as *Pillar of Fire* or *Romeo* it is a highly interesting, a very special piece and a notable credit to the season. *Undertow* tells a story which appears to happen more in a young man's mind than in objective reality. The first scene presents quite realistically an image of his birth and his later interrupted breast-feeding. In the second, he stands, a shy and gentle adolescent in an imaginary city and watches with increasing excitement the suggestive actions of passersby. Other figures, innocent ones, which include a sort of innocent "brother" of his own self, try to divert his attention; and he, too, would like to ignore the horrid excitement he feels. He even persuades a girl, as excited as he, to join him in a kind of prayer meeting. But she breaks away, she invites his passion, and in an irresistible paroxysm of desire he strangles her. The next scene, set against a backdrop of clouds, shows him frenzied with terror and alone, while some of the previous characters, with a noncommittal air, stroll past. He realizes his guilt, he sees his innocence lost in the symbol of a balloon that escapes from a child's hand. And as he becomes conscious of the town once more, this very child, whom he had scarcely noticed before, points an accusing finger at him; the other characters, whether good or bad before, join her and point at him. An outcast, as if going to his execution, he walks slowly and resignedly off.

The theme of *Undertow* is that of an adolescent's neurosis, the terrifying dilemma which presents to him the act of manhood as equivalent to murder. The hero of the piece cannot find the normal solution of this, according to psychology, normal dilemma; the image of murder is so powerful in him it dominates and petrifies him, and in his impotence he kills. But despite Hugh Laing's completely sincere and sustained impersonation of the adolescent, the motivation does not convey itself to the audience, one doesn't identify oneself with him. The trouble is, I think, that the decisive initial scene, presenting a bloody birth, brilliantly shocking though it is, does not seem to be a part of the hero's inner life, it is not placed anywhere in particular. Later, at the climax, after the shockingly instantaneous murder (brilliantly duplicating the birth image) we see the hero trying to escape in vain an unseen force mightier than he; but we should have to see this antagonist of his moving in an active shape on the stage to know what the hero knows and feel as he feels. Because *Undertow* lacks such a physical release of opposing forces, it remains intellectual in its effect, like a case history, and does not quite become a drama of physical movement.

Indeed one keeps watching the movement all through for the intellectual meaning its pantomime conveys more than for its physical impetus as dancing. Its impetus is often tenuous. But its pantomime invention is frequently Tudor's most brilliant to date. The birth scene, an elderly man's advances to a prostitute, an hysterical wedding, drunken slum women, several provocative poses by the hero's victim, and quite particularly the suggested rape of a vicious little girl by four boys, these are all masterpieces of pantomime, and freer, more fluid, more plastic than Tudor's style has been. Brilliant too is his individualized use of the dancers and wonderful the way each one of them rises to the occasion. *Undertow* is worth seeing just for Miss Alonso's horrifying bit; and though not a successful drama, it suggests in many details that Tudor's style is more powerful at present than ever before—*April* 15, 1945.

A BALANCHINE MASTERPIECE

CONCERTO BAROCCO, the Balanchine novelty of the current Monte Carlo season at the Center, is an unpretentious and good-tempered little ballet and it is also the masterpiece of a master choreographer. It has only eleven dancers; it is merely straight dancing to music—no sex story, no period angle, no violence. It does not seem to be trying to win your interest, but before you know it it has absorbed your attention and doesn't let it go. It has power of rhythm and flow; in a wealth of figuration it is everywhere transparent, fresh, graceful and noble; and its adagio section is peculiarly beautiful.

Concerto Barocco was recognized as a masterpiece at once when it was shown here in dress rehearsal four years ago by Lincoln Kirstein's American Ballet. It had just been created then for the Rockefeller-sponsored South American tour of that company. And though this ballet tour has recently been spoken of as one of Mr. Rockefeller's inter-American mistakes, as a ballet critic I can say that in showing *Concerto Barocco,* he was showing our neighbors choreography of the best quality in the world—showing a United States product that no country of western Europe could have equaled. A mistake such as that does anyone honor.

It is a pleasure to report that the Monte Carlo production of *Barocco* is excellent both in the dancing on stage and in the playing in the orchestra pit. Unfortunately though, the piece has in the present production been given a backdrop of meager, dirty blue and a set of harsh black bathing suits for the charm-

124

ing girls. Meagerness and harshness are not in its spirit; some of the wonderful clarity in its spacing is dimmed; and in so poverty-struck a frame, the rich title of the ballet strikes one as absurd.

But *Concerto Barocco* comes by its fancy title quite honestly. The name might lead you to expect an evocation of Baroque dancing or Baroque mannerisms; still what the title actually promises is a Baroque concerto, and that is just what you get. Balanchine has set his ballet so happily to Bach's *Concerto for Two Violins* that the score may be called his subject matter. The style of the dance is pure classic ballet of today, and the steps themselves follow the notes now strictly, now freely. But in its vigorous dance rhythm, its long-linked phrases, its consistent drive and sovereign articulation, *Concerto Barocco* corresponds brilliantly to this masterpiece of Baroque music.

The correspondence of eye and ear is at its most surprising in the poignant adagio movement. At the climax, for instance, against a background of chorus that suggests the look of trees in the wind before a storm breaks, the ballerina, with limbs powerfully outspread, is lifted by her male partner, lifted repeatedly in narrowing arcs higher and higher. Then at the culminating phrase, from her greatest height he very slowly lowers her. You watch her body slowly descend, her foot and leg pointing stiffly downward, till her toe reaches the floor and she rests her full weight at last on this single sharp point and pauses. It has the effect at that moment of a deliberate and powerful plunge into a wound, and the emotion of it answers strangely to the musical stress. And (as another example) the final adagio figure before the coda, the ballerina being slid upstage in two or three swoops that dip down and rise a moment into an extension in second—like a receding cry—creates another image that corresponds vividly to the weight of the musical passage. But these "emotional" figures are strictly formal as dance inventions. They require no miming in execution to make them expressive, just as the violin parts call for no special schmalz. And this modesty of stage presence combined with effects so strong and assured gives one a sense of lyric grandeur.

The adagio section is the only movement with a lyric expression. The introductory vivace is rather like a dance of triumph, strong, quick and square; while the concluding allegro is livelier and friendlier, with touches of syncopated fun and sportive jigging. Both these sections have sharply cut rhythms, a powerful onward drive and a diamond-like sparkle in their evolutions. There are, for instance, many lightning shifts in the arm positions and yet the pulse of the dance is so sure its complexity never looks elaborate. The ten girls who execute the little chorus and the two girl soloists are precise and quick and their grace is wonderfully natural. They are all so earnestly busy dancing, they seem more than ever charmingly young, and their youth gives an innocent animal sweetness to their handsome deportment—*September* 16, 1945.

DANCER'S PARTY

COMEDIA BALLETICA, the new ballet the Monte Carlo presented last night at the City Center, was applauded by the audience with enthusiasm. But though it was danced with frequent brilliance, and though a promising work, I thought the piece as a whole an unsatisfactory ballet. It marks, however, the big-time debut of a young local choreographer, Todd Bolender, in whose gifts many young dancers have great confidence.

The title is a fancy one for a work that is so unpretentious in manner. *Comedia Balletica* is a dance ballet for five dancers, set to Stravinsky's *Pulcinella Suite*. Against a somber little cut-out in false perspective, representing, one guesses, some sort of ballroom that is being used for rehearsal, the dancers—Miss Boris, Miss Marie-Jeanne, Miss Tompkins, Mr. Danielian and Mr. Bolender himself—appear in conventional ballet costume. They present themselves to the audience, sit down on stools, take turns in solos, duets and ensembles, changing seats at each conclusion. It is a sort of party, a party of professionals, each does his or her turn as an entertainer.

The style is straight ballet with an ironic sharpness and quickness in timing suited to the acerbity of the orchestra. The fun as you see it, though, is rather like that of a little clique of professionals indulging in acid gossip. There is no ill-humor in it, it is clean and lively, but it is not as intelligible and charming to an outsider as to the performers and the jokes seem all pretty much alike.

Brilliant in this tight intramural manner are, for instance, the quick quivers of Marie-Jeanne's solo, or the Spanish spurt of Miss Boris in the minuet, and both were brilliantly executed. As well danced were Danielian's sharp-footed solo and Bolender's more easy-footed one. And Miss Tompkins had an adagio intentionally clipped in rhythm. But this variety in tightness is not boldly enough differentiated to make one enjoy the various flavors. And the sharpness needs the contrast of longer, more flowing phrases to make it carry. The connecting passages are wooden instead of being relaxed. Mr. Bolender is highly inventive in many details, but it strikes me he has missed the Neapolitan amiability, the naturalness of Pergolesi's flow which Stravinsky's score embroiders in such violent and witty color. The music is a pretty fancy joke, but it is a larger joke than the ballet—*September* 18, 1945.

LOW-BROW CHARM

ON STAGE, the new ballet which Ballet Theater presented last night at the Metropolitan, put its audience in a good humor partly by the adolescent liveliness of its execution, partly by the clearness with which it played up a good old-fashioned trooper's fairytale. *On Stage* is Michael Kidd's first big-time work as a choreographer. It is low-brow in sentiment, ambitious in size, and its dance invention as such is not very striking. But as theater the piece creates a friendly atmosphere and projects an obvious charm.

On Stage is a Chaplinade about a handyman in a theater (Mr. Kidd) and a little girl in pink (Janet Reed) who auditions for a ballet master (John Taras) and fails because she is nervous. The audition comes in the midst of a ballet rehearsal on stage, and its painful failure is covered over by the entrance of the company's tough grand ballerina (Nora Kaye) ready for action. The handyman and the little girl watch the rehearsal proceed, and soon, first one and then the other, both are daydreaming of how beautifully they could do the star parts. After the company has been dismissed and the stage is empty, the handyman tries to cheer up the little girl by pranks which gradually lead to dancing. At the moment she has lost all self-consciousness he manages to call back the ballet master, the company crowds back too, and all applaud her. She is accepted into the company, she waves goodbye gratefully to the handyman, and he is left alone, as Chaplin used to be, privately pleased with his adventure.

The big dance scenes, as you can see, have a realistic excuse; they are mostly the parody of a classic ballet, which moves from rather obvious jokes to vigorous evolutions, parodistic in their rudeness of style rather than in their invention. And this vulgarity of dance style which sets the tone of *On Stage* is in keeping with the sentimental hokum of the story. Far more subtle are Kidd's funny pranks and Miss Reed's downcast features.

But in the dancing itself, though the detail is unsubtle, there is a plain vigor in the arrangements that shows Mr. Kidd's latent strength; some of the static groupings too are attractive without emphasis. The gifts he shows are all for the present more suited to musical comedy than to ballet; but they are real ones. And as he took his final bow, he made a little gesture of "I'll be seeing you," which the audience clearly approved of.

The new score of *On Stage* by Norman dello Joio is good plain theater without being distinguished. Its sentimental close was most effective. The set by Oliver Smith is discreet and attractive and gives the action clarity and freshness. Alvin Colt's costumes, too, are plain and clear—*October* 10, 1945.

BAD MOMENT

SEMENOFF'S *Gift of the Magi,* Ballet Theater's novelty last night at the Metropolitan, is foolish corn and a big dose of it. It is both inept as a ballet and absurdly blown up as a production. Lukas Foss's score (the most lively element of the show) is constantly ambitious and overheavy. Raoul Pène du Bois's décor is sentimentally coy and ponderous on stage. In this clutter of disproportionate trimmings Semenoff's stage action dribbles along meagerly, jerkily and slowly. Pantomime points and dance rhythms are equally weak and the sentiment saccharine. Nora Kaye and John Kriza danced the leads admirably, and watching them one regretted the waste of their brilliant talents. It was all a bad moment for ballet and a long-drawn-out one.

Gift of the Magi is a story ballet that follows and clumsily embroiders O. Henry's short story of the same title. On Christmas Eve, Della Young sells her hair and Jim Young (her husband) sells his watch, each wanting to surprise the other with a fine Christmas present; she buys him a chain for his watch, he buys her combs for her hair. It is the pathos of young white-collar life, of taste without money. But O. Henry ends not in pathetic frustration, but with a rising little apotheosis of young love; and that is the point of the title. Semenoff however drags out the frustration until it subsides, exhausted. Luckily for him, Kriza and Nora Kaye saved the ending—as they had the beginning—by their personal charm and their sweetness of characterization.

One might have expected an O. Henry ballet to be American in atmosphere and flavor. There was nothing in the action that recalled New York in particular or real life anywhere, for that matter.

Foss's score for *Gift of the Magi* is program music in the grand manner. It describes everything, though nothing very intimately, and it changes its subject every few seconds without the least hesitation or loss of breath. It makes lots of big noises, some of them sour—*October* 16, 1945.

THE POWER OF POETRY

B ALLET THEATER covered itself with a real glory at the Metropolitan last night by bringing back to us Balanchine's *Apollo* and by dancing it completely beautifully. *Apollo—Apollon Musagète* is the title of the Stravinsky score —has been performed in New York now and then by various companies during the last ten years, and each time its serene and sensuous poetry has won it a spontaneous acclaim. It is an untarnished masterpiece. Last night, too, there were bravos, and not bravos merely for the virtuosity but for the poetic beauty of the dancing. For myself, seeing *Apollo* last night has left me—for the first time in the current season, I'm afraid —happily and unreservedly enthusiastic.

Enthusiastic about the piece, which moves me and delights me each time I see it; enthusiastic about last night's performance in which Alicia Alonso, Nora Kaye and Barbara

Fallis were brilliantly delicate, brilliantly strong, and André Eglevsky magnificently powerful. Virtuoso they were, all four of them—Alonso's extensions, Kaye's speed and Eglevsky's sweep were in detail dazzling; but the sweet earnestness, the classic modesty, the poetic naturalness of all four throughout the piece made one forget the unhappy tendencies to a more foolish kind of solo showmanship that seems to be creeping more and more into Ballet Theater's everyday performances. Last night Ballet Theater was dancing seriously again, and beautiful was the result.

Apollo is about poetry, poetry in the sense of a brilliant, sensuous, daring and powerful activity of our nature. It depicts the birth of Apollo in a prologue; then how Apollo was given a lyre, and tried to make it sing; how three muses appeared and showed each her special ability to delight; how he then tried out his surging strength; how he danced with Terpsichore, and how her loveliness and his strength responded in touching harmony; and last, how all four together were inspired and felt the full power of the imagination; and then in calm and with assurance left for Parnassus, where they were to live.

Balanchine has told this metaphysical story in the concrete terms of classic dancing, in a series of episodes of rising power and brilliance. Extraordinary is the richness with which he can, with only four dancers, create a sustained and more and more satisfying impression of the grandness of man's creative genius, depicting it concretely in its grace, its sweet wit, its force and boldness, and with the constant warmth of its sensuous complicity with physical beauty. *Apollo* is an homage to the academic ballet tradition—and the first work in the contemporary classic style, but it is an homage to classicism's sensuous loveliness as well as to its brilliant exactitude and its science of dance effect.

What you see on stage is strangely simple and clear. It begins modestly with effects derived from pantomime, a hint of birth pangs, a crying baby, a man dancing with a lute, and it becomes progressively a more and more directly classic dance ballet, the melodious lines and lyric or forceful climaxes of which are effects of dance continuity, dance rhythm and dance architecture. And it leaves at the end, despite its innumerable incidental inventions, a sense of bold, open, effortless and limpid grandeur. Nothing has looked unnatural, any more than anything in Mozart sounds unnatural. But you feel happily the nobility that the human spirit is capable of by nature—*October* 23, 1945.

BALANCHINE'S APOLLO

BALANCHINE'S *Apollo* is a ballet so simple in story, so rich in dance imagery, so exciting in invention, I should like to describe a little what happens. The piece calls for a string orchestra to play the Stravinsky score and for four superb dancers; it has beyond that only three small parts, no chorus, almost no scenery. It is quite unpretentious as theater. The scene is on Delos, Apollo's birthplace, and the action begins a moment before his birth, with Leto, his mother, high on a rock in a sharp ray of light, tossing grandly to and fro in the labor of a goddess. Then Apollo appears standing wrapped rigid in swaddling clothes. Two nymphs bring him forward and he bawls infant-like. The nymphs begin to unwrap him, but with a godlike vigor before they are done he makes a ballet preparation and whoosh! spins himself free. Free, he makes a grandly clumsy and baby-like thrust and curvet or two, and the prologue is over.

When the lights come on again, he is grown to boyhood and alone. The nymphs have brought him a long-necked lute and he tries to make it sing. But his solitary attempts, first entangled, then lyrical, then determined, look inconclusive. Three young Muses appear and the four of them dance together. They dance charmingly and a little stiffly, reminding you of the inexpressive seriousness and shy, naive fancy of children. But as they end, the boy gives the three girls each a magic gift, a scroll of verse to one, a theater mask to the second, a lyre to the third. And holding these emblems of poetry, each seems to be inspired beyond her years. The first girl dances flowingly with an airy and lyric delight; the second bounds with dramatic speed, with sudden reversals of direction as if in mid-leap; just at the end one hand that has seemed all through to be holding a mask before her face seems to sweep the mask away, and she is herself again and frightened. The third muse, Terpsichore, invents the most adventurously brilliant dance of all, boldly cutting her motions in startling divisions, as if isolating the elements of her art, without in these diamond-clear stops breaking the cumulative drive. She combines suspense with calm. And as she ends, Apollo gently touches her bright head. But, the dance over, she ducks away like a child and runs off.

Then Apollo, his strength awakened, dances by himself, leaping in complex virtuoso sequences, in a grandly sustained sweep of powerful motion. It is no show-off number, it is a masculine surge of full dance mastery. Terpsichore returns just as he ends and together they invent a series of adagio surprises, extremes of balance and extension, boldly large in line, boldly intimate in imagery, and ending with a tender and lovely "swimming lesson" that he gives her. And now all three Muses dance together in darting harmony and dance inspired by poetry's power, swinging from Apollo like birds, curving from his body like a cluster of flowers, driven by him like an ardent charioteer; and ending, when immortal Zeus has called through the air, in three grand accents of immolation. Then calmly and soberly, in Indian file, all four ascend the rock of the island and a chariot comes through the sky down toward them as the curtain falls. They will go to Parnassus where they will live ever after.

You see as *Apollo* proceeds how from a kind of pantomimic opening, it becomes more and more a purely classic dance ballet. More and more it offers the eye an interplay of lines and rhythms, of changing architectural balances the edge of which becomes keener and keener. In this sense *Apollo* conveys an image of increasing discipline, of increasing clarity of definition. It grows more and more civilized. But the rhythmic vitality of the dance, the abundance of vigor increases simultaneously, so that you feel as if the heightening of discipline led to a heightening of power, to a freer, bolder range of imagination. Since the piece is about the gods of poetry, and how they learned their art, it seems, too, to be describing concretely the development of the creative imagination.

And as the dance images grow more disciplined, more large and more vigorous, they also grow grander in their sensuous connotations. As Apollo and the little Muses grow up, the intimate contact between them seems to develop from an innocent childlike play to the firm audacity and tender inventiveness of maturity. Suggested in no sense mimically but purely by dance architecture, the range and richness of *Apollo's* sensuous imagery is marvelous; and because of this consistent honest but unself-conscious sensuousness the "abstract" classicism is at no point dehumanized or out of character with the dramatic situation. So for example the taut ballet extension of a girl's leg and toe—used in *Apollo* as an insignia of poetry itself—grows increasingly poignant to watch as the piece proceeds; and you experience everywhere the cool sensual luminosity of civilized art.

So *Apollo* can tell you how beautiful classic dancing is when it is correct and sincere; or how the power of poetry grows in our nature; or even that as man's genius becomes more civilized, it grows more expressive, more ardent, more responsive, more beautiful. Balanchine has conveyed these large ideas really as modestly as possible, by means of three girls and a boy dancing together for a while.

But the immediate excitement of watching does not depend on how you choose to rationalize it. *Apollo* is beautiful as dancing and gloriously danced—*October 28, 1945.*

INTERPLAY

ROBBINS' *Interplay*, once in Billy Rose's *Concert Varieties* and now a success in Ballet Theater's repertory, is of serious interest both for being young Robbins' second work and for being, of all the ballets by American-trained choreographers, the most expertly streamlined in dance design. *Interplay* looks like a brief entertainment, a little athletic fun, now and then cute, but consistently clear, simple and lively. You see four boys come out and then four girls and all eight join in improvised games (such as follow-the-leader) done in dance terms; there is a boy's joking show-off solo, and a duet with a touch of blues sentiment in the air, and then all eight together play another game, competing in leaps and spins with the effect of a collective speed-up finale. It looks rather like an American outdoor party where everyone is full of pep and naively rough and where the general unfocused physical well-being is the fun of the occasion. Still, watching how the dancers behave to each other, it isn't always clear if they represent twenty-year-olds being cute or maybe ten-year-olds on their good behavior.

But leaving aside the subject matter (which the program doesn't clarify either) what immediately captures your attention is the pace of the piece, the clear drive of its dance impetus, and the athletic verve of the cast—a perfect cast in which Harold Lang is especially brilliant. The physical spring of the athletic phrases obviously suits the dancers and the impetus of the movement obviously suits that of the score as well; and the whole continuity is perfectly clear to the eye as dance architecture. There is nothing subtle about the dance— nor about the score, Gould's *Concertette*, for that matter; the texture and the expressive accents are commonplace; but nowhere does the piece break down and become fragmentary, fussy or thick. And this is a serious achievement. Robbins alone of our native choreographers has grasped at one stroke that the basis of ballet logic is a view of time and space as a closed entity. The time of a ballet is that specified by the

musical architecture of its score and the space is that of the
stage area as a static whole. These two architectural frames of
reference, so to speak, give to the mazes of a ballet its coherent
and cumulative distinctness. And the cumulative distinctness
in spacing and timing *Interplay* has in action is of serious
ballet quality.

Not of serious ballet quality is *Interplay's* specific dance
technique. Robbins does not show the resource of deploying
the body unself-consciously, of a sustained and natural soaring
and sailing; the foot positions are only approximate and this
spoils the buoyancy and sharpness of floor contact and of
phrase construction; he tries for vivacity by again and again
overspeeding pirouettes; his jokes are sometimes too coy; he
does not distinguish between the timing of pantomime and of
dance gesture; and the accents of the dance are likely to be
energetic thrusts expressing a shot-in-the-arm vigor rather than
an individual response to a dramatic moment.

But perhaps Robbins feels that both the score and the subject matter of *Interplay* call for a general vigor rather than for
a modulated and individual grace. The characters of *Interplay*
seem to be urban middle-class young people having a good
time, who know each other well and like being together but
have no particular personal emotions about each other and no
special keenness of response. They know about sex as a jive
joke or as a general blues sentiment; they don't know it as an
individual focus of passion. From a hint of personal sincerity
they turn untroubled and vague with a coltish playfulness,
expert in strength but blunt in edge.

In this unpersonal aspect of *Interplay*, there might be the
poetic subject matter of an American flavor of sentiment. And
Robbins has, I think, a poetic love for the air of rudeness and

unresponsiveness in our national manners. But in *Interplay* he has glossed it over by a general mutual amiability that is humanly unconvincing and a bit goody-goody; he has for the moment confused love of America with flattery. Such criticism is nonsense if *Interplay* is taken as passing entertainment; but not if it is taken as some sort of serious ballet. And the intellectual vigor, the clear focus of its over-all craftsmanship, suggests—as *Fancy Free* suggested in another way—that Robbins means to be and can be more than a sure-fire Broadway entertainer, that he can be a serious American ballet choreographer —*November 4, 1945.*

ANTI-BROADWAY HIT

GRAZIANA, the new piece at the Metropolitan last night, was Ballet Theater's final novelty of the season, and turned out to be the one most cordially approved of by ballet first-nighters. What is striking in this success is that *Graziana* has none of the zippy Broadway showmanship Ballet Theater has been trying to deliver to its public. *Graziana* is straight academic classicism, without apologies, without vulgarity, without straining for attention. It isn't very interesting; but the ballet audience seemed to be saying demonstratively that it prefers its ballet straight and not Broadwayized, and that it approves highly of a young man who seems likely to produce what it prefers.

The young man is John Taras, a soloist in the company

whose first ballet *Graziana* is. It is an ambitious effort—no less than setting a Mozart violin concerto (K 216) with four soloists and thirteen supporting dancers. They appear against a neutral blue drop in dance costume and dance ballet very well; and that is all that happens. The title is simply a word to identify the piece with.

Taras' approach to classic dancing is completely direct and aboveboard, with no nervousness or evasion. But though there is considerable variety in the steps, there is not much variety in dance expression. The figures are clear and they change without confusion. But one does not get a lift out of varieties of lightness, of speed, of rhythm, out of effects in spacing and timing. *Graziana* solemnly misses the expressive quality of its score, the Mozartian animation in grace and intimacy of sentiment, and hints boyishly at such qualities only in mild Balanchinisms. But young Taras is nowhere fussy or strained. He has happy moments of his own (in the transition to the adagio, and in the adagio foursome); and the public is clearly ready for more of his work—*October 26, 1945.*

EXTRAORDINARY FASCINATION

THE Ballet Society, New York's new subscription organization for producing ballet and opera, opened with startling brilliance on Nov. 20, presenting to its subscribers Ravel's one-act opera, *The Spellbound Child,* and a new Balanchine ballet, *The Four Temperaments.*

The audience, an experienced one, welcomed the executants and welcomed *The Four Temperaments* in particular as a novelty of extraordinary fascination and power.

In its flavor *The Four Temperaments* is unlike any other Balanchine work. In form it is a half-hour dance ballet, without plot or locale, set to Hindemith's score of the same title (originally commissioned for it). The score consists of a set of three long themes, first stated directly, then varied four times. These variations, called "Melancholic," "Sanguinic," "Phlegmatic" and "Choleric," follow in their plan the four temperaments (or humors) of Hippocratic and medieval physiology. And the plan of the choreography scrupulously observes the musical plan. But the ballet as one watches it can better be described as a suite of dances of amazing richness and variety that illuminate an exceptionally powerful thick-flowing score.

The ballet holds one spellbound by the constant surprise of its dance development; by the denseness and power of the dance images which the figures on stage create from moment to moment. One seems to be watching innumerable novel dance possibilities realized without the least hesitancy in the drive or the least awkwardness in the continuity. The continuity is like nothing one has seen and it looks completely self-evident.

Unpredictable and fantastic the sequences are in the way they crowd close the most extreme contrasts of motion possible —low lunges, sharp stabbing steps, arms flung wide, startling lifts at half height, turns in plié, dragged steps, réverences and strange renversés; then an abrupt dazzle of stabbing leaps or a sudden light and easy syncopated stepping.

Neither sequences nor figures look familiar. The grandiose force of these crowded large motions seems to correspond in its accents to the dense tensions of the score's counterpoint, and the unexpected continuity (as the phrases evolve) to the score's smooth melodic surfacing.

But it is the pressure and shift of the musical as well as of the dance images that is the heart of the piece; no choreography was ever more serious, more vigorous, more wide in scope or penetrating in imagination. And none could be more consistently elegant in its bearing—*December, 1946.*

3
Dancers in Performance

PLEASURE IN THE GRAND STYLE

AMONG ballet stars Danilova has a special gift. At the height of a classical variation, while she is observing all the restrictions of the grand style, she seems suddenly to be happy to be dancing, with a pleasure like a little girl's. It gives her a sort of natural grace that is unique.

Last night, appearing in *Nutcracker,* which the Monte Carlo Ballet presented at the Broadway Theater, she showed this wonderful quality once more. Her assurance was remarkable, too. She was ably assisted by Youskevitch, who was himself dazzling in his variation in the final scene.

The production of *Nutcracker* was, however, hardly worthy either of the sweetly fanciful and famous score, or of the touching flavor the ballet as a whole can have. The first scene especially was rudely done. Some years ago, in the de Basil company's production, this scene particularly had much more of the real E. T. A. Hoffman domestic charm that is the point of it. But it is a great pleasure to see the piece again; it remains one of the great classics of dancing—*May 22, 1943.*

BOISTEROUS, THEN BEAUTIFUL

SATURDAY NIGHT'S performance of Ballet Theater at the Lewisohn Stadium was a full success. The first two ballets (*Capriccio Espagnol* and *Three Virgins and a Devil*) have the boisterous qualities that register most easily in the open air. *Giselle*, the third ballet, is anything but boisterous. But the passionate precision of Miss Markova in the lead made its subtle values intelligible a block away. It was a startling experience to see so delicate, so intimate a piece appeal without effort to an audience of ten thousand. It was a triumph for Miss Markova as a theater artist.

Capriccio Espagnol in Massine and Argentinita's choreography is a lively arrangement of Spanish regional and Spanish gypsy dances. It does not try for the special strictness of real Spanish dancing. The steps are authentic, but the rush and swirl of movement is Massine's. Massine has the secret of the sure-fire number for a large ballet company, and *Capriccio* is a happy example. Massine himself appeared in the part of the Gypsy, a role he does more sharply than anyone else. Miss Kaye was his gypsy partner; her lightning turns, her hip shakes, her wrist movements in the air were vividly temperamental.

Three Virgins, Miss de Mille's little satire on virginal vanity, makes all of its jokes very clearly. The dances slip from old country dance forms into burlesque bumps and bits of Lindy steps (Flying Charleston, Suzie-Q and Pecking). The meaning of the pantomime is unmistakable. The five dancers were all excellent; and particularly Miss Karnilova, in the longest part, proved herself a masterly dance comedian.

These two ballets are meant as light entertainment. But *Giselle*, that followed them, is a tragedy. It is a hundred-year-old classic, in which the great dancer Carlotta Grisi conquered Paris in 1841. The theme was inspired by two Romantic poets; the plot was fixed by a successful librettist and the choreography, credited to Coralli, is probably largely due to one of the greatest of choreographers and classic dancers, Grisi's husband, Perrot. The ballet is still danced in Paris, London and Leningrad. And all the great ballerinas of the past have appeared in it.

Though so brilliant a history may add to the prestige of a ballet, all this seems remote from Amsterdam Avenue, 1943. But it is not prestige, it is its quality that keeps *Giselle* alive. The story of the ballet has poetic reality. The dances are in a large, open style. They are not intended primarily as exhibitions of virtuosity, they are meant to tell a tragic story and create a mood. And the score of *Giselle* by Adam is direct and animated; the more closely one listens, the more one notices how carefully made it is. But above all *Giselle* gives a great ballerina a superb chance to captivate, to dazzle and to touch the heart. *Giselle* is the Lady of the Camellias, the Violetta, of the dance.

Miss Markova succeeded in the role on Saturday as completely as she already had at the Metropolitan. She captivated, dazzled, and touched. In the mimed passages—for instance, the conventional gesture of madness, staring at the audience with hands pressed to frame the face—she is somehow thrillingly sincere. In the dance passages of the first act, she is gay and light with a sort of chaste abandon; in those of the second, she is partly unearthly like a specter, partly gracious as a tender memory. It is as hard to color correct academic dancing with emotion as it is to give emotional color to correct bel canto. Miss Markova makes it seem the most natural thing in the world.

One reason she succeeds is that one sees every detail of the movement so distinctly. The movement of other dancers is apt to look fuzzy or two-dimensional in comparison to hers, which looks three-dimensional. Only the greatest dancers have this, so to speak, stereoscopic distinctness. Markova also has a complete command of the impetus of dance movement. She hits the climax of a phrase—say, a pose on one toe, or a leap—without a trace of effort or excess drive. The leap, the pose, seems to sustain itself in the air of its own accord.

She does not strain either in movement or in theater projection. She is so straight upright, so secure, that she does not have to thrust her personality on the audience for an effect; the audience is happy to come to her. This makes her dance seem personal, intimate, even in the open air—*June* 28, 1943.

TWO AMBITIOUS YOUNG DANCERS: ROSELLA AND JERRY

THE Ballet Theater's Saturday night program at the Metropolitan contained *Petrouchka*, *Dim Luster*, *Pas de Deux* (from *The Nutcracker*) and *Bluebeard*. The news event of the evening was Rosella Hightower's dancing in *Pas de Deux,* which was of exceptional brilliance and classic finish.

This time her poses were completely plastic and her timing of the dance phrases was sure. She gave the sense of finishing one phrase before the next: of fulfilling one impulse and completing it before the next impulse alters the figure of the dance. It is astonishing how rarely dancers are able to have so clear a control; a control which Miss Markova, of course, possesses to a phenomenal degree.

Because of Miss Hightower's technical brilliance, her naturally forthright manner of dancing was more than ever attractive. And Eglevsky, her partner, was at his very best, too; not only technically superb and magnificently simple, but with that large open-heartedness that he alone brings to classic dancing. His warm and loyal manner toward Miss Hightower added a great deal to the freshness the whole dance had; and in her spontaneous delight, Miss Hightower looked really radiant. It was a great pleasure to see her in this final triumph at the close of a season in which she has been so remarkable.

In *Petrouchka* Jerome Robbins took the title part. In distinctness and energy of gesture he couldn't have been better; he is a highly intelligent dancer, and he can make the meaning he intends his dance to have completely clear. I liked, too, the slight comic quality he keeps in this often exaggeratedly pathetic part, and I liked his make-up. But Robbins sometimes seems to like to jump about for the sake of jumping; and he forgets then not the meaning of his gesture but the illusion of the stage—that is, the reality of a character and of a story. I thought he was too anxious to get across to the audience, too eager to please; he would be more effective with more reserve. Technically, the gesture looks as if it started in the limbs, not

as if it arose in the trunk and had the full strength of that;
Massine, whom Robbins imitates so extraordinarily well,
keeps the main expressive force in the torso—even in this puppet role. Robbins is evidently a dancer of remarkable talent,
and the style he is developing promises a great deal of originality—*November* 8, 1943.

TRIBUTE TO YOUSKEVITCH

THE Ballet Russe de Monte Carlo closed its spring season
at the City Center Saturday night with a program con-
sisting of *Etude, Cuckolds' Fair, Pas de Deux Classique*
(danced by Alexandra Danilova and Igor Youskevitch), and
Red Poppy. It was the *Pas de Deux* that was the event of the
evening, and it was Seaman Second Class Youskevitch—dancing on the last night of his shore leave—who made it so.

At the moment Youskevitch is at the peak of his classic
style. His style is calm, rich and elastic. It is completely correct. You see easily what the action is, how the trunk takes the
main direction of the dance and how the limbs vary the force
and the drive by calculated countermovements. The changing
shape of the dancing body is vigorously defined. The weight
of the body and the abundant strength of it are equally clear;
and the two aspects blend gracefully in the architectural play
of classic sequences. The distribution of energy is intelligent
and complex. In his leaps, for instance, the noble arm positions, the tilt of the head sideways or forward, make you

watch with interest a whole man who leaps; you don't watch, as with most dancers, only the lively legs of one. And while most dancers leap for the sake of the bound upward only, Youskevitch (like Markova) leaps for the entire trajectory, and for a mysterious repose he keeps as he hangs in the air.

The completeness of his dance education is unique among our classic male dancers. His rhythm is free, his characterization economical, his lift gracious. His stage presence has none of that hard insistence on attention that breaks the illusion and the flow of a classic ballet. It is unanxious and gently confiding. True, he has neither blazing temperament nor dazzling edge; at times I find his romantic miming a trifle too politely eager; I prefer Franklin's Hussar in *Danube* to Youskevitch's. But, if Igor hasn't every quality imaginable, I, at least, know of no dancer anywhere who is nearer than he to perfection.

And now he is returning to his base, it is hard to think how the Monte Carlo can long continue as a first-class company without him—*May* 1, 1944.

JANET REED: LEARNING TO STAR

AT THE Metropolitan last night, Ballet Theater presented *Fair at Sorochinsk, Pas de Quatre, Fancy Free,* and *Tally-Ho.* Young Janet Reed danced Cerrito in the second ballet, one of the passersby in the third, and the wife in the fourth—three star parts and three very different roles on one program. It was a tour de force and red-headed Miss Reed carried it off with determination.

As a dancer, she is a born soubrette: petite, active, bounding, sharp, malicious and strong. She is in her element in character parts where the gesture counts and the speed makes a point. Her fault on the stage is that she often has a tendency to force both in her movement and in her projection; the first breaks the continuity, the second isolates her own part from the general atmosphere and meaning of a ballet. Forcing, except in farce, destroys the dancer's dignity.

Last night she was not quite in her best form, judging by her Cerrito and her passerby. I had not yet seen her in the lead in *Tally-Ho,* which she was dancing in place of Miss de Mille for the second time last night. Miss Reed's dance technique is superior to Miss de Mille's—the steps are more distinct and rapid, she is more at ease in the lifts. One misses, however, the sense of legato phrasing that Miss de Mille showed.

Miss de Mille, by lifting her chest and tilting back her head easily, by understressing her arm gestures and steps, gave the sense of a woman in the relaxed full flower of her thirties; she was also happily aware of her husband's presence, and happily at home in it. She projected not only her own role but their joint role as a couple. (And Mr. Laing, as the husband, does the same thing very beautifully on his side.) A happy marriage and the dignity of a happy wife are the focus of the story, even though the point gets insufficient expression in actual dancing. This crucial overtone Miss Reed does not convey.

A quieter approach, and movements timed just a trifle behind the beat might help Miss Reed. And a sense of repose might help her, too, to give the feeling of being in the open air in summer, that Miss de Mille so beautifully conveys.

A young dancer so obviously talented and intelligent as Miss Reed is can be forgiven for such misjudgments; stage assurance is not learned without mistakes—*May* 2, 1944.

BALLET THEATER'S GLORY

ALICIA MARKOVA in *Giselle* is Ballet Theater's greatest glory. Last night was the second of three performances of *Giselle* on this season's programs; and it was a gala evening at the Metropolitan. Miss Markova danced once again with incomparable beauty of style—dazzlingly limpid, mysteriously tender.

There is no other dancer whose movement is so perfectly centered, and who controls so exactly the full continuity of a motion from the center to the extremities. There is no other dancer whose waist and thighs are so quick to execute the first actions that lead to an arm gesture and to a step; or who diminishes the stress so precisely as it travels outward along the arms and legs. It is this that gives her dancing figure its incomparable clarity, its delicacy and its repose. It is this, too, that makes her dance rhythm so clear to the eye and so full of variety.

This superlative dance intelligence makes her dance fascinating, both as pure motion and as motion to music. The fragility of her figure, the dramatic conviction of her characterization give her dance another and equally strong expressivity. Her physical and intellectual concentration confer on her a mysterious remoteness and isolation, and this tragic dignity makes her expressions of tenderness extraordinarily touching.

All her qualities, of dancing, of mime, of presence, find a perfect use in the part of Giselle; the extraordinary effect Miss Markova creates in this part is obvious to the thousands who watch her, whether they are familiar with ballet or not. Last night again she received a unanimous ovation.

The costumes and set of the first act—dating from the early days of Ballet Theater when *Giselle* was taken as a cute period piece—are still a blot; in time we may get a new décor, and let us hope it will be Berman's projected one for this piece—*May* 6, 1944.

MARKOVA IN SYLPHIDES

ON LAST night's program of Ballet Theater at the Metropolitan the great Alicia Markova—whom we are not to see in ballet next year—appeared in *Sylphides* and in *Pas de Quatre*. There was no trace of the indisposition that had made some of her earlier appearances this spring uneven. Though she is perhaps not yet as strong as she was before her illness last fall, her dancing yesterday was again immaculately beautiful.

In *Sylphides* one could admire again the limpidity of her phrasing—how delicately she seems to let the musical phrase impel and lift her, and then how gently the impulse in her subsides into repose. Without blurring a detail of her steps, she can subordinate them to a retard or an acceleration of impetus. No other dancer can make her runs on toe or half-toe as exact and yet transfer her weight as imperceptibly. In complex sequences, it is the complete elasticity of her ankle and instep that gives her so light a step; but it is her keen sense of rhythm, her dance imagination that make the most of her exceptional technique. And what is uniquely Miss Markova's own is the rare grace of spirit which her dancing figure communicates—*May* 20, 1944.

HIGHTOWER INTO SWAN

ROSELLA HIGHTOWER, blossoming into New York's favorite among the younger classical dancers, gave a quite exceptionally fine performance as the Swan Queen in *Swan Lake* at Ballet Theater's Saturday matinee at the Metropolitan. Dimitri Romanoff too, as her Prince, was remarkable in the poetic quality of his miming and of his support, a quality which John Kriza, as the Prince's friend, shared with him. The emotion of *Swan Lake* comes from the sense of a mysterious understanding that exists among these three characters— and between them and the enchanted Swans. And it is only out of their simple acceptance of a moonlight transfiguration that the bravura "arias" of the ballerina can take on their real poignancy. Saturday's performance was a touchingly sincere one, and Miss Banks as one of the Swans was lovely, too.

Miss Hightower was superb in the great adagio, better than

she has ever been in it before. Her phrasing was sustained, classical and lucid. All through the piece her slow gestures had a beautiful repose. The quicker ones, at which she usually excels, seemed too hasty by contrast. But in her second allegro solo she was again very brilliant indeed. It is a great pleasure to watch her growing into a complete ballerina.

Swan Lake was followed by *Fair at Sorochinsk,* in which Jerome Robbins substituted for Anton Dolin as the Devil. As the striking rapidity of the part is based on toe-work, Mr. Robbins, who doesn't, like Mr. Dolin, use toe-shoes, had a hard time making much of it. The exuberant climax of the Fair scene as usual went over in a big way; the subsequent quiet dances of the boys and girls have lost a little of their charming bloom because the dancers no longer start their phrases a fraction behind the beat, and in addition end the phrase too hastily.

The third number on the program was *Barn Dance.* I think that the orchestra in this has become too brassy for the attractive parlor style of the score; though of course the dances on stage are brassy if they are anything. In *Barn Dance,* however, Nana Gollner and Paul Petroff give their best performances of the season. Miss Gollner is ravishing to look at, and both of them are amusing and vivacious; the absence of sustained phrasing, that has for me spoiled their classic work this season, is no drawback in this high-pressure romp—*May* 21, 1944.

RIABOUCHINSKA AND OTHERS

THE general impression over the week end is that Ballet Theater is headed up again. Sunday night's performance at the Metropolitan was lively and accurate, the best evening so far. The new *Waltz Academy* looked as it should have on its opening night, gay, unpresuming and beautiful. Miss Alonso was dancing with a new animation in her perfect neatness; Miss Gollner with a new simplicity in her fine feats, a directness we have waited for for two years. And the audience enjoyed the charming piece and the company cordially.

The bill included the "Pas de Deux" from *The Nutcracker*, danced by Toumanova and Dolin. Miss Toumanova, with a prettier coiffure, this time superimposed a different manner on her dazzlingly perfect leg action, smiling and giving ecstatic little tosses of the head before big effects. I imagine a great classic choreographer like Balanchine could best correct the miscalculations of manner that mar her superb capabilities.

Sunday afternoon's *Sylphides* and Saturday night's *Aurora* billed both Toumanova and Riabouchinska, the guest celebrities of Ballet Theater. Miss Riabouchinska, though no great technician in movement, has so warm and true a presence, so clear a sense of the musical enchantment that surrounds her, and so keen an instinct for a natural characterization, that one watches everything she does—even her faults—with pleasure. Her greatest fault is a tendency to raise her shoulders too much, which gives her torso a dumpy look. But when you see her dancing with the happy absorption of a little girl, you

155

wish other dancers in classic pieces would learn from her to believe in their imagination.

In *Sylphides* she seems to be one of the chorus dancing by accident; in the *Bluebird* she is a sparkling princess with a wonderful blue bird of her own; in *Graduation Ball* she is a little girl, mischievous, sweet natured and well mannered. She creates a magic world around her; a very rare dancer indeed.

Graduation Ball on Sunday afternoon brought Harold Lang in Lichine's part, and he danced it with a fine natural charm and clarity, perfectly in character. He is developing particularly well this season. This piece is, happily, losing the strident stress that spoiled it at first—*October* 16, 1944.

VIGOROUS GHOST

MISS TOUMANOVA with her large, handsome and deadly face, her swordlike toesteps, her firm positions, her vigorous and record-high leg gestures—and with her bold and large style of dancing—by nature makes a very different figure from delicate Miss Markova, whose star role in *Giselle* she undertook for the first time last night. Dancing at the Metropolitan as guest of Ballet Theater in the familiar Ballet Theater version (including Mr. Dolin as the star's partner), Miss Toumanova was very striking and was properly cheered. But Miss Markova's Giselle is still incomparable.

In Toumanova's performance, this Markova fan missed the sustained otherworldly floating quality and the calm completion of each pose and phrase that were Markova's specialty, and that helped make this ballet in particular extraordinarily thrilling. But Miss Toumanova not only gave her best performance of the season, she showed some of her dramatic gifts as well as her technical ones. She sustained the first act and built up an atmosphere of threat that might well lead into the second. And in the second act she gave her supported adagio section a very interesting sensual overtone, that might, if developed in the role, add to this whole act an unusual (but perfectly possible) macabre intensity.

Later in the second act, at the allegro climax, in the famous series of little leaps on both toes, Miss Toumanova leaped too far to keep her lightness, and she did not reach a sort of desperate quality she may have intended. In the lifts that follow she was too large for Dolin quite to create an effect of lightness. Indeed, Dolin's overpowering assurance in the part is now becoming his most serious qualification; he has to substitute a theatrical pose for dance brilliance. But he supported Miss Toumanova very handsomely.

The company was excellent indeed in the second act; here Miss Hightower as the Queen was at her very finest, with magnificent leaps, beautiful arm gestures—*October* 17, 1944.

TOUMANOVA'S SHOW

DAZZLINGLY handsome to look at in "Black Swan," effervescently and girlishly temperamental in *Three-Cornered Hat*, Tamara Toumanova sustained and put across last night's Ballet Theater show at the Metropolitan as a star performer should. Ballet can be more gracefully poignant and the Spanish style more controlled; but last night one was happy in the vigorous theatrical impetus Miss Toumanova gave both pieces she appeared in.

"Black Swan" is the grand pas de deux from *Swan Lake* Act 3. The most correct version of the duet was the Monte Carlo's of 1941, danced then by Toumanova and Eglevsky, and a performance unparalleled that was. Mr. Dolin's present version is a straight bravura exhibition number, and Miss Toumanova rose to the occasion. The grand abundance of force she had in all she did was stunning; and her accurate line, her half turn recovery from a deep back bend, her ballones and circle of turns—each effect was driven home magnificently. The house rightly gave her an ovation.

The same duet in its context in *Swan Lake* has an overtone of vicious evil; it can be danced with more reference to the ballerina's partner and projected less hard at the audience. It is more moving that way. But done as Miss Toumanova did it—a brilliant feat of unique prowess—it affords an honest theatrical thrill; and no other dancer could have delivered it with such physical magnificence.

Mr. Dolin was Toumanova's partner, and what he did was neatly done. His showmanship put it over successfully.

Three-Cornered Hat, with Toumanova and Massine in the leads, and David Lichine as the Governor, had a star cast. Here Miss Toumanova was very touching in the brief hand-fluttering solo after the Miller's arrest; and if her Spanish is awkward in the arms and vague in the feet, if her silhouette is diffuse—as Massine's even now is not—still the way she plays her role with conviction and dances with impetuosity brings back a long-lost freshness to this excellent little ballet. The

Picasso drop and costumes are each time a joy to see. One wishes Ballet Theater would also restore the Picasso front curtain. Lichine was amusing and discreet, though he does the role as impish comedy without any Spanish dignity to give it an extra sharpness—*October 24, 1944.*

BALLET QUINTET

MIA SLAVENSKA, notably beautiful ballerina at the Monte Carlo during a number of its notable pre-war seasons, appeared yesterday afternoon at the Ninety-second Street Y. M. H. A. with her present pocket company of four soloists. It was the first recital of the subscription series held there annually, and the intensely dance conscious audience present applauded generously.

The level of dance execution, if not the level of dance invention, deserved it. And the special audience was delighted to "discover" a new soloist—Joseph A. Harris, a boy of evident talent and schoolboy charm. His one solo stopped the show.

The program was well planned for variety: it brought classic numbers, interpretive-symphonic ones and costume character episodes—including the bravura variation of Mr. Harris (staged by Vincenzo Celli). The styles vary, the costumes do, and the program is well paced. How to achieve variety and pacing with only five dancers is a very difficult feat for the choreographer and an exhausting one for the company, too, to pull off.

Yesterday the choreographic intentions were reasonable and the execution was meticulous and animated throughout. But Miss Slavenska and her partner David Tihmar, who between them have set the new numbers, are inexpert at dance arrangement. Miss Slavenska's numbers convey the impression that the heroine is being badly treated by the men in the story, for no particular reason and with no particular consequences. In Mr. Tihmar's "Spirituals" Negro religious fervor looks like an exhibition of suffering—indicated by bending double; and Negro joy becomes a flirtatious jittering.

Both choreographers have ideas, but they try to impose them on dance steps, instead of taking them as a point of departure for rhythmic and dynamic dance sequences. Because the ideas don't fit the movement the gesture looks sentimental and the dance impulse unfree. The choreographers don't rely enough on a sense of how a dance phrase takes shape, how it builds into the next and follows a bodily impulse. As a result the dances look crowded, airless, sometimes ingenious, but uncommunicative; they also look like a reduction for small company of a larger work instead of a work concisely planned for few performers.

Technically, however, Miss Slavenska is a true ballerina and yesterday she was in excellent form. Her stage personality too was straightforward, serious and modest. Neatness and agreeable personality as well as good looks characterize her company; and Miss Keane's natural breeziness, Miss Vaslavina's warmth add to the friendly tone of the performance. Such excellent dancers as Miss Slavenska and her group could make a serious artistic success if they appealed to a first-class choreographer to set their dances—*November 27, 1944.*

INTERNATIONAL'S FAREWELL:
EGLEVSKY—MONCION

BALLET INTERNATIONAL closed its season at the International last Saturday night. Both last Saturday's and Friday's performances showed that the company, for all its mistaken timidity in production, has acquired a following of friends and showed also how steadily the inexperienced ensemble has improved.

Saturday's biggest applause went to André Eglevsky, a great dancer and established star who that night was dancing his best, as he does not always seem to have the heart to do. *Brahms Variations*, which he appeared in, is an exacting, ungrateful and crabbed ballet, and its decoration is so awkward that the dancers look like several flavors of ice cream melting messily over the stage. Just the same, the piece is the only one in International's repertory that makes use of Eglevsky's phenomenal ability.

In the first part he stars by being the calmest in motion of all the busy dancers; in the second, by having the most powerful drive. The absurdly twisted arm and head positions required of him, the protracted poses, the sudden dartings—none of these can break the grand continuity of his dancing. The piece is especially a leg-action ballet: Eglevsky's leaps and steps are models of every variety of resilience. Fine, too, are the small entrechats, in which his calves, beating against each other, rebound with the taut quiver of a plucked string.

Eglevsky is an established great star; a star in the making is young Francisco Moncion, who Saturday appeared as Tristan in Dali's *Mad Tristan*. Moncion is the first dancer in the four Dali ballets since 1939 to create a stage character who remains convincing in the frenzy of the impressive set; and plenty of ballet's best artists have been in the other three. Moncion as a character dancer is the happy discovery of the season.

Looking back over the season, the agreeable side has been the general seriousness of the dance company. Of the novelties, only *Mad Tristan* was produced on the professional level of our other two ballet companies. But people who dropped in at the International much as they might drop in at a neighborhood cinema for a quiet evening have found the general tone pleasant, modest and acceptable. That is more than one hoped for after the first performance—*December 25, 1944.*

GLIMPSE OF MARKOVA

THERE are only two real ballerinas in the country; the senior one is the great Alexandra Danilova and the junior one is the great Alicia Markova. Miss Markova, appearing last night with Ballet Theater at the Metropolitan in two of her former ballets, *Romeo and Juliet* and *Pas de Quatre*, transformed this sadly disoriented company at a stroke into the splendid one it was during her marvelous final week with them last spring. She did it by showing them the quiet simplicity of a great style, by believing completely in the piece she was performing. They glowed, they danced, they were all wonderful.

Miss Markova's delicacy in lightness, in rapidity; the quickness in the thighs, the arrowy flexibility of the instep; her responsiveness in the torso, the poise of the arms, the sweetness of the wrists, the grace of neck and head; all this is extraordinary. But her dancing is based on a rarer virtue. It is the quiet which she moves in, an instinct for the melody of movement as it deploys and subsides in the silence of time that is the most refined of rhythmic delights. The sense of serenity in animation she creates is as touching as that of a Mozart melody.

She is a completely objective artist. Who Markova is, nobody knows. What you see on the stage is the piece she performs, the character she acts. She shows you, as only the greatest of actresses do, a completely fascinating impersonation, completely fascinating because you recognize a heroine of the imagination who finds out all about vanity and love and authority and death. You watch her discover them.

Markova's Juliet is a miracle of acting. Every nuance of pantomime is poignantly clear and every moment is a different aspect of the cumulative tragedy. Her shy loveliness in the balcony scene, her moment watching Romeo die—but one would like to enumerate them all minute by minute. And the restraint of them all, the slow-motion continuum from which they each arise as dance gestures and which flows so steadily through the whole hour-long ballet are wonders to have seen.

The entire performance of *Romeo* was everywhere a glory. Laing, that beautifully poetic dancer, was an inspired Romeo. Mr. Orloff as Mercutio was distinguished indeed. And at the end when Markova and Laing with the great Sir Thomas Beecham, who conducted the score with miraculous fluidity, and Tudor the choreographer (and Tybalt in the piece) took a joint bow, the enthusiastic audience applauded our quartet of British genius with the sincerest enthusiasm.

Later Miss Markova's Taglioni in *Pas de Quatre* was—as it used to be—a delight of sweet wit and stylistic brilliance. But I must add a word of sincere praise too, for the semi-novelty of the evening, Argentinita with her enlarged company in *Café de Chinitas*. It is her best creation at the Metropolitan— in style, in sequence, in atmosphere—and it is fine to have it in the repertory. The Dali set and front curtain are grandiosely handsome, and the dancing (and Miss Miralles' fine singing) have true Spanish charm and distinction—*April 9, 1945.*

DANILOVA AND RHYTHM

ALEXANDRA DANILOVA, dancing in Balanchine's *Mozartiana* on the Monte Carlo's program Monday night at the City Center, showed us once again how touchingly personal the grandeur of a true ballerina is, and how a ballerina's noble clarity of execution, her mastery over the many resources of dance rhythm, can make her formal steps and phrases seem poignantly unique and spontaneous, like a happy event in real life.

In all the severity of exact classicism Danilova's dancing rhythm fills the time quantities of the music to the full; it does not, like the rhythm of lesser dancers, jab at a stress and then drag for a moment till the music catches up. Stress and release in all their variety are all equally vivid, equally expressive to watch. And in watching her, you feel, in the sustained flow of Danilova's rhythm, the alert vivacity of her personal dance imagination, the bite and grace of her feminine temperament and a human sincerity that makes an artist both unpretentious and great.

The performance of *Mozartiana* was in every way charming. Franklin, Danilova's partner, danced with his happy flow of dance vitality and his wonderful generosity as a partner. Miss Etheridge was very fine indeed in both her numbers— the beautiful "Prayer" and the Gypsy dance. Mr. Zompakos and the virtuoso chorus of eight girls (Maria Tallchief particularly) were light, exact and full of verve. The piece was, as usual, a complete success—*September* 11, 1945.

FRANKLIN'S NEW CLASSICISM

IN GENERAL, the Monte Carlo as a dance ensemble has not reached the happy pitch it had last winter, but Frederic Franklin as rehearsal master has done a remarkable job in getting a large repertory with a dozen new dancers and several new productions successfully launched in the very first week.

And Franklin's personal achievement this season as a classic dancer is striking, too. His line is large and open, his deportment is convincing, his execution is clean, his support is sure and easy. He has variety of attack and he ends with assurance. Though he has no startling brilliance or Slavic subtlety, he dances with a continuity of rhythm and a clarity of phrasing that are rare indeed. Franklin's dancing always makes perfect sense; like a true artist, he is completely at the service of the role he takes, and his straight delight in dancing, his forthright presence and openhearted nature give his version of the great classic roles a lyric grace that is fresh and sweet.

Excellent he was as Danilova's partner in two traditional classic ballets, in *Coppelia* yesterday afternoon and in last Wednesday's *Nutcracker*. Danilova, who is again magnificent this fall, was particularly so in both of these pieces. Indeed, her dancing of the grand pas de deux in the last scene of *The Nutcracker* would have been an event in any season.

Though we have often seen the part in recent years, it has never been as luminous in grandeur and as delicately sensuous in feminine grace; the exquisite variation was as astonishingly personal in its correctness as the ample adagio. And if only for the sake of this great passage, the Monte Carlo should rehearse other parts more carefully—*September* 17, 1945.

YOUTH AND OLD GISELLE

ALICIA ALONSO danced Giselle Tuesday night with Ballet Theater and both Havana and New York crowded into the Metropolitan to cheer, in enthusiastic ballet fashion, Markova's heiress-apparent in the company. Young, unaffected and often very brilliant, the performance was, on Alonso's part and on André Eglevsky's, who danced the great partner role of Albrecht magnificently. Both of them broke through the familiar Markova-Dolin interpretation with a sincere youthful fervor of dancing and of love that even the mystery beyond the grave could not repress. You can imagine how the audience cheered.

Alonso is a delightfully young and a very Latin Giselle, quick, clear, direct in her relation to her lover. She is passionate rather than sensuous. She is brilliant in allegro, not so convincing in sustained grace. Her plié is not yet a soft and subtly modulated one and this weakens her soaring phrases. She has little patience for those slow-motion, vaporous effects that we Northerners find so touching. But there is no fake about her, no staginess. Her points, her young high extensions, her clean line, her lightness in speed, her quick balance are of star quality.

Her first act was the more distinguished of the two in its dramatic interpretation. She is no tubercular ballerina-peasant but a spirited girl who stabs herself. The dance-solo was hidden from me by late-comers, but loudly applauded. The confrontation scene and the mad scene were convincing, simple and large in their miming. In the second act the first whirls were thrilling, and the famous passage of lifts with the following solo of échappées and spins stopped the show by its cumulative bold, clear speed. If there was little that was spectral in the second act, there was nothing that was not vividly young and straightforward.

But it was Eglevsky's dancing in the second act that was a superb revelation to those New Yorkers who have only seen Dolin in it, of what this part is really like. Eglevsky's grandeur of rhythm, his magnificently easy elevation, his masterful, clean and unstressed beats, and even more than that his modesty and young sincerity show how stagey, fidgety and

absurdly weak, technically, Dolin's Albrecht has recently become. Eglevsky's "fish-leaps" (pas de poisson) near the end
were beautiful indeed. And though he is clearly happier dancing than miming, and though the more difficult the passage
the more beautifully he dances it, there is in his naive acting
none of the empty showmanship of Dolin's. The way Eglevsky sustained an atmosphere of remoteness in his second act
solos showed that these passages can heighten the mystery of
the second act and need not smash it in pieces as Dolin does
each time he gets set for a solo. Eglevsky's Albrecht is something for ballet lovers to see.

The Ballet Theater company danced *Giselle* Tuesday with
a happy and spontaneous animation, particularly the first act
ensembles, and the second act scene with Hilarion. Their interest in the mad scene, done so differently this time, was
vivid, and the general support they gave Alonso made the
company charming, too. I hope we shall have many more such
bright Alonso-Eglevsky *Giselles—October* 24, 1945.

UPS AND DOWNS—AND KRIZA

BALLET hungry New Yorkers continue to crowd into the
Metropolitan, and Ballet Theater serves them performances that vary from rude or slipshod to superb, from non-
descript to imaginative without warning. The valiant company struggles sometimes against overwork, sometimes against
underrehearsal, sometimes against feeble choreography and al-

most constantly against the quite unexpected noises the conductor and orchestra are contriving for it in their pit. Just the
same some performances come off with verve and brilliance
The public accepts everything that happens with the best of
good nature and is grateful for ballet even with handicaps.

Thursday night the orchestra played the most extraordinary
things during *Apollo,* and yet the dancers, particularly Eglevsky and Alicia Alonso, were often magnificent. Pity it was the
sold-out house hadn't justified the management in paying for
an hour's additional orchestra rehearsal.

The music seemed much better in *Firebird,* but in *Swan
Lake* Mr. Horenstein started out with a record-breaking tempo
that left no time for dancing at all. It was Nora Kaye's only
Swan Lake of the season and it was a pleasure to see a careful,
serious and accurate interpretation. Consistently brilliant she
was last night only in the last rapid solo; at other times she
often could not in shoulders and head find the completion of
the dance phrases that so often must subside in an arabesque.

The recent repertory has seen in the men's roles the
changes enforced by Hugh Laing's departure. Michael Kidd
has taken the most hectic ones—those in *Pillar* and *Undertow.*
Both ballets are among the few that the company as a whole
still does with real care, and Kidd, though he cannot be expected to grasp at once the constantly shifting rhythms of his
long roles, does not mar them. The darting motions he does
with amazing speed, but he still misses the consistent sensual
legato and the imaginative grasp of evil that Laing had.

Harold Lang substitutes in *Aleko* but misses the sinuous
independence the part requires. Romanoff in *Tally-Ho* is not
as convincing a husband nor as real a sweet-natured intellectual as Laing, but he is agreeable. He is too eager in Tudor's

part in *Lilac Garden,* but excellent indeed as the hero in *Pillar.*

But it is the lyricist John Kriza who in the character parts he now takes shows the finest new character talent in the company. True, in *Romeo* and *Lilac Garden* he has not the suppressed drive of Laing. But neither does he force the facial miming, or the speed; he takes each part large and easy. Easily and charmingly, too, he handles the low-brow comedy of Hermes in *Helen;* and superbly the sensual high comedy of the Prince in *Tally-Ho.* Here in *Tally-Ho* is at last an American male dancer who is not self-conscious in acting an evil character; Kriza is elegant, unstrained, and adult in his characterization, and never works it for farce laughs as a less sincerely imaginative dancer would do. Kriza's development both as a first-class classicist and as a first-class character dancer is one of the really happy features of this Ballet Theater season —*November 2, 1945.*

MARKOVA THIS SEASON

BALLET THEATER'S season, which closes tonight, has been very successful commercially, but artistically it leaves a disappointing impression, and one of its unexpected disappointments has been the lessening of Markova's marvelous magic. Sunday night in *Romeo* and the night before in *Giselle* she was an exquisite figure to watch, clearly Ballet Theater's loveliest dancer. But she who in her own miraculously fragile way used to illuminate the meaning of an entire ballet and spread a radiance over the rest of the cast and the entire stage, seemed too often to be upstaging the company and to be dancing her own steps merely to look as deliciously graceful as possible, not for the sake of a larger dramatic expression. This has often been her failing this season.

Graceful she still is, and incomparably so, in the lovely bearing of the head, the beautifully effaced shoulders, the line of arms and wrists, the arrowy ankles and feet. Her variety in speed, her general exactness of positions, the limpidity with which she reveals the contrasting accents in direction of a dance sequence without breaking the smoothness of its flow are all of ballerina quality. Her leaps, her way of soaring and gliding, her wonderful lightness in downward motions are unique. But one notices that she tends this season to preserve these graces by lessening the vitality of her dancing, by understating the climaxes. It is as though a singer were to get the mannerism of taking fortissimos in half voice, a kind of crooning in ballet.

One sees climaxes this season (in *Nutcracker* and *Aurora*) that are tricked out with flicks of the head in pirouettes, with flicks of the wrist in poses; one notices (in *Giselle,* too) the wrists beating time in sustained passages, and broad smiles held throughout a classic number. She seems, no doubt unconsciously, to indicate a discourteous aversion to dancing with Eglevsky and Kriza; and in dancing with Dolin she sometimes gives the effect of a private understanding between them—as is customary and proper in exhibition ballroom dancing but hardly in great classic roles.

These are no doubt inadvertencies which can be blamed on her year's absence from serious ballet. But they are unfortunate mannerisms in a great ballerina. They give an impression of sufficiency that is especially not in keeping with Markova's shy style. And though the audience still applauds her wonderful moments of grace, it does not now thrill to her performance as it used to and as it will again when she gives herself wholly to her parts. I don't doubt that so great an artist will soon tire of the effects she now toys with—*November* 5, 1945.

4

Seasons in Retrospect

THREE NEW CHOREOGRAPHIES

I IMAGINE that our two big ballet companies could—at almost no cost to the management—add considerably to the prestige and to the interest of their seasons, if they were able to produce now and then a special program entirely by new choreographers; danced say, by their less known dancers, in practice costume and to piano accompaniment. Unfortunately the heavy touring schedules of these companies make such a project impossible because the dancers haven't the free time to rehearse extra novelties. It is a pity; whether such studio matinees produced remarkable works or not, they would find an interested special public, they would vary the dancers' routine, and best of all they would give young choreographers—and big ballet needs them for the future—a chance to develop. How is a choreographer to learn except by trying?

In practice, however, it has always been the small unglamorous companies, on a semi-student basis, who have tried out most of the new choreographers. Though the execution is often rough, the performances are very valuable to the ballet public and the ballet industry. Among our best known choreographers, Agnes de Mille and Eugene Loring began with small groups;

so did Tudor in England and Balanchine in Soviet Russia. There is every reason to suppose that such small ballet companies are a necessity to the sound development of ballet in this country.

The American Concert Ballet is just such a group, a new one that has begun by showing us the work of two new choreographers, Mary Jane Shea and Todd Bolender. It also brings a new piece by William Dollar, whose last New York ballet was the *Concerto in F* at the Metropolitan some years ago; and in addition, it dances Balanchine's *Concerto Barocco*, which had not yet been produced here.

Miss Shea's *Sailor Bar, 1943* is to my mind the most interesting of them. It is a realistic scene in a sailor bar—a place something like the sailor bars of the East Fifties or West Sixties. Sailors come in, meet their girls, they dance, they fight, they leave again. One sailor and his girl are the chief characters, and on the other side of the stage you see a young man and a young woman represent their ideal selves. As the sailor and his girl come closer to having confidence in each other, the ideal selves, too, have more contact; for a moment the gesture is even the same for both pairs; then the boy and girl in both pairs draw apart again, unable to believe in one another.

The psychological action is credible and the realistic gestures look astonishingly familiar. What is interesting is that they have not been stylized to fit in a definite dance style, they keep their natural contour and impulse; what has been stylized is the weight, the flow and tempo of the motion.

In this way held poses (such as sitting), slow motion (as if dazed), normal dance steps and representational gestures keep their familiar realistic value, but they also combine into dance sequences. The sequence of the girl climbing on the table, the long climax of the sailor dancing with two girls, quarreling with the one he likes, knocking her down, and being beaten up by two other sailors—these are excellent as continuities of movement. (And for once a fight in dance form and realistic costume didn't look silly.)

Not so successful are the two ideal selves. They are carefully directed in an abstract dance style, and seriously thought out; but they manage to say no more than what the realistic figures tell us already in a more convincing way. As ideal dance figures I should have liked to see them move with greater force and freedom than the realistic ones; their movement might have emphasized (where it barely suggested) the quality of spreading into space that differentiates abstract from realistic dancing, and it might so have heightened the restrictedness of the other figures. But as a whole, Miss Shea's first piece shows a very original dance intelligence, and a notable absence of false dramatics. And she uses the music she chose with exceptional adroitness.

Mr. Bolender's *Mother Goose Suite* tells several Mother Goose stories to a little girl, and it has a feeling both solitary and intimate, like that of a child's day-dream. I liked how the movement seems to wait a long time and then flare up all at once; or how sometimes the space is very empty and then peculiarly crowded. I liked the tree that once picked up a little girl and carried her to a garden seat; and the slow clouds. But I wished the chief character had danced more, and that the many slow arm movements had held my interest better. The piece seems almost to make a virtue of indecision; but it has a quality of timing that is not derivative and serious workmanship is evident throughout.

Mr. Dollar's *Five Boons of Life* was the most fluent of the choreographies, but to me the least convincing. It is the kind of ballet I like, it has lots of dancing; but though it begins very well indeed, after a while the dances do not seem very different one from another, the effect becomes one of repetitious agitation, and one loses interest. But like the other two ballets it is a perfectly honest piece of choreography, it is planned for dancing, not for an exhibition of stage personality.

The dancers performed all these ballets satisfactorily. Some of them are, I imagine, students, others are appearing in current shows and some have appeared in solo roles in ballet. They are unequal in talent but they all dance straight: their bearing is clear, their acting is, in the best sense, modest, and the effect is one of general good style, with excellent individual moments.

The performance of Balanchine's *Concerto Barocco* was much less exact and able than that of the other pieces. It is a wholly admirable ballet. Its coolness and its simplicity are not in the current fashion; its musicality—for instance in the lifts in the second movement or in the percussive effects of the toe steps—is very bold indeed. I hope the piece will be seen often enough so that its noble qualities can become familiar; for the moment its lack of affectation and the natural look the dancers have in it seem to puzzle the audience.

The American Concert Ballet has made an intelligent and very attractive debut—*November* 21, 1943.

THE BALLET OF OUR METROPOLITAN
OPERA

CHRISTMAS DAY the Metropolitan gave the Polovtzian dances from *Prince Igor* as a ballet in a new choreography by Laurent Novikoff. Many of the steps and gestures were like those in the old Fokine version of *Prince Igor* (some of this material has an ethnological basis) but the choreography did not produce the effect of savagely brilliant force that Fokine's ballet does; the new dances were neither clear nor bold. They suffered, too, because Fokine's masterpiece has so often been executed by first-rate companies. It was foolish of the management to exhibit its choreographer and its dancers at such a disadvantage or to risk such comparisons. Had we been shown four or five "concert" dances, presenting the best dancers in their best light, the result might well have been pleasing. As it was, a great deal of hard work went into an embarrassing performance.

Embarrassing too was the rest of the production. The score was played mechanically. The singing chorus was placed in a way that crowded and dwarfed the dancers. The hundred costumes were so ill assorted in color that the stage looked like a dollar tie-counter pawed through by Christmas shoppers.

It is a good deal pleasanter to speak of the Fourth Act ballet in *Carmen*. Miss Svetlova's toe dance with fan and mantilla and in a brief ballet skirt—I imagine this is some 1870 kind of ballet Spanish—was an amusing novelty and didn't look out of place at all. It was also the best dancing I have seen at the Met. Amusing too was the mock bullfight that followed her number: and after that the ensemble flung itself into the finale with delight. A good deal of this vivacity was due to Beecham's conducting; at another performance, where he didn't conduct, the ballet was much less lively.

I also liked the incidental dance in *Lucia*; it was simple, but spirited and neat. Of the ballets for *Tannhaeuser, Samson and Delilah,* and even *The Bartered Bride,* the best I can report is that they were routine opera-ballet numbers, orderly in execution, but with foolish figures and dowdy costumes.

One may regret that the choreography at the Metropolitan has no freshness in movement, and regret that the young dancers seem to have no one who can awaken their vitality, who can teach them style and a clean line. But one can understand why the management prefers a routine ballet to a lively and stylish one. A lively ballet company is as much trouble to an opera manager as an infatuation is to a middle-aged man. When opera managers go overboard for really good dancing, they are in for extravagances, misunderstandings, recriminations and triumphant premieres. For a man who is running singers and musicians besides, it is a terrible strain. So one can accept our present "well meaning but not very able" Metropolitan ballet (so Paul Bowles called it) as a modest substitute for a glorious inconvenience—*January* 2, 1944.

WHERE ARE THE NEW SERIOUS
BALLETS?

THE April "war" between Ballet Theater and the Monte Carlo would have been more exciting to watch if it had been a competition between artistic directions instead of a competition for customers. There were plenty of customers everywhere, so both companies won. Ballet Theater, of course, had the smash hit, *Fancy Free*, and it had all through the smarter public. But it didn't allow its great choreographer, Mr. Tudor, to produce a new serious work; nor had the Monte Carlo allowed its guiding artist, Mme Nijinska, also a great choreographer, to create a serious new piece. Though the dancing was often superb and the audience got its money's worth, neither company can boast of a new production an intelligent citizen can get excited over; with all their rich resources neither company produced anything as remarkable as Martha Graham's *Deaths and Entrances*.

Ballet Theater has given native-born choreographers a chance as long as they would entertain. The Monte Carlo has tried to get the foreigners to be cute. No doubt the heavy touring schedules of both organizations make it impossible for them to rehearse with concentration. And no doubt the general public likes light pieces. But it is striking how the daily public here in town responds to the heavy ones, the abstract ones, the classic ones. Both companies underestimate the intelligence, the sensibility and the curiosity of the public. And they have no faith in the special power of a disinterested creation. One can't win an artistic victory without taking an artistic chance. And without such a special kind of victory no amount of success can counterbalance the decline of prestige.

Artistic prestige is ballet's chief economic asset. In order to survive ballet has to keep in competition with the classics—as contemporary serious painting, music and poetry do. It can't compete with commercial entertainment. This is not a matter of snobbishness, it is strictly a money matter. Ballet is too extravagant an apparatus to exist without subvention, public or private; it is as extravagant as a museum, or a symphony orchestra. In their artistic policy all of these enterprises must sell themselves to the kind of money that can pay for them—in their case the solid fortunes of trusts, foundations and states. Once our ballet succeeds in interesting such money, it can stop living from hand to mouth and present itself in its proper splendor.

And it is the solid world of the classics and of their serious contemporary competitors—representing as it does long-term artistic capital—that is most congenial to such long-term fortunes; while the world of commercial entertainment—strictly short-term artistic capital—normally appeals to short-term fortunes as a congenial field for their erratic spending.

But there is a simpler argument in favor of a disinterested artistic policy. It is that a ballet is a company of artists and that artists lose their vitality when they cannot feel around them an atmosphere of artistic conviction.

For the moment success is enough to give our dancers vitality. And though I feel that the glamor of momentary success is no solid foundation on which to build an American ballet, I am full of admiration for their freshness, their earnestness and their unremitting intensity. Their own artistic integrity is unimpeachable—*May 7,* 1944.

A FAULT IN BALLET THEATER'S DANCING

EACH Ballet Theater season, the more often I go, the more I admire the company. As a group, they are gifted, strong, conscientious, untiring dancers; as individuals they are lively, attractive young people. Each season, as the weeks pass and they recover from the strain of touring and from the interruption of ballet classes on tour, you see first this one and then that one begin to blossom in their dancing. Just now they are better than ever, and among the soloists warm-hearted Miss Hightower, Miss Alonso and Mr. Kriza are often even strikingly expressive. And yet, despite all this, the general tone of Ballet Theater's dancing has long had a tendency to seem heavy-footed and wooden. Watching Miss Riabouchinska and the illusion of animation she gives, I wondered what the technical secret of it might be.

For in the technique of a step, leap, or a lift most of Ballet Theater's company is far more accurate than she is. She fakes and she has no tautness. But when she dances she has a miraculous instinct for the atmosphere of a piece, so that her number fits naturally into the poetic illusion of it. Her dance makes sense in terms of the piece and it also makes natural sense as a dance. Her naturalness in action comes from the fact that she shows you so clearly the sustaining impetus, the dance impulse which carries her lightly through from beginning to end. Because the impetus is exactly right she strikes you as dancing her whole number on an impulse, spontaneously for joy of it.

Ballet Theater, by comparison, looks as if it tried manfully to do its duty. It doesn't dance as if dancing were easy; it doesn't quite seem to believe that a dance is a joy in itself. Instead of letting the number take wing and deploy in the make-believe atmosphere of the piece, Ballet Theater is afraid to let it go at that, it "theatricalizes" a dance by mugging or glamorizing. Often it acts as if a dance were an argument, a string of points to be put across by fair means or foul. It hits hard one step or gesture, goes dead and then with an effort begins the next one. You don't feel that the waist and the thighs are ready for dancing ahead of the feet and arms, the slight knee and ankle bend which connects steps isn't agile; the muscles around the small of the back aren't quiet enough. And so the feet stick and the arms drag. I am of course drawing a caricature here, but though I exaggerate the failing it exists.

Ballet Theater has, I think, trained itself too little in the physical basis for continuity in dancing and it has not trained, either, the instinctive gift for it that dancers have. They have not been trained to sense accurately the dance impetus which will best carry them through all the detail they are called on to perform, which will give it coherence and expression. But it is when he discovers the appropriate impetus for his part that the dancer begins to look light and natural and captivating.

Unfortunately Ballet Theater's repertory doesn't suggest lightness and naturalness to a young dancer. In spirit, its nineteenth-century revivals are often too self-conscious; its light modern pieces are often too smart-alecky—they comment on comic characters self-consciously from the outside. And in technique Tudor's complex serious ballets are obviously hard to dance with spontaneity. Spontaneity in dancing requires, among other things, personal changes of pace which animate the prevalent rhythm, but Tudor's main rhythm is hard to get hold of, it has no beat or lilt. So it is difficult for the dancers to sense where their instinctive changes of pace (their rubato) would be proper. Much rehearsed, *Romeo* and *Lilac Garden,* thanks to the brilliant example of rubato that Markova and Laing have given, have recently been danced with a striking increase in animation. And the company is dancing the new *Waltz Academy* with a new naturalness, too. It gives hope that Ballet Theater will plan its future repertory (and its future ballet classes) with an eye to remedying its faulty tendencies in dancing.

Ballet Theater is our strongest dance company. Its accuracy and its steady drive are quite exceptional. But it might look lighter and more spontaneous and more unself-conscious. As a company it still needs more of the physical sincerity, the warmheartedness that it admires readily and generously when it sees its own home-grown ballerina, Rosella Hightower, dancing—*October* 29, 1944.

ABOUT TOUMANOVA AND BALLET THEATER

WHAT really thrills in Toumanova's dancing is its horizontal and downward drive—the velocity with which she travels perfectly stiff, the force with which she rams her squared-off toe shoe into the floor, the solid slowness with which her free leg deploys its mass from the leg she stands anchored on. These are thrills where her prowess and her dance instinct coincide. She can simulate the motions of airiness—she did it perfectly in her second *Giselle* performance and in *Sylphides* —but she does not sustain for any length of time the impulse upward, the lyric breathing on which these roles are based. On the contrary you see her natural genius in *Tricorne,* when she sits down grandly and massively like a Roman river deity on the floor and waits for the Farucca to begin. The true ex pression of her dancing comes from her passion for the floor and its rhythm is one of pressure and explosion. The tone is an unexpected one in ballet, it even recalls Mary Wigman at her best. Toumanova has some of Frau Wigman's scorn for the amenities of the theater, her force of self-isolation on stage, her hectic smashing rhythm. A ballet in which Toumanova could oppose her record feats and her quasi-Wagnerian gran- deur to the airiness of the rest of the company would be com- pletely sensational; what she needs is a choreographer to show her as she is.

She has, I believe, been presented this season mostly as she is not. Unable to use her natural expressiveness, she has impro- vised a fake stage personality and with that, with her unfaked acrobatics and her face, she has been wowing the customers in the old vaudeville way.

Mr. Dolin as her partner in classic numbers, equally unable to prove his real theater virtue, has resorted to the same vaude- ville attack. He is not technically a classic dancer any more. He can get applause, to be sure, merely by looking lovingly at his own right hand or by doing a leap (entrechat) in which his feet paddle in the air like Donald Duck's; but this is no proof of his classic technique, it is a proof of his genius and experience as a showman. Dolin is a first-rate showman and comedian. His natural wit, enthusiasm, great charm and sense of caricature give a parody point to everything he does; they assure him of an immense success on the speaking stage, and those of us who sincerely admire him would like to see him add a fresh legitimate glory there to his former great glory in ballet. It is distressing to see two artists as fine as Toumanova and Dolin, both miscast, competing in a ballet number as to which will be the more audience conscious and stagey.

High-class vaudeville is not ballet. Ballet Theater is a company of very fine dancers. If the management encouraged their native sincerity as artists, if it encouraged sincerely poetic dancing above vaudeville auto-exhibitionism, the management would be astonished both how its neglected classic ballets would increase in value and how its intellectual prestige would soar —*November 5, 1944.*

BALLET INTERNATIONAL TWO WEEKS OLD

BALLET INTERNATIONAL, our new company, has several strong points which should not be overlooked. In the first place, it is a resident company. The dancers will not be exhausted by touring and their regular training will be less interrupted. Ballet dancers are athletes and they respond to a reasonable hygiene as much as other athletes do; they are also artists, and artists need a quiet place where they can work and they need an unconscious participation in the daily life of a city as anybody there lives it. A resident company can eat and sleep at home; it can practice and rehearse with concentration; it can be happy and unhappy in the same familiar drug store or elevator. International already shows a trace of the easy family feeling sensible working conditions induce. There is a serious and cheerful tone on the stage that a ballet company should have; there is no desperate anxiousness for personal applause that stage people resort to, as to a drug, when their vitality and self-respect are low.

But good points at International have been obscured by bad mistakes in artistic judgment. Of the nine pieces shown so far even the four more or less interesting productions—*Constantia, Sentimental Colloquy, Sebastian* and *Sylphides*—have not been satisfactorily produced all around. The general impression of the repertory to date is that the new choreographies begin well, but instead of developing further they turn repetitious; the choreographers needed more discerning encouragement to go on. The new orchestrations of old scores are not dry, but they tend to banalize (and rather sour) the music they set out to amplify. Hardly any of the new costuming is properly calculated for the small stage; it takes up too much room. The cut is awkward (*Swan Lake* bodices) or conceals the gesture (*Sebastian*), or suggests foolish associations (*Constantia*), or the colors break up the dance (*Brahms Variations, I*). The problems of orchestral balances, of how a lot of costumes will add up in dancing, of how drawing and color in a drop create or destroy space on stage—these technical problems are outside of the professional experience of Broadway because they are vital only in ballet production. And so instead of commissioning Broadway stylists, International might have appealed for new scores and sets to the composers and painters in town who are perfectly familiar with ballet production from experience with ballet here and abroad; their boldness and accuracy would have started the new repertory right.

When International started, the town was looking for a bold venture and it found a timid one. What we expected and missed was a clear sign of artistic direction, of intellectual drama and decision, of the nerve that creates style. Style can be created only at a risk, it is a form of courage, it is an exposed and often indefensible position. Stylishness even in the serenest classicism has a now-or-never edge and thrill, and even at its most playful it doesn't ask for a second chance. International has not been bold in style—*November* 10, 1944.

BALLET INTERNATIONAL'S SEASON

LOOKING back on International's recent season, its luckiest stroke was the discovery of the very great gifts of young Francisco Moncion. He had been doing classic as well as dramatic parts for some time in successive Kirstein companies, and a year ago his Sailor in Miss Shea's very interesting *Sailor Bar* had been especially remarkable. At the beginning of this season with International his parts weren't grateful ones. But later on in the male leads of *Sebastian, Mute Wife* and *Mad Tristan*— three wholly different styles of movement—he showed that he is the most gifted American character dancer (if one may use the term for dramatic characterization in ballet) to appear—"the best thing that has happened," as Mr. Van Vechten, our greatest ballet critic, said to me, "since Hugh Laing came along."

Moncion, well trained as a classic dancer, strong and manly, is like a modern dancer in the freedom with which he can use torso, arms and neck. But his exceptional gift is his intense imaginative sincerity. He creates a character completely, and he has power, musicality and humor. His leg gestures when the thighs separate are not as clear as the others, and his feet can get a more expressive support from the floor, but his instinctive dignity in expression will teach him best. A fine dancer who believes in dancing more than in himself is a wonderful thing and we can look forward to many seasons of growing pleasure in Moncion.

Sebastian and *Mute Wife*, in which Moncion made his mark, also showed the other dancers at their best. In the first, Miss Essen, though she has not the powerful, open line or the rhythm needed for a Swan Queen, was perfect as the Courtesan with a perverse young softness, a girl sincerely kind in little ways. In *Mute Wife* one saw young Guelis leaping up and hoped he might soon learn to be elastic above the waist. Among corps dancers, Miss Blum, Miss Shea were bright and cute, and one noticed a girl of quite exceptional grace and individuality, Miss Garfield, of whom her fellow dancers, too, prophesy great things. Among featured dancers in other pieces I admired Marie-Jeanne very much with her classic openness and rapidity in the thighs, her clear rhythm, and regretted her reticence in yielding motions and gestures above the head—and sometimes a little neglect of line in the instep. There was William Dollar, whom I like for his musical delight in dancing when he is in form, but whose mannerism of relaxing his loins in the air and his neck in poses has cost him the popularity he long since deserved; and forthright Miss Patterson, musical Miss Golovina, Maslova, Geleznova, and from the corps Miss Hill, Mr. Beard, Mr. Raher,

Mr. Armstrong. International's company is still not homogeneous and it is a bit heavy, but it is talented.

But International's great dance attraction was of course the superbly easy, clean, classic virtuoso, Eglevsky. Unfortunately, he was not well presented. One would have thought that International, faced with showing a green company in an untried repertory on a shallow, narrow stage under inadequate lighting facilities, would have built its first season around Eglevsky, and built it to some extent around its unusually fine orchestra. Instead, it wasted both these exceptional features by pretending to have as well all the other resources for ballet in the grand manner, which it too clearly didn't. International's personnel as well as its plant suggested a repertory of ballets in the concert style, small individualized ensembles, novel music, decoration planned to make the stage look freer. As gifted and experienced a choreographer as Nijinska might perhaps have given the company several striking concert-style ballets, had she been told to. The limitations of the form might have led to a freshness of conception and ideas, qualities that would have given vitality to the whole enterprise. And the small stage would have turned into an organic advantage—*December* 31, 1944.

THE MONTE CARLO NOW

THE Monte Carlo in the season that closes tonight at the Center has shown us wonders: a buoyant and direct classic style, a string of Balanchine productions featured as they should be, and in Danilova an incomparable ballerina who is both the queen and the visible heart of the dancing company about her. No wonder that the spirit on stage has been high, with so much reason for a clear artistic conscience. The company's spirit has won out over obvious defects—the sad spots still in the repertory, the fewness of experienced dancers, the absence of Youskevitch, a war-time need of men and the abominable visibility at the Center Theater. In respect to the theater, I find it scandalous that the Center administration has once more neglected to lower the fence of footlights that cuts off the dancers' feet for orchestra patrons as far back as row R; and absurd that the legs (side pieces) of the scenery are often hung in a way to make the small stage narrower than it need be. Just the same the dancing has been the happiest to watch in town for some years—unselfconscious in its manner, clear in its rhythm, fresh in its animation, light in its spring.

The new classicism which the Monte Carlo has accepted is the secret of its happy transformation. Classicism, in one sense, is a method of keeping clarity, continuity and dignity in vigorous dance movement. Though it limits the dancers' movements, so complete a classic master as Balanchine finds within these limitations an inexhaustible variety of dance figures, of rhythm and of human meaning. And the classic style as Balanchine understands it gives the dancer a means of personal expression without asking him to be an exhibitionist or to hypnotize the audience. There are no doubt other methods by which dancers can show their human dignity in their relation to an audience, but Balanchine's is a successful one. When they observe his classicism, dancers look clear and light, youthful and buoyant, and their personality that comes across is easy and fresh.

It has been astonishing to see how such thoroughly experienced dancers as the great Danilova, Franklin, Krassovska and

Lazovsky have all revealed their best qualities under his influence. As for the younger soloists, they have seemed to be bursting into bloom like forsythia all over the stage. My favorite has been Mary Ellen Moylan, whose graceful intrepidity and air of candor make me think of those demure ballet heroines who a century ago leaped from the top of a twenty-foot scenic waterfall into the arms of a partner. With Moylan's arrowy exactitude a special gift of hers is the young pliability of her straight back, and with it her instinctive grace in effacing or moving forward a shoulder or turning out an arm in its socket. Straightforward Maria Tallchief has not yet Moylan's grace of shoulder and she is now and then tempted to try for a solo effect when dancing with others, but her thrilling decisiveness and her brilliant legs are magnificent. Miss Boris, more experienced, has shown a scintillating clarity and a rich variety of dramatic temperament. All three do biting and beautiful toesteps. Imaginative Miss Etheridge, Miss Goddard, Miss Chouteau, Miss Razoumova, Miss Riekman have often been remarkable. Mr. Danielian, certainly the most brilliant American in leaps and beats, continues to gain admirably in classic rhythm and deportment. His weakness (like that of most young dancers) is a lack of expressive power in the connection between arms and torso. Far less brilliant than he, Magallanes has not this weakness and his handsome line as well as his miming is easy and natural. Bliss and Corvino are clearly gifted dancers too, and Talin is remarkably so whenever he doesn't jut out his chin in an unfortunate way.

I rather think that the young dancers of the company have been dancing far better than they know how, and if in one sense that is the only way to dance, in another it means that to strengthen their gifts they need most to keep on dancing in the fortunate direction they have taken. I hope they will bring us as many new Balanchine productions next year as this. That would assure their style and their deportment in all the rest of the repertory (their manners are still rude in the first act of *Nutcracker,* in the ensembles of *Gaité* and *Danube,* where good manners aren't solidly built into the choreography). And next year's repertory should by all means allow retiring *Frankie and Johnny, Scheherazade, Igrouchki, Red Poppy.*

The Monte Carlo, as our first clearly classic dance company, has given us a happy season, it has regained its artistic prestige, it has won discerning friends, and it has awakened great hopes for the future. It can be proud of its wonderful achievement in the last five months—*March 25, 1945.*

THE TOUMANOVA PROBLEM

BALLET THEATER'S current season closes next Sunday; judging by the improvement the company has shown this last week the final one may well be brilliant. Thanks to *Undertow* the company's spirits have recovered and so has attendance. During the first fortnight, however, Ballet Theater looked generally demoralized. Poor its houses were, due to a general slump in theater business, but an experienced company is not bowled over by a week of poor houses. I shouldn't wonder if Ballet Theater's jitters are serious and are due to an aggravated case of ballerina trouble. Ballet Theater often seems like a tight little republic of soloists; though they once accepted Miss

Markova as their queen ballerina, they have not accepted Miss Toumanova as her successor. And miscast as she has been—in absurd novelties, too—she has had the misfortune of not being fully accepted by the public either. Since she dominates the classic repertory, however, everybody is under an unhappy pressure, the general style of the company suffers and the public is disappointed.

If this is so, it would seem that the solution would be to run Ballet Theater without a queen ballerina until one emerges by public recognition of her merit. Miss Alonso, Miss Hightower, Miss Kaye have all been granted a joint first rank with Miss Toumanova and Miss Gollner by ensemble and public alike— in fact, despite the billing, this season has turned out to be more Miss Alonso's than Miss Toumanova's. It would be fine to see all five of them taking turns in starring.

Miss Toumanova is no doubt a more striking figure than the others. Her fascinating prowess is even more startling than in the fall, her aura of fanaticism, the impression she gives of devouring the stage, suggest how thrilling she might be in a part suited to her. Even in the way she is now presented, as an athletic prodigy of incomparably powerful leg gestures, she supplies a special excitement welcome on special occasions. It is only in her current false position as the central dynamo of the company that she is lost.

For in classic ballet the queen ballerina of a company is its central dynamo; she sets the style, she exemplifies it at its most completely expressive. It is through watching her that the audience understands the style of a piece, and the style creates the poetic illusion in which the drama becomes real. She projects not only her own role, but the entire world of fancy in which that role becomes dramatic, in which everybody and everything on stage can play a part. Stage stars of all kinds project such imaginary worlds; Miss Holm and Miss Merman, for instance, do it in musical comedy; Miss Cornell and Miss Taylor in spoken drama. In ballet Miss Markova showed this quality pre-eminently two weeks ago in *Romeo,* Miss Kaye showed it last Monday in *Lilac Garden* and Mr. Laing has it very strongly among male dancers. It is a quality that ballet language recognizes by saying that a real ballerina dances not a part but a ballet, not the Swan Queen but *Swan Lake.* I imagine that if Toumanova had shown this quality as steadily as Markova used to—as convincingly for the general ballet public—they would crowd to see her and give her similar ovations. And for myself, I notice she often gives me the impression of a phenomenal sleep-walker moving isolated among dancers who are performing a different piece.

Her isolation comes, perhaps, from the special nature of her dance style, which has little in common with that of the other dancers, for all its apparent classicism. Her blocklike torso, limp arms and predatory head position, her strangely static and magnificent leg control set her apart from the others. Her action looks not like what everyone does, done more subtly and naturally (which is a ballerina's function), but it looks like something radically different from her classic surroundings. It makes her seem less a classic heroine than an outcast.

And sometimes one wonders if Miss Toumanova doesn't play up her gift of chilly isolation on stage for an effect of exotic glamor, for a solemn impersonation of the foreign ballerina as Hollywood would type the part. It seems a foolish pose for her to take. Danilova, Krassovska, Riabouchinska, all as Russian as she, are all of them far too busy dancing to emphasize their Russianness among the Americans who surround them. But perhaps forcing her all at once into the position of top ballerina with Ballet Theater—instead of letting them gradually become acclimated to one another—has been the real cause of a "Toumanova problem." Now, as I see it, the problem both threatens to disrupt the company and misemploy this great dancer's native genius—*April* 22, 1945.

BALLET THEATER'S SEASON

LOOKING back on the two recent ballet seasons, I find that the Monte Carlo at the Center left an exhilarating impression despite its faults and Ballet Theater at the Metropolitan, despite its merits, left a depressing one. Wondering why so strong an array of dancers and a number of fine performances should leave a ballet lover depressed, it struck me that Ballet Theater's season had seemed like a number of disconnected efforts that had no guiding conviction to give them coherence and collective power. The performances of individual dancers had often been very fine, but too often they had had no dance contact with the rest of the ensemble on stage. Everybody did his job, but each worked for himself. Too often I missed the collective inspiration in dancing, the mutual dance response, that had been so exhilarating at the Monte Carlo. Ballet Theater was slick, but not inspired. And most of its fine moments reminded me of the fine moments of a good jazz soloist playing with a high-class commercial band; slick the band is and it has a showy punch, but it can't pick up the animation of his rhythm.

The expressive virtue of any dancing is its rhythm, and its rhythm is felt only in continuity. Lightness and heaviness, the start and stop of a gesture or step, the thrust and return of a limb form the alternating rhythm of dancing, its stress and non-stress. But the two elements must not be so different in interest that they cannot combine into a continuity; and so to be able to combine them a dancer learns light-footedness, elasticity and grace.

Classic dancing is our most expressive development of dance rhythm. It builds long continuities (or phrases) of movement that offer the audience variations of bodily impetus clearly set in relation to a fixed space. And these long phrases of movement convey the specific meaning of the ballet—its drama. As the impetus of successive phrases of music suggest to the hearer a particular quality of emotion and thought, so the successive phrases of a ballet suggest to the observer a particular quality of human action. When you watch a girl moving about a room you sometimes guess what the quality of movement "means." It is not that she expresses herself by making handies, she does it by the rhythm of her actions. We often understand animals that way and they us. And in love we all know how dramatic such a moment of understanding is. It seems to tell more than any words and say it more irrevocably. And this is the natural phenomenon on which the art of ballet is built as a convincing human expression.

I think it was this power of expression through rhythm that I missed at Ballet Theater so often this spring, for, as a company, their dancing was convincing only now and then. It seemed somehow too heavy-footed, overstressed, discontinuous. I think it did, because they defined the stress of the gesture emphatically but took no interest in the unstressed part. Perhaps they were thinking of dancing in terms of key effects rather than in terms of a continuous melody. But they missed giving the exhilarating sense of dance rhythm, that only the projection of a complete movement—stress and non-stress—can begin to create.

One can see that while it is possible for a dancer to smash the stress of a gesture at the public, he cannot do the same with the gesture's weaker phase. A complete movement (both parts of it as a rhythmic unit) gets its carrying power by a different attack—by being projected in relation to the stage space and the other dancers. This method has an air of modesty that doesn't catch the public as quickly, but it has the advantage of drawing the audience steadily into the illusion of situation and character which can exist only back of the proscenium. That is why the dramatic illusion and the dance illusion of ballet are broken by the punch of the hyper-active showman and are secured by the gentle-mannered and luminously calm ballerina.

If Ballet Theater's fine company would aim for the continuity of movement of classic dancing and for the rhythmic power such dancing has, it wouldn't need to worry whether the ballet craze is over yet in America or not—*May* 13, 1945.

BALLET RUSSE DE MONTE CARLO
DISTRACTED

THE Ballet Russe de Monte Carlo opened in New York September 4th in a distracted state with too little illusion of grace or style. During the course of its twelve-day season at the City Center the company had brighter moments and the big news was the dancing of Ruthanna Boris, who showed she deserved further ballerina parts. But the disappointments of the season remained too great. The repertory had been exposed to view in a ragged state to ragged music; Danilova, owing to a knee injury, hadn't appeared at all; Maria Tallchief, injured too, had had to stop dancing after a few days; and the only novelty had been Ruth Page's *The Bells*. Such a string of misfortunes was disheartening to watch. *The Bells*—choreography by Ruth Page, music by Milhaud, décor by Noguchi—claims in a pretentious program note that it "parallels the psychological development" of Poe's well-known poem. Incidentally, the program doesn't bother to quote the poem correctly.

The Bells is a piece that goes on for half an hour being puerile in public. First there is a good deal of blithe maidenhood on toe. Then a young man in yellow comes in and the heroine and he have a nice long wedding. After a while, the corps waves some cloth between them and they look unhappy. In due time enter the King of the Ghouls, a young man with a headdress. Our hero abandons his bride to stamp around with the newcomer, and this offends her. She takes to an umbrella. Everybody suffers more and more and works hard at it. By now everybody is tangled up in black streamers and in each other and so eventually everybody gets down on the floor except the King of the Ghouls, who, after breaking up one happy home, stands menacing the audience. The program book says this indicates "Beauty divorced from Truth and . . . the Moral Sense."

Not that *The Bells* is incompetent in its own manner. Cut down to ten minutes it would be an unusually good stage show at a movie palace. It has lots of different steps, difficult lifts, pretty line-ups, smooth transitions, an anodyne story, and even a dash of what in stage shows passes for modern dance. No doubt its dance ideas and its expressive passages are never anything but girlishly cute; its characters gesticulate in clichés of love and despair, its dances beat time to the music and have no surge or freedom of dance rhythm. But that is what the audience in a movie house expects of the stage show.

To Poe lovers in the dance public, not *The Bells,* but the mysteriousness of Balanchine's *Night Shadow*—a novelty of last season—is recommended. Mysterious is the interaction of its elements: the vapid ballroom dances; the winsome exhibition numbers that have a perverse and cruel undertone; the elaborate, encircling artifices of the coquette's pas de deux; the directness and space of the sleepwalking scene; the massed mime chorus in unison at the end. The progress of the piece is "romantic"—it is disconcerting, absurd and disproportionate; but its effect when it is over is powerful and exact. It gives you a sense—as Poe does—of losing your bearings, the feeling of an elastic sort of time and a heaving floor. As a friend of mine remarked, "When it's over, you don't know what hit you." *Night Shadow* bears no resemblance to the recent Balanchine "classic" pieces—no resemblance to their firm dance lilt and their formal transparence; though it is not a mimed piece, its effects are related to mime effects.

At the opposite pole from *Night Shadow* in form and in sentiment is the reconstruction by Danilova and Balanchine of Petipa's *Raymonda,* which the Monte Carlo also introduced last spring. Not only its air of leisure but its candor and sunny clarity are qualities unusual nowadays. It is difficult at first to be so unnervous, so relaxed and unresentful as this long and peaceful ballet invites you to be. The surprise is that it can be so long and so peaceful without turning foolish or false in sentiment. *Raymonda* has an easy amplitude and graciousness in good spirits; there is a sweetness in the air like that of a large, happy, well-mannered and gifted family living on a large, old-fashioned summer place. And you feel in it, too, the family note that distinguishes so pleasingly the Monte Carlo company itself.

There is, I am told, little of the original Petersburg *Raymonda* in this version, though the most fantastic dance invention, the ballerina's third-act Czardas on toe is authentic Petipa, and Petipa's, too, is the large, bold force of the male pas de quatre in that act. But all through this American *Raymonda*, the resourcefulness in simplicity, the vitality of dance rhythm, the clarity in plastic contrasts, the grand relief of the human figure are in the honest Petipa manner. The dances are by no means easy to do, for a blurred or unintelligent movement shows up at once. Everywhere they look as if it felt good to dance them and it feels good to watch them. With all their profuse variety there is not a mean gesture to be seen for a whole hour. Some people find this escapism, but as a conception of society it strikes me as revolutionary.

Without Danilova to dance them, her great parts looked pale and some fine passages meaningless. Franklin too was not at his best without her. Magnanimous and buoyant lyricist as he is and an excellent actor, he seemed a little tired and distressed and his style suffered; he looked as if he were counting for everybody else on stage and keeping a weather eye out for everyone's mistakes. In Danilova's parts, Krassovska, lovely and sweetly feminine when she can be yielding and modest, lacks the authority in development, the vitality and variety of dance rhythm that make grandeur lively. Marie-Jeanne, fantastically sharp in *Imperial,* excellent in *Night Shadow,* was on the other hand lost in *Baiser,* in which her intention to look soft and sweet made her slur the steps, vaguely wave her arms and miss the drama. Tallchief was wonderfully fascinating at moments, but her bad ankle restricted her.

A dancer who was constantly a pleasure to watch was Boris. Her lovely figure, her bearing and balance, her line, her clean, swift steps and harmonious ease, her reliability in every part were very remarkable. Her best part was *Serenade* where she showed a sense of what she seems still a little to lack—a wider scope in rhythm, a bolder timing of main accents and a more elastic change of speed which will sustain and join the phrases of a dance in what in music is called a period. Young Chouteau, as careful though not nearly so finished, but clear and intelligent in her dancing, seems to me to have very great possibilities. There isn't space for more, but one should at least mention Tyven's excellence this season, Goddard's Nelly, Magallanes' noble support, especially in *Barocco,* young Weaver's cleanness, Kokic's Wrangler, Bliss's Roper, and above all Danielian's really superb dancing in *Raymonda.*

Watching the dancers in good and less good performances, and considering the handicaps the management imposed on them this fall, there is no doubt that with a little planning the company can show again the light, clear, intelligent dance style they specialize in and that ballet lovers have justly admired them for—*November,* 1946.

BALLET THEATER WINS

NEW YORKERS never spent so much money on ballet as in October and it was a pity they didn't get a dazzling season. The novelties of interest were only two, both of them given by Ballet Theater—Jerome Robbins' new piece, *Facsimile,* and a new staging of *Giselle* danced by Alonso and Youskevitch and decorated by Berman. Comparing the two rival companies, Ballet Theater's season was a very pleasant one as a whole, though distinctly uneven; but it set a superb standard compared to that of the Original Ballet Russe which was cluttered with shabby performances and shoddy productions. The Original's was far the poorest Met season in ten years, even though it included Markova's beautiful Giselle.

The Original had not been here since '41. For five years it toured Latin America, repeating its pre-war repertory, changing personnel, recasting roles. Such as it was, the company remained committed to the Franco-Russian Ballet Russe tradition. For its return to New York, however, a dozen or more dancers, raised in or acclimated to our own different standards, were quickly added; Markova and Dolin, Eglevsky, Hightower, Antonia Cobos, George Skibine, Francisco Moncion were put in as extra stars; four New York choreographies, plus *Giselle,* Dolin's *Pas de Quatre* and standard pas de deux were hastily stuffed in among the repertory. The ballet grab-bag that resulted had no collective vitality or style. It was the added dancers and choreographies that gave the Original season what bright moments it had; but the Ballet Russe contingent far outnumbered them, and in their dilapidated state offered one dismal sight after another.

There were times when these pre-war Ballet Russe productions evoked a ghost of the company's pre-war grand manner—evoked as in a parody the former sweep of phrase, the former temperament, the former gift for color and impersonation. The old effects failed now because the technical basis for them had rotted away. The usual dancing of even the principals—such as Stepanova, Moulin, Morosova among the ladies, or Toupine (a dancer of great gifts), Dokoudovsky, MacKenzie among the men—was rudely forced or vague in rhythm, in line, in step; it was thick in the shoulder, heavy in carriage, lacking in courtesy and emptily emphatic in stage presence. That there was talent buried under these ruins only made the spectacle more morbid. If the Ballet Russe section of the Original is to be revivified as a company, it will take a year of rigorous classwork and a new repertory to do it.

Danced without grace of any kind, the pre-war repertory was no pleasure to see. Massine's *Fantastique,* for instance, looked merely hectic and brutal; Fokine's *Paganini*—despite its often large-scale rhythmic continuity—merely complacently mawkish in sentiment. The Original also displayed two lengthy 1946 novelties. One, Psota's *Yara* had a pleasing Brazilian score and décor (Mignone and Portinari) but no dance interest. The other, Lichine's *Cain and Abel,* stressed manly Body Beautiful poses by two rugged boys in tiny trunks, and sexy entanglements with two girls called Good and Evil; Cain and Abel also bumped around together on the floor a good deal and perspired freely. A wit called it "Tarzan in a Turkish Bath" and the orchestra played *Siegfried* to it.

Fresh and quite clear by contrast were the non-Ballet Russe

productions added here under local direction, and with non-Ballet Russe dancers to set the style. The only new piece among them was John Taras' *Camille* (score, Schubert-Rieti; décor, Cecil Beaton), described as a dream of the dying Lady of the Camelias. The graceful and cool correctness of its dance invention and bits of mime made it an agreeable though an excessively slight ballet. Markova danced the title part delicately and the first dim glimpse of the set was remarkable. On the other hand, seen in any relation to its subject matter, *Camille* was preposterously virginal.

The Original's two super-stars were guest artists, Markova and Eglevsky. Markova danced more carefully, elegantly and imaginatively than last year. Like last year she diminished, wherever possible, high leaps, high développées, large displacements, all that required unusual physical strength. But within this diminished scale of dance values her control of momentum, the limpidity of rhythm and gesture were as miraculous as ever. That her dramatic genius has found no big part since Juliet—and is now restricted to Giselle—is a great loss, greater as the years hurry by.

It is a loss too that, since his triumph in *Apollo* last year, no new part has been found that suits Eglevsky's special large and deliberate soaring rhythm. The magnificence of his force at present is unequaled among dancers. He was unusually meticulous this season; but an entrechat with his back to the audience (in his Black Swan variation) was an impolite error.

Eglevsky's leaps and Markova's Giselle had long been Ballet Theater attractions; to make up for losing them this year, Ballet Theater offered two of its three finest new features—the new production of *Giselle* with Alonso; and Youskevitch as regular classic premier. Where Eglevsky's virtuosity is one of forthright power and breadth, Youskevitch's in the same great passages is one of elegant and even insinuating grace. Youskevitch's art of plastic harmony (of contra-posto) can give his strength a sort of mild luster; his miming is unmannered; his support is superb; his courtesy and his modesty charm and his bows are in good taste. These were his first weeks of real ballet in more than three years, and his achievement in general was excellent.

Ballet Theater's new *Giselle* which he danced in was, though unfinished, an event of importance. Formerly it was only Markova's piece, now it is on the way to becoming the whole company's. Alonso's Giselle is young, lovely, much more carefully worked out than last year. In the crucial second act she is stronger than Markova in many virtuoso feats; none the less Markova is still dramatically more thrilling. One watches Alonso imitate to perfection several of those touching "Victorianisms" of Markova's that are close to mincing; they are effects that suit Markova's figure but not always Alonso's. (Alonso's head, for example, when she holds it forward is not fragile enough to be innocently wagged.) Markova, too, attains expressive effects by a sovereign evenness of momentum, which makes her motion seem floating and her lift seem under a spell (as when, for instance, the unbroken impetus at the start of her lifts prepares for the vaporous descent). Alonso tends to a more sforzando-edged attack and it sometimes breaks the continuity of her characterization, too. (So, in *Giselle* as in *Swan Lake,* she can first look a bit too consciously familiar in the arms of her lover and then start away a bit too willfully, twice breaking the spell.) Alonso's Giselle is a brilliant effort still incomplete; when she gains full dramatic power, she will have found an over-all dance impetus (or attack) for the part that suits more intimately her own genius as a dancer. (Incidentally, Alonso's bows "in character" are unfortunate.)

The new production aimed in many details for clarity of motivation. I was sorry it missed motivating through Myrtha Giselle's return to dancing stage center after her flight with Albrecht to the cross—and this, the beginning of the climax, was the point at which the dramatic continuity broke down. The "love death" climax of *Giselle* was best conveyed years ago in Serge Lifar's version and his own rise in elevation toward the end, like an ecstatic possession, was magnificent.

Marvelously dreamloaded and miasmic in atmosphere, in subject matter, color and perspective were Berman's backdrops; beautiful too were his two front curtains (all superbly executed) and several costumes. On the other hand, the Willis looked interesting but too substantial and the chorus costumes in act one were a mistake. As a whole, Ballet Theater's production was a real theater event, full of imagination, amplitude and devotion to a central tradition of ballet.

Robbins' new piece, *Facsimile* (score by Leonard Bernstein, set by Oliver Smith, costumes by Irene Sharaff) is an earnest satirical image of a flirtation between an idle woman and two idle men. You see how these people by anxiously pretending they feel a mutual attraction, get themselves into an awkward *amour à trois* tangle, which turns viciously hateful as the frenzy rises. At a momentary stalemate that postpones the climax, the woman stops the action with an hysterical cry. Politely the men stop. Humiliated but polite, the three leave separately and the stage is empty.

To pretend to be sexy is a farce situation and Robbins hasn't missed the jokes. But he has given his characters a spasmodic grasping drive that indicates they are passionately pretentious. The devouring drive of vainglory is a tragic subject. But *Facsimile* doesn't go that far. Its characters stop prematurely; after the embarrassing cry there is no further development, no shock of terror, no fury, disintegration or resolution. And so the disaster remains pathetically trivial.

Though timid in that more serious sense, the stage craftsmanship of *Facsimile* is immensely capable. There is no padding, no hesitancy, no drop, no blur. Though made up of fragmentary, often constricted gestures, the continuity is unbroken, the placing sharp, the rhythm bold, the musical tact remarkable. So is the cartoonist wit; and remarkable as dance invention is the long main climax. *Facsimile* is a big step forward by an honest, exceptionally gifted craftsman. It was excellently performed by Robbins and John Kriza and with consummately rich brilliance by Nora Kaye. The set was intelligent, remarkable in the opening light; the score trivial and efficient.

Ballet Theater's other novelties, Ashton's *Patineurs* and Lester's *Pas de Quatre,* two ten-year-old charm numbers brought back from England, were pleasant and in good taste but too slight. Ashton should be invited over to rehearse some of his serious pieces with our companies.

The attractive general character of Ballet Theater's season was due to the return of a happier, more homogeneous company atmosphere. Though smaller and not quite so strong as once, it is still as pretty a company and, despite overwork, it managed generally to look fresh and crisp.

The management has restored the company's collective harmony and morale; the dancers are fresh, bold and strong; it looks like a good opportunity for some conscientious technical development—*December,* 1946.

5

Events of Earlier Seasons

NOCES

NOCES in the choreography of Nijinska (revived this spring by the Monte Carlo Ballet) is, I'm sure, one of the finest things one can see anywhere. And if I could think of higher praise I would write it.

Noces is noble, it is fierce, it is simple, it is fresh, it is thrilling. It is full of interest. It is perhaps an indication of the heroic age of Nijinsky. There is a realness in the relation of dance and music like a dual force, separate but inseparable. The movements, odd as they are and oddly as they come, often in counter accent, are always in what theoreticians call "motor logic"; that is they are in a sequence you get the hang of to your own surprise, and that has a quality of directness when performed. Amazingly few movement-motives are used, and only the clearest groupings and paths, making the rhythmic subtlety obvious by contrast. That all these movement-motives should be accentuating the direction into the floor leads to such interesting results as that ballet dancers more familiar with the opposite direction do these movements with a curious freshness; that the leaps seem higher; that further, the "pointes" get a special significance and hardness (almost a

form of tapping), a hardness which all the performers by the
way had not understood; and, as a further example, this
general downward direction gives the heaped bodies a sense
further than decoration and the conventional pyramid at the
end, the effect of an heroic extreme, of a real difficulty. This
sense of the realness of what is being done is underlined by
the constant use of people at rest contrasted with people dancing, in the last part people actually at rest on chairs. How
often in other ballets have people stood about while others
danced without adding by their contrast, because the contrast
was not being used. And the stillness of the whole company
at the end after all their frenzy is a climax of genius. During
the whole last scene, the climax is a sort of steady expansion,
as thrilling and inevitable as for the intelligence the motion
from the particular to the abstract—*May-June, 1936.*

AFTERNOON OF A FAUN

D URING the last six weeks New York has been a pleasant place for a person who likes ballet. I have seen one
absolutely first-class piece, Nijinsky's *Faun;* Berard's sets for
the *Symphonie Fantastique,* the second and third of which are
as good as the best ever made—probably the best we'll see all
winter; and then a new dance group that is full of freshness
and interest, the American Ballet Caravan. I have also seen
other things I liked more or less, or not at all, and I have not
by any means seen everything that has been done.

The revivals of the de Basil Ballet Russe are as carefully rehearsed and as freshly executed as its novelties. Last year's *Noces* and this year's *Faun* are things to be very grateful for. The *Faun* is an astonishing work. After twenty-three years it is as direct and moving as though it had been invented yesterday. It gathers momentum from the first gesture to the last like an ideal short story. From this point of view of a story, the way the veil is introduced and reemphasized by the nymph is a marvel of rightness. From the point of view of visual rhythm the repetition of the nymph's gesture of dismay is the perfection of timing. It is, of course, because so few gesture motives are used that one can recognize each so plainly, but there is no feeling of poverty in this simplification. The rhythmic pattern in relation to the stage and to the music is so subtly graded that instead of monotony we get a steady increase in suspense, an increase in the eyes' perceptiveness, and a feeling of heroic style at the climax.

It is true that most of the gestures used have prototypes in Greek reliefs and vase paintings, but, in addition to that intellectual association with adolescence, the fact is that when the body imitates these poses, the kind of tension resulting expresses exactly the emotion Nijinsky wants to express. Both their actual tension and their apparent remoteness, both their plastic clarity and their emphasis by negation on the center of the body (it is always strained between the feet in profile and the shoulders *en face*)—all these qualities lead up to the complete realization of the faun's last gesture. The poignancy of this moment lies partly in the complete change in the direction of tension, in the satisfying relief that results; and the substitution of a new tension (the incredible backbend) gives the work its balance. But besides, the eye has been educated to see the plastic beauty of this last pose, and the rhythmic sense to appreciate its noble deliberateness. That it is so intensely human a gesture, coming after a long preparation of understatement, gives it, in its cumulative assurance, the force of an illumination. This force of direct human statement, this faith in all of us, is the astonishing thing about the *Faun*. It is as rare in dancing as in the other arts. These last moments of the *Faun* do not need any critical defense. But they have been so talked about that I am trying to point out for intellectuals that they are not a sensational tag, but that the whole piece builds up to them, and reaches in them an extraordinary beauty.

The de Basil company danced the *Faun* beautifully. Lichine in the title role excelled. It is a part that demands exceptional imagination, as well as great plastic sense. And Lichine had besides these a fine simplicity—*November-December*, 1936.

LINCOLN KIRSTEIN'S AMERICAN BALLET CARAVAN

THE intelligentsia turned out in full for the All-American Evening of Kirstein's American Ballet Caravan, they approved the whole thing vociferously and they were quite right. There was a happy community feeling about the occasion, a sort of church-social delight, that would have surprised the out-of-towners who feel New York is just a big cold selfish place, where nobody has any interest in anybody else. The ballets—*Showpiece* by McBride and Hawkins, *Yankee Clipper* by Bowles and Loring, and *Filling Station* by Thomson and Christensen—taken together show that an American kind of ballet is growing up, different from the nervous Franco-Russian style. From Balanchine it has learned plasticity, and openness, and I imagine his teaching has fostered sincerity in these dancers as in others he has taught. But our own ballet has an easier, simpler character, a kind of American straightforwardness, that is thoroughly agreeable. None of these ballets is imitative or artificial, and there is nothing pretentious about them. Hawkins shows us a good-humored inventiveness, Loring a warmth of characterization, and Christensen a clear logic of movement that are each a personal and also specifically American version of ballet. I think this is the highest kind of praise, because it shows the ballet has taken root and is from now on a part of our life. And the dancers themselves have an unspoiled, American, rather athletic quality of movement that is pleasant. As a group they are first-rate in their legs and feet and in the profile of the arms. I think they still lack an incisive stopping; and the expressiveness across the shoulders that will shed light through the correctness of movement; but their improvement in the last two years has been so phenomenal that these reservations aren't serious. At present the boys steal the show, especially Christensen with his great ease, and Loring with his human quality, but they don't try to steal it; and Albia Cavan and Marie-Jeanne show they intend to catch up with them. But one of the very good things about the Caravan is its homogeneity as a group. And I congratulate them all wholeheartedly, just as the audience did—*March-April,* 1938.

LEONIDE MASSINE

M ASSINE is certainly brilliant whether he appears as a
performer or a director. He knows how to keep things
going, how to make them look like a lot, how to get a big
hand. He can get away with murder. If one took him seriously, he would be guilty of murdering the Beethoven *Seventh*,
the Fioretti, and even tender little Offenbach (though there
wasn't much of Offenbach left in that new orchestration).
There is of course no reason for taking Massine seriously, he
doesn't mean to be, he doesn't mean to murder. Like a ciga-
rette company, he is using famous names to advertise his
wares. But I cannot help resenting it, because they are names
of living things I have loved. It is hardest to bear in the case of
the *Seventh*, where the orchestra is constantly reminding me
of the Beethoven original.

Trying however to put aside this private resentment, I still
am disappointed. Well, I'll exaggerate, and be clearer. I could
see a kaleidoscopic succession of clever arrangements, but
there was no thrill in the order in which they came. There
was no sequence in the movement that awakened some kind
of special feeling, some kind of urgency. It all occupied the
eye as long as it lasted, and left no reality, no secret emotion
behind. I missed the sense of growth and interplay, of shifting
kinds of tensions, the feeling of drama almost, that makes the
best choreography mean much more than a string of effects.
As a pictorial arranger Massine is inexhaustible. But dancing
is less pictorial than plastic, and pictures in dancing leave a

213

void in the imagination. They arrest the drama of dancing which the imagination craves to continue, stimulated by all the kinetic senses of the body that demand a new movement to answer the one just past. Until a kind of secret satisfaction and a kind of secret weariness coincide.

This dramatic progression of different qualities of movement is what means so little in these ballets. Take the *Seventh*. Every gesture is visually clear, but every gesture is at the same pitch, hit equally hard. The picture changes, but the tension remains the same. It's all very agitated. There are sometimes more, sometimes fewer people on the stage; they get on top of each other, lie down, run around, jump, crouch, whirl, pose, wave, or huddle, and they never give any sense of getting closer together or farther apart, of getting lighter or heavier, more open or more shut in, more soft or more hard. It is showmanship with a vengeance, it is a drill of automatons. Notice Massine's use of ballet technique. The extended silhouette is used as though it were a constant, like a military position; with none of the thousand subtleties of direction and intensity with which Balanchine gives it so much variety and purpose. And consequently with Massine it breaks in the middle, in the small of the back, instead of growing out from there by reaching up and down in a thousand human ways.

Because Massine's tension is static he can never make us feel the curious unfolding that is like tenderness. Like a Hollywood director he gives us no sense of human growth (there isn't time), he keeps everything at a constant level of finish, everything is over as soon as it starts. He has no equivalent for mystery except to bring down the lights. So the *Seventh*, though danced with fervor and transfigured by the most wonderful sets and costumes in the world, leaves a sense of cheapness; and if you remember the mystery of Beethoven dynamics, it is unpleasant. *Gaîté Parisienne* seems just another empty Review number. Where sex is a convention and not an emotion. Smarter of course than Broadway, and marvelously danced. And *St. Francis* seems a slinky posturing, a Sacharoff-Kreuzberg parody of illuminated Books of Hours and Minnelieder, with a grand finale of anthroposophic chorus girls—*November-December*, 1938.

DEVIL'S HOLIDAY, CAPRICCIO ESPAGNOL, GHOST TOWN

THE Monte Carlo, which I am always happy to see, began the season with a new ballet Diaghileff would have been proud of: *Devil's Holiday*. And Massine, who has been the Diaghileff for this production, deserves equal praise. I have seen it three times and I like it better each time. Everything about it is full of zest, sincerity, freshness, and charm. Tommasini, as Mr. Martin so well said, seems to have had the time of his life writing the music on Paganini themes, and the variations in the first half of the last scene struck me as particularly beautiful. Berman, from whom we had wonderful drops for *Icare* last season, has given us five more which are as brilliant as any baroque Burnacini, but full of a contemporary intimate and personal sentiment, and also scenically discreet; and his costumes are the most wonderful imaginable—just look at the two Servants of the Devil, at the Devil's horrible disguise, or the farandole in the last scene, like a fashion show in heaven. (Judging from the published sketches the drops were not as well executed as they should have been—especially the landscape—nor all the costumes, but even so they were wonderful.)

And I am delighted too with the new choreographer, Frederick Ashton, the young Englishman who several years ago did the dances for *Four Saints*. His style is original, and originality usually looks awkward at first or unnecessarily complicated, or arbitrary, or something. His at first looks jerky, and you miss the large simple phrases you have come to like in Fokine, or the expert mass climaxes of Massine, or the incredible long moments of extension and tenderness of Balanchine, like speech in the silence of the night. But you can praise all that and still praise Ashton too. If he derives from anyone it is, I think, Nijinska, with her hasty almost shy elegance, her hobbled toesteps. He derives too it seems to me from the kind of awkward and inspired dancing that young people do when they come back from their first thrilling ballet evening and dance the whole ballet they have seen in their own room in a kind of trance. The steps do not look like school steps (though they are as a matter of fact correct), they are like discoveries, like something you do not know you can do, with the deceptive air of being incorrect and accidental that romantic poetry has. But how expressive, how true to human feeling the dances are. The perverse solemnity of the betrothal guests, the noble and pathetic stiffness of the betrayed betrothed, the curious frenzy of cruelty after the scandal; these are real emotions. The lovers' dream dance is restlessly hurried like a dream in which you know you are only dreaming; and what a final and brief conclusion it has into a deeper sleep. Like a Sitwell poem, the Hunting number is fussy and witty to heighten the lonely and frantic despair of the lost lover, interrupted by a diabolically hysterical substitute love. And the last scene is a whirl of inventions, of young eagerness that can hardly stop for the tenderness it dreams of, and that is tender without knowing it. A choreographer who can call up so many sincere emotions, who keeps a steady line of increasing interest (and animation) throughout a long ballet, and does not fall into conventional tags at important moments is a real rarity who is worth being enthusiastic about, and, what is more, worth paying for a ticket to see. Personally the only part I do not care for is the fox's dance, which however gets a laugh and a hand.

Devil's Holiday is probably difficult to dance and it is danced very well by everyone. The type of expression is not mimetic, but like that in classic ballet, in which the entire personality illuminates a role that the dancer has to conceive without the aid of detail. Danilova is particularly fine, of course; Krassovska is brilliant; and Franklin is magnificent. Platoff, of whom I think very highly as a dancer, was good but not as good as he generally is. All the dancers in the divertissement of the last scene were splendid.

As to the other novelties: *Igrouchki* (Fokine) is a doll-skit in the Chauve Souris style, which looks a little silly blown up to the proportions of an opera stage. *Capriccio Espagnol* has the benefit of Argentinita's exhaustless repertoire of regional steps, and of Massine's equally exhaustless repertoire of effective theater. Most of it is pleasant to watch and the end is one of those bang-up finales that are indispensable to ring the curtain down if you have a lethargic audience. Massine has a solo, and in it he makes the other men look like little boys.

The showmanship, the bite of his stage presence is superlative; look at the slow curling of his hands as his dance begins. It is inaccurate to call such a dance as his Spanish in the specific sense (see the difference in stance, in the relation of the partners, in the casual interruption of dancing) and foolish to compare him with a real gypsy, who would probably have no gift for dominating a crowded stage and would hardly be visible at that moment to an ordinary audience. (Eglevsky, the new star, is very agreeable in this ballet; he has the world's finest plié, which delighted me in *Swan Lake;* his *Spectre de la Rose* was more brilliant than Guerard's but less distinguished. Theilade was fine in the *Spectre,* too.)

Ghost Town won an ovation. Rodgers' music is Rodgers at his own best; it is catchy, and unpretentious, and keeps going, and I enjoyed the clarity of it. It also sounded repetitious and orchestrally sour and melodically saccharine, but that is not the point; it does say something of its own. The set and costumes (du Bois) too are musical comedy, and yet they have a callow freshness that isn't fake. The Picasso, the Derain, the Berman or Berard decorations all have space under wonderful control; and their colors even during dancing stay in place, so to speak, and don't mess up the stage. There is nothing of that in this du Bois, which is obviously awkward and keeps going all the time all over the place, without rest or coherence; but it's not an imitation any more than the Rodgers is. You can call it vulgar, but in its own way it is sincere.

The choreography, which is Platoff's first work, strikes me as much more interesting than either the music or décor, although it is even less orderly. It too keeps going all over the place, messes up dances by realistic gestures, by awkward spacing, and operatic arm-waving. But there is an exuberant energy in it. There are also, even at a first view, bold details, such as the double action of the two rival groups of prospectors, which are remarkable and very promising for the future; the second Mormon entrance and Ralston's dance of jubilation looked especially good too. But I think better than any detail was a something direct in the whole attack. It was not an imported atmosphere. For the first time the Broadway audience felt at home at the Ballet Russe; and before anybody knew it the Metropolitan itself turned out to be only two blocks from good old Times Square—*October-November,* 1939.

POKER GAME AND BAISER DE LA FEE

BALANCHINE'S *Poker Game* (set to Stravinsky's *Jeu de Cartes*), revived this fall at the Monte Carlo, is a ballet in a minor genre but it is as good ballet as one can possibly have. And it creeps into your heart as unpretentiously as a kitten. To be sure its range is limited. It is no more than a new twist to the animated doll subject, which by nature is witty, ironical, appealing and playful, and rather likes to stay within the bounds of pleasant manners. Ballet certainly can have a wider range if it chooses; and *Petrouchka,* even though it starts with the doll idea, does choose. *Poker Game* doesn't, and yet it succeeds in becoming a "minor masterpiece." I think when you see it, you will notice yourself how easy it is to look at, how agreeably it shifts from group to ensemble or solo, with an unexpectedness that is never disconcerting; how lively the relation is between still figures and moving ones; how distinct the action remains; how clear the center of attention, or the division of interest, so your eye does not take to wandering on its own and confuse the rhythm intended.

But besides being easy to look at, what you see is amusing. The steps emphasize a kind of staccato and a lateralness that may remind you of playing-card figures; many of the steps you recognize as derived from musical comedy. But the variety, the elasticity of dance impetus, the intelligent grace are qualities you never get in musical comedy routines. Nor does the musical comedy routine allow everyone on stage to project intelligent and personal good spirits. *Poker Game* by allowing the dancers just this makes you feel as if you were for a while in the best of company, with everybody natural and everybody interesting.

It is Balanchine's merit that all this is so. He keeps the dance placed in relation to the actual stage frame, which gives it a common sense point of reference. He has the sense of timing, the sense of distances, which makes the movement distinct. He has the wit which makes it amusing and the invention both plastic and rhythmic to keep it going in a lively way. He has the good sense to keep the numbers to their obvious subject: you see the Durante-like Joker egging on the silly Queens against the Aces; you distinguish between Jacks and Kings, you can tell who is winning or losing, and he does not make either too serious for the other. The subject in other words remains real and aboveboard; and the emotion it leads to, whether witty or sentimental, kept in relation to this subject, does not take on a faked or a private urgency.

But Balanchine has a profounder choreographic gift. His

steps no matter where derived are steps that a ballet dancer specifically can do and do best; steps a ballet dancer can be brilliant in. His rhythms however complex are grateful to ballet dancers. He seems never to violate the real nature of a dancer's body, the part native, part trained, relation of trunk and arms and head and feet; so that no matter how odd the movement required, the dancer still remains himself, and does not congeal to an impersonal instrument. And so the choreography does not violate the dancer's best gift, which is his natural human warmth. It is a fact that Balanchine has been able to make the same dancers seem real and true in his ballets, who have seemed conventional or stupid in others. All these qualities being the best qualities of choreography there are, make a good Balanchine ballet as good ballet as you can get. It is true his style is very complex, and some people don't like complex dancing. There is also a joyous irony in his tenderest pathos, and irony in sentiment seems subversive to good people who like to think that sentiment is something comfortable, secure. But this issue does not arise in *Poker Game*.

I found the entertaining music of *Poker Game* wonderful to listen to; and thanks to the play of counter-rhythm and counter-dynamics on the stage, easy to follow. (The light orchestration, obvious accents and sharp eighth notes seemed helpful for dancing, making counting easier.)

I cannot resist adding by way of footnote that I urge you to see and see again the Balanchine-Stravinsky *Baiser de la Fée*, now also in the Monte Carlo repertory. Unlike *Poker Game* it is ballet at its grandest. It has a range of expression that includes the brutality of the peasant dances, the frightening large mime gestures of the fortune-telling scene, the ominous speed-up of the wedding party, the hobbled tenderness of the bridal duet, the clap of thunder entrance of the veiled Fairy, the repulsive dissolution of the last scene; all of it fascinating and beautiful. Its images of destiny, its tragic illuminations are as convincing as any I know in literature; but the lightness, the grace with which these dramatic scenes develop is peculiarly Balanchinian. *Baiser de la Fée* is poetic theater at its truest.

Looking back on this season and the repertory as a whole, the dancers seemed better than ever in technique and verve. But I am disappointed that Danilova and Massine are still the only artists who seem to have got over the limitation and the prejudice of being invariably juvenile. Maybe I do Rostova, Lauret and Krassovska an injustice; and Markova—whose second act in *Giselle* was so miraculous last year—showed real warmth this time as Queen of Hearts. But I believe that she and Franklin and Eglevsky are greater dancers than they have dared to prove in their repertory this season. I missed in general the performer's passionate and uninhibited belief in his part, which can give to a dancer the most luminous theater presence in the world—*November-December*, 1940.

(A Year Later)

I am shocked to find that the last scene of the *Baiser de la Fée* has been mutilated. The slow rope climbing in its finale used to open up, both in style and emotion, an obscure and terrifying further perspective, which set the proportion of everything that had gone before; just as the music here does. This year the rope ladder has been cut and there is some creeping around on a ramp, which can't look other than stupid and is completely ineffective. The substitution is an act of vandalism. Whoever is responsible for it should be watched; he is dangerous—*November-December*, 1941.

GRADUATION BALL

LICHINE'S *Graduation Ball* is in its type just an operetta to Strauss music, the stock item every company offers. But Lichine's piece, without visible effort to be special, turns out to be a pleasant surprise. You may think you are looking at the same old thing, but you don't feel as if you were. The very first waltz strikes you right away as a little human scene. And the show-off "Perpetuum Mobile" which is a feat of new steps and trick technique, doesn't impress you, it delights you as spontaneously as the best Lindy Hop does. *Graduation Ball* has its weak spots too, but they do not seem important because you feel the piece directly as a whole, you feel its whole-hearted impulse before you judge its detail.

Though *Graduation Ball* is ballet comedy, the conventional marionette gestures that belong to the type have almost disappeared. In modern ballets they have not often been amusing; they have not often been jokes of character, but only professional jokes of dance style. Dancers think them terribly funny, but no one else does. Lichine's numbers, instead of being made up out of smug references to what is supposed to be funny, are the actions of real dance characters in a plausible situation, they are real dancers with all the exuberance of dancing. Such direct humor puts *Graduation Ball* in the best class of comedy, which Massine's recent comedies, for all their wit, do not reach.

Character dancing is not like lyric dancing. Lyric dancing is concerned with the secret reality of proportions in space; to

223

character dancing space is more practical, it's a question of having room enough. The lyric effect is lovely. But its method (under the absurd name of modern and abstract) has become so canonized in the last two decades that it is now the only respectable way to do choreography whether one has the gift for it or not. Lichine's gift is too concrete to get very far among secrets; and it is a pleasure to see him drop what he could continue only as a respectable convention. You can forgive him his plain floor patterns, his unrefined spacing, his lack of subtlety for the sake of the true gift he gives free play to instead. Lichine is not "translating ideas into terms of dance," he is dancing in the first place. His mistakes are not correctible according to another choreographer's style; the impulse is too original, an originality so spontaneous you get the happy feeling he can go on inventing forever, that he draws not on his taste but on a world he was born with, a whole world new to us.

Graduation Ball, though by nature a minor piece, struck me as proving Lichine's gifts most conclusively. Of his other pieces, *Protée* seemed like a grave finagling of nothing much. *Francesca da Rimini* was empty in its elaborate love scenes, but it had a few fine group moments, which suggested that life in a thirteenth-century castle was actually brutal, crowded and public. Lichine's version of *The Prodigal Son* was more convincing as a busy night on the waterfront than as a parable. The action parts were lively, striking dances; but the lyric parts, the scenes of warning, of remorse, of reconciliation were mostly dumb show and not interesting at all. In our hearts, as in the parable, forgiveness is more wonderful than sin and lends sin its wonderful horror. Lichine doesn't manage to say this, and it isn't the kind of emotion he can express. Instead he shows us concrete human actions, a concrete story in dancing. But what makes him a choreographer of real importance is his exuberance of physical rhythm, his exuberant impulse to dance—*January-February*, 1941.

COTILLON

BALANCHINE'S *Cotillon* (score, Chabrier; décor, Berard) is the classic in dancing of the later School of Paris and it is to me the glory of the Original's repertory. This piece profoundly affected the imagination of the young people of my generation. It expresses in a curiously fugitive and juvenile movement the intimacy, the desolation, the heart's tenderness and savagery which gave a brilliant unevenness to our beautifully mannered charm. The thirties had not only a kind of Biedermeier parochialism, they had also insight into the eternity of a moment of grace. We are all out of them now, and it is strange to see now that what we then believed is still as true and absorbing in itself as any subsequent discovery—*January-February*, 1941.

BALUSTRADE

B ALUSTRADE with a Stravinsky score and a Tchelitcheff
décor was a ballet in the Diaghileff tradition, a collaboration of first-class artists where one can expect to feel movement, look and listen with the same degree of sensibility. In
such collaborations you can see the poetic quality of dancing
better, because all the different aspects of the spectacle have
been made by people who believe in its poetry. When there is
only one artist working on a show at a time, there is mostly
something pathetic and provincial about the theater; one feels
too sorry for him to pay undivided attention. At any rate it is
a fact that such collaborations created the Diaghileff tradition;
the tradition that dancing can be as poetic (or if you prefer,
as serious) as any other art; the tradition that painters and
musicians should not give up their character when they work
for dancers; the tradition that a dance evening is a natural
pleasure for a civilized person.

Balustrade is danced to Stravinsky's Violin Concerto, music
that seems to me easy to go along with from the rhythmic
side. The choreography too is easy to go along with from the
rhythmic side as it is full of references to our usual show dancing, the kind you see anywhere from a burlesque to a Hollywood production number. I noticed two elements or "motifs":
the upstretch on the downbeat; and one knee slipping across
the other in a little gesture of conventional shame. The first
syncopic element Balanchine enlarges into the liveliest and

226

lightest ensemble dances; the second element—one of gesture
—he elaborates into a long acrobatic trio in which all sorts of
"slippings across" are tried—of legs, of bodies, of arms; and this
trio ends by a separation, the girl looking reproachful, the boys
hanging their heads in shame. How strangely such a concrete
moment tops the abstract acrobatics before it; a discontinuity
in one's way of seeing that is bridged by the clearness of placing and the sureness of timing.

Balustrade is complex (or "contradictory") in this way as
the eye adds up its successive phases. Its novelty is that it is
not complex at each moment in the manner we are accustomed to. The individual dance role has almost no countermovement, no angular breaking of the dance impulse or direction. The impulse is allowed to flow out, so to speak,
through the arms and legs, which delineate the dance figure
lightly, as it were in passing. As they do in our show dancing.
This is all something else than the "European" style of the
thirties. There is in this new "undissonant," "undeformed"
or "one at a time" way of dancing a kind of parallel relation to
Miss Graham's new modern-school manner in *Letter to the
World*. Once more, dancing like any living art has moved
ahead of what we had come to think of as the modern style;
and this time without even any manifestos to warn us.

I must add that in *Balustrade* the costumes are elegant but
annoying. Though they have imagination and a sort of super-
Hollywood pruriency, the materials are such that after the
first minute or so they look like a wilted bunch of rags cutting
the line of the body at the knee, obscuring the differentiation
of steps and messing up the dance. And the trio costumes look
too publicly sexy, they take away from this erotic dance its

mysterious juvenile modesty. Still it was right of the management to take a first-rate painter for a work of this kind; an artist's mistake is infuriating, but not vulgar—*March-April*, 1941.

BLUEBEARD

THE reorganized Ballet Theater presented a season that was timid and on the musty side. Only one new feature was a real pleasure: the presence of Alicia Markova, the great English dancer. The management had commissioned no new American choreography, or score, or set. It did not even offer a new piece by its own Antony Tudor, one of the most interesting choreographers in America; and even abandoned the best of his previously presented works, *Dark Elegies*. This season's novelties were Dolin's version of *Aurora's Wedding* called *Princess Aurora*; a revival of Nijinska's *Beloved*; a piece called *Slavonika* which was nothing, and a *Bluebeard* which at least was a new work by Fokine.

Beloved (1928) has a very beautiful and interesting score, a Milhaud free rendering of some Schubert and Liszt, and it has choreography in Nijinska's "amateurish" or "primitif" ballet style, which I found oddly poetic in the whole effect of it. And Markova's dancing of a Romantic Muse ("half in love with easeful death") is terrific. *Slavonika* was one of those washouts that are natural in any theater routine and harmless. And it did have costumes by a talented local designer, Alvin Colt. Unluckily they were in a dressed-doll style that is fine

for revue but too cute for ballet: and the lace-trimmed stage
looked like a Christmas window at McCutcheon's, giganti-
cally blown up.

Bluebeard, the Fokine-Offenbach farce, was something of a
hit. The choreography tells a very complicated story with admirable clarity, and it is full of effective gags, a little in the
manner of a college show. In this collegiate style Dolin dances
charmingly, and everybody around is pretty busy. I was sorry
however that the Offenbach love lyrics which contrast with the
action had been cut down to short bits, and that the dances
set to them were conventionally nice instead of really poetic.
The result was more like the mechanical balance of Sullivan
than the delicate equilibrium of Offenbach. It seems to me
that Offenbach's humor, like Mozart's, is poised on the suggestion that false love and true love are not as different as one
might wish; they are both of them really tender. The joke isn't
that romantic love is just a fake, and therefore ridiculous; the
joke is that romantic love is real and real love is full of incon-
gruity. I am sorry that neither Massine's *Gaîté* nor Fokine's
Bluebeard conveys the fragrance of this tender irony that
makes Offenbach a real friend. For in neither ballet is anybody
ever really in love, neither with the right nor the wrong person. The music is better in *Bluebeard* however, than in *Gaîté,*
because the original orchestration (which is perfect) has been
less tampered with. The décor of *Bluebeard* by Vertés, the
fashionable magazine artist, is fussy and boring. There is no
color and no shape which stays alive longer than a couple of
minutes. There is no sense of air or space. A few of the costumes are pretty. Mr. Vertés is fine in his own profession. But
to do a ballet set a man must make a decoration one can look
at for at least fifteen minutes steady and still be interested in;

it is obvious that this is just what a serious painter spends his time trying to accomplish. It is among serious painters that ballet designers should be looked for. This is a responsibility of a first-class management—*January-February, 1942.*

PILLAR OF FIRE

BALLET THEATER celebrated its first season at the Metropolitan by putting on the first large, completely serious and poetic work it has ever created on its own initiative. Tudor's *Pillar of Fire* (score, Schoenberg; décor, Mielziner) is the one really good ballet that has been launched in New York since the de Basil company's *Balustrade.*

The audience watched *Pillar of Fire* almost breathlessly. For me, I see the dancers continuously transforming and contrasting their dance, as if no possibility open to them were to be left out. And the moving effect of the piece is that all this real complexity and power seem barely able to cope with the shadowy, immense space of the stage above them that becomes, as you watch, vast and real as the doom of fate. It seems to shut down from all sides on the dancers. Tudor is a master in what the painters call negative space. It gives the movement a peculiar privacy, as if it took place in an immense silence.

In point of dance style, *Pillar of Fire* is a work of originality and precision. The devices used are dramatic ones: Brief phrases urgently interrupted—they re-emerge and do amplify; gesture that tends in or braces itself against a direction, an imperative direction in which the dance is driving, urgently into an imminent future. It is the thrill of needing, not the delight of having. And the need is so intense, so unrelieved, it is unbelievable in any but a private faith.

Or looking at the style statically as a complex of devices, you see it employs three separate techniques of body carriage, of body tension. The ballet technique—firm, with gesture flowing controlled, with taut leaps and high lifts; a kind of modern-school technique—flexible, with impulsive gesture explosive as jitterbugging, loose low leaps, low lifts; and third, a technique of the body as in everyday life, modest, unstraining, as if at ease. Absorbing are the variations of these three seen simultaneously in adjustments of speed to delayed movement, of diving into space to holding back, of tautness to being relaxed.

But there is another aspect of the choreography that gives me a more convincing intimate pleasure. This is that the technical devices don't have the effect of tricks, the effect of them isn't that of professional symbols of style or pattern or meaning. While you watch the dance, the eye sees everything plain. If Tudor uses a grand jete, with high carriage and legs spread taut in the air, the carriage, the taut legs don't tickle you as a gadget would, they are a direct act. And if two dancers are close together, the knees, the hands, the shoulders, what they do to each other, how they mix—this is what holds your attention, the actual moves made. You don't have to make allowances as if anatomical facts were to be glossed over, as if you were for the sake of ulterior generalization to ignore one left arm, or the place where you know an organ is. In other words, at every moment you see the dancer as a person, as a man or a woman dancing; not as an unhappily defective instrument of a choreographer's flights of fancy. This is honesty in dancing. It makes not theoretical perfection the paramount issue, but the merely intensified expressivity of a dancer's movements over our common movement. In sequence all of it—the dance—has an emotional effect. And this effect is real and poetic thanks to the continuous certainty of the physical impression all along. Here is an example: It happens to one side of stage front, as if painfully placed. The frantic heroine leaps and the passionate young man she wants but does not love catches her in a split in mid-air firmly between the legs with both hands, catches her close to him at the level of his waist; for an instant she hangs against him, rigid as in mid-leap and caught. This is a technical device, a concrete act, and an image all at once. The audience watches spellbound, shocked and moved at the same time. Such a moment would be merely vulgar in the unpoetic theater.

The dancing of *Pillar of Fire* is perfect. Of course the dancers of the Ballet Theater are very good indeed; but they don't always look as good as that. Tudor, like Balanchine, is one of those rare choreographers who make dancers look technically superb and accurately expressive. I have never seen Miss Kaye, Miss Chase, and particularly Miss Lyon look quite so wonderfully interesting. Laing is always remarkable.

As for Tudor's musicality, like Balanchine's again, it is a marvel worth seeing. The seams of the music are never patched over by the dancing. At climaxes Tudor may use arrested movement, at other times he holds back or hurries the steps ahead, but music and dance seem to have equivalent phrasings that don't get in each other's way, and don't double for one another either. The score (it is *Verklaerte Nacht*) comes out limpid and clear. Incidentally the orchestra sounded very good too.

I do just the same have a reservation about the ending of *Pillar of Fire*. Here the dance becomes so subdued, it turns static and the effect is indistinct. The heroine seems still sad and strained. It is rather a sense of exhaustion and retrospection (as it is in the music, too) than a sense of fulfillment; though the latter would be expected from the story's happy ending and the (rather over-warm) Threshold-of-the-Future lighting effect that ends the piece. I was bothered by this discrepancy, and then retrospectively fell to wondering if the real subject of the piece isn't "Nevermore" despite the story. But though I was confused the happy end does not really carry, anyway. The long tortured and humiliated parts stay with you, not comforting, but very moving in their pathos—*May-June*, 1942.

ELEPHANT POLKA

IT WAS the Circus that this spring played the trump card of ballet, beating the Operahouse Gang at their own game by putting on a Balanchine-Stravinsky novelty. It was also the world's first elephant ballet, and it was a fine number. The elephants do all their charming old tricks and one new one— the classic adagio pirouette supported by the partner. The elephants are lively and feminine, and the many pretty girls with garlands are very exact and very pleasant. Balanchine as usual has deployed counter-rhythm, asymmetry and adagio invention. And there is none of that drill-sergeant emphasis on uniformity that destroys the real flavor of dances by animals or athletes. The Stravinsky *Polka* is a bit jumpy, but he's an old friend, we're glad to meet up with him, and even if we can't quite make out what he's saying in the general din, I'm willing to give him the benefit of the doubt. "There goes Igor," as *The New Yorker* reports the band saying.

There was a Chinese wirewalking number with a completely beautiful flowertable, that made me think how sumptuous the Circus would look if the whole décor could be designed and executed by Chinese. The Bel-Geddes color is all aniline and it's like playing in one key very loud for three hours—*May-June,* 1942.

RODEO

THE ballet season (Ballet Theater and Monte Carlo Ballet sharing a month at the Met) has not been very startling but it has been unusually pleasant. Both companies danced almost constantly at dance pitch, which had never happened before. The audience was less jittery and more cordial. People didn't seem to come to ballet because they "must" see it, they just naturally were there, and the house wasn't any too big for them. A few older people may have wished for a little more nervous stylishness in the air. But I had the impression that the elegance we are headed for is a less quivering, a less immodest and more amiable one.

The success story of the season was the Monte Carlo's all-

American *Rodeo.* I never heard so friendly an enthusiasm as on the opening night. The noise didn't have the harsh fierce sound of a demonstration, either artistic or regional. It sounded like a sincere pleasure, easy and full and sort of homey.

The effect of the ballet, as a friend of mine said, is like that of a pleasant comic strip. You watch a little coy and tear-jerky cowgirl-gets-her-cowboy story, and you don't get upset about it. What you are really recognizing is what people in general do together out West. Somehow the flavor of American domestic manners is especially clear in that peculiar desert landscape; and that is its fascination. The dance, the music, the décor (Agnes de Mille—Copland—Smith and Love) each are drawn to that same local fact with affection; and so they have a mysterious unity of a touching kind. They also have the unity of being each one of superior workmanship. It is a modesty of the work that their relationship otherwise looks quite casual.

Choreographically, too, *Rodeo* looks like something improvised. Its truest and luckiest overtones come from style-mixtures. For instance, the long first and third scenes to full orchestra are made up of stylized pantomime, plot, gags, and stylized folk-dance effects. But the brief second scene has none of that. It's a fast cowboy dance or running-set—a real one—danced just to hand-clapping and some calling. By themselves the other two stylized scenes would turn cute and corny. But, thanks to the little interlude, you feel as if continuing through the others, the long silence and the cheerful loneliness of the real place. It's a fine effect; and it also escapes the sourpuss these-are-my-roots claptrap.

The dances proper which take up most of the time are full of quick invention, lively and very attractive; the best we've had on the prairie subject and the best Miss de Mille has done. The ballet was danced very handsomely, with an accurate sense of what American movement (and the pokerfaced expression it has) is like. It was no trouble at all to the Ballet Russe. What I particularly liked about Miss de Mille in the lead was how— by imaginative projection—she gave a completely clear sense of the West as a place she had lived in, quite independently of anything she did. It gave her performance the extra dimension of style; and the audience took to her completely. The drawing and sense of space in the drops by Oliver Smith are remarkably fine too.

Well, there was a dispute whether the ballet imitated *Billy the Kid*. It didn't. What in *Billy* is local color, in *Rodeo* is the main subject. (*Billy* was revived by the Ballet Theater afterwards. The score sounded fine but was played slowly and roughly. Gibson, as Billy, is of course a better dancer than Loring; on the other hand he hasn't Loring's command of the dramatic pause. The spacing of the figures as well as the flavor of the movement has not the old clear focus; and the Sheriff has lost his mysterious quiet. Not enough rehearsal)—*November-December*, 1942.

ALEKO

THE one big-time novelty of the Ballet Theater is Massine's *Aleko*. It has the only Paris-school décor of the season, by Chagall, and besides giving the satisfaction and having the fine presence of a great painter's work, it is also beautifully executed.

The ballet is Massine's finest since *Fantastic Symphony*. It has lots of his expert stylization of local color (in this case, Russian gypsies and peasants), lots of his stylized dance-pantomime, lots of his ballet counterpoint (different dancers doing different things at the same time). It has as prize plum a long last scene with the breathless melodramatic thriller rush that Massine does better than anyone. And it even has an admiring bow or two in the direction of Tudor choreography. For me however it has also plenty of the qualities I dislike in Massine's work—an agitation that seems senseless, a piling up of scraps of movement and bits of character like so much junk from Woolworth's, patterns but no room for them, accent and meter but no rhythm and flower of phrase. The duets are bizarre without intimacy, the man has to jerk from one position to another by turning his back awkwardly on his partner. For me *Aleko* has a real subject only in its décor, the dance is just a hectic show and whenever it slows down it goes flat. Well, the public at any rate loves the hubbub of it, and it loves the junk. Anyone can very well love all the dancers of it, they work as hard as possible and everyone dances his or her best.

It is quite right for the management of Ballet Theater to be developing its better dancers by rotating the solo roles. I hope it can also do something to give the ensemble more real style. (The Monte Carlo still is the better company in that respect.) A sense of style in the ensemble is what really brings a ballet to life. Style is the expression of the secret meaning of the piece as far as it relates to the individual dancer; in that way it is the dancer's deportment. In another way, it is the question of giving a phrase of dancing an edge or vivacity by timing the point of emphasis—as in reciting poetry. Virgil Thomson, who saw a performance of *Swan Lake* in which Markova was magnificent, told me that in the old days with the magnificent Doubrovska in the part he had not had so sharp a sense of a distinction between star and chorus; in style they were related to her style, they were all enchanted swans. The ensemble of the Ballet Theater are accurate technically, they are lively and pleasant and goodlooking. But nobody has yet taught them classical deportment, which is delicate and grand and personal; it also allows the girls a special femininity which would be interesting —*November-December*, 1942.

BALLET IMPERIAL

BALLET IMPERIAL (Balanchine-Tchaikovsky-Doboujinsky; danced by and created in '41 for Kirstein's American Ballet) was the single full-length ballet offered at the New Opera and it is the most brilliant ballet of the season. In intention it is an homage to the Petersburg ballet style, the peculiarly sincere grand manner which the Imperial Ballet School and Petipa evolved. We know the style here from the choreography of *Swan Lake, Aurora's Wedding* or *Nutcracker*, even of *Coppelia*, though all of them have been patched out; we know it from glimpses of grandeur in the dancing of the Russian-trained ballerinas; from photographs, especially of the young Pavlova and the young Nijinsky; and from the legend that persists and which is distinct from the Diaghileff legend. Balanchine of course knows it thoroughly from having been trained

in the actual School. But even with little knowledge homage
to this manner is natural for a dance lover. The Petersburg
style was the one that vigorously continued our whole tradition
of serious dancing during the increasing barbarism of 1850–
1900. It was also the solid foundation for the extraordinary glory
of ballet in the Diaghileff era, a glory which still pays the ex-
penses of our ballet companies. And there is another attraction
toward it more compelling and more personal: it is the force
of the mysteriously poignant images of the style—an expressive
force which keeps returning them to the mind. And they so return, even after the context of them is gone and their outline
altered, marked among other images by their singularity of expression.

Such images spontaneously arising are *Ballet Imperial's*
theme. It does not reproduce the period as a decorator would.
You don't find the fairy-tale plot, the Swans, the dance variations strung on a story. Instead there is a backdrop that makes
you think of the concrete St. Petersburg, and in front of that
a brand new ballet with lots of novel steps. Actually you see a
stage full of dancers who, say, arbitrarily disappear, who re-
appear in peculiarly rigid formations that instantly dissolve, or
else stop and stand immobile. You see the vivacity of the star
set over sharply against the grand pose of the ensemble; or else
the solo dancer lost and still, while the full company hastens
happily. You watch the solo partners discover each other, two
individuals in the noncommittal cheerful society of the company; you follow their touching individual response. And afterward you see them alter their natures from having been tender
personages to being star performers, an inexplicable duplicity
that leads to no heartbreak but culminates instead in the general dazzle of a virtuoso finale for everybody all over the stage

at once. So described, *Ballet Imperial* might be a typical Petersburg ballet. But the fact is that each of these typical effects is arrived at by so novel a technical procedure that it comes as a surprise. We feel the effect first, we recognize the feeling, and from that we remember the old effect. One might say the new effect is as fresh as that of the Petersburg ballet was in its own time. Or that the past and the present seem to happen at the same time as they do in the drama of personal memory.

As dancing, *Ballet Imperial* is full of freshness. In point of form, it is an abstract ballet interpreting Tchaikovsky's *Second Piano Concerto*. Interpretive dance reveals one of the structural aspects of a piece of music—Fokine is apt to show how the periods sit, Massine goes for the tangle of musical motives. Balanchine draws our attention to the expressive flow under the syntax and we have a vivid sense of the free musical animation. I was delighted in *Ballet Imperial* how the *Concerto*, a show piece I had thought forced, came to life and sounded fresh and direct. The dance focuses the interest like a good musician's playing: certain moments get an imperceptible emphasis, a long passage is taken in at a swoop, another is subdivided; and thanks to a happy interpretation the piece comes out as good as new.

In dance steps and dance figures Balanchine has always been inventive. But most people think of his choreography as full of specifically poignant detail—quick thrusts backward and sideways, odd pauses, hobbled leaps, extraordinary group poses, indecently upsidedown lifts. Most of us recall how his dancers have looked torn in three directions at once, and so were we, and it was wonderful. *Ballet Imperial* has a certain oddness, but it isn't in that earlier manner in the least. It does have a slow middle section, a very beautiful one (it's in a free style of ballet movement derived from classic pantomime) which has for sentiment the pathos of a love story. A boy and girl find each other, they misunderstand, become reconciled, and lose one another. The tone is intimate. But there is not one indecent image or lift. The gestures are easy, the figures simple. And at the end the movement is brushed away, and the solitary "frustrated" emotion left in the air is very simply succeeded by a general comradely liveliness of tone in the next section, a long finale which like the long opening section has no pathos at all.

And in the slow pantomime part as well as in the rapid other two parts one comes to notice how the detail of gesture does not run counter to the main line of movement. It is not an accent, it does not draw attention to itself. The arms are easy, the dance is lighter, faster, more positive, presents itself more openly. The dance figures throughout are readily grasped. Balanchine maintains interest by an extraordinary flickering rapidity of dance steps and quick shift of dance figures. I found the speed, perhaps because it is still unfamiliar, at times confusing; but the positive style was unexpected and it had a pleasantly fresh aroma. And the brief solos in the last section reminded me of the bold large manner Petipa seems to have had, where the dance stands out so plain you see it right off with delight and you don't stop to think of the choreographer.

I was sorry the ensemble performing *Ballet Imperial* had the weakness that young dancers always show—an insufficient power of projection. It is hard to feel them if you watch from the back of the house. Looking at this question in another way, in inexperienced dancers the movement never quite comes to rest; so that the dynamic scale is a bit blurred, and the movement does not lift to its flower, shine, and subside completely, leaving a completed image in the mind. This is rhythm in dancing (as distinct from musical rhythm) and it is what gives to

dancing the air of style. It is a quality of expression independent of choreographic or virtuoso effects (or of characterization)
and much more communicative than they are. To have it a
dancer must be unusually sturdy and self-possessed. But as
Ballet Imperial progresses the dancers do give you a sense of
dance style. You begin to feel it in the air. You see it as vivacity
and then you recognize that the freshness of movement comes
from their personal animation. And you realize in the end how
badly you missed, in the celebrated ensembles at the Met this
fall, an air of intelligence that the sense of style gives to dancing. I remember too that dancers Balanchine rehearses, whether
stars or students, always tend to show their natural dance intelligence. They have an indefinable grace in dancing that seems
to come natural to them, that seems extemporaneous. They look
not so much like professionals, they look like boys and girls who
are dancing.

Balanchine has an extraordinary gift for bringing performers
to life on their own personal terms, so that the unconscious
grace that is in each one of them can shine out in the work
they do, giving it the momentary and mortal expression of
beauty. The plan of a choreography is a great pleasure. But it
is the brilliancy of young dancers entirely in the present, the
unique liveliness of each dancer caught entirely in the present
instant that at once, we all know it, will be past and irretrieva-
ble forever—it is this clear sharp sense of our own natural way
of living that makes a moment of ballet speak to the complete
consciousness; that makes choreography look beautiful. As
Balanchine's has again and again—*January-February,* 1943.

ALICIA MARKOVA
AND ROMEO AND JULIET

THE great event of any Ballet Theater season is the dancing of Markova. And this season she danced even more wonderfully than before. She appeared night after night, and even in two ballets on the same program. Once the papers said she had fainted after the performance. There is only one of her. I very much hope she is gratefully taken care of and prevented from injurious overwork.

When she dances everybody seems to understand as if by sympathy everything she does. And yet her modesty is the very opposite of the Broadway and Hollywood emphasis we are used to. A Russian girl I know who works in a defense plant brought along her whole swingshift one Sunday into standing room. They had never seen ballet, and they all unanimously fell in love with Markova. Markova has the authority of a star, but her glamor comes from what the English so well call a genuine spiritual refinement.

Watching her critically in Petipa's *Swan Lake,* in Fokine's *Sylphides,* in Massine's *Aleko,* or in Tudor's novelty, the *Romeo and Juliet,* I am constantly astonished how she makes each of these very different styles completely intelligible in its own terms. None looks old-fashioned or new-fangled. Each makes straight sense. Her new Juliet for instance is extraordinary. One doesn't think of it as Markova in a Tudor part, you see only Juliet. She is like no girl one has ever seen before, and she is completely real. One doesn't take one's eyes off her, and one

243

doesn't forget a single move. It doesn't occur to you that she is dancing for an audience; she is so quiet. Juliet doesn't try to move you. She appears, she lives her life, and dies.

One of the qualities that strikes me more and more in Markova's dancing is her dance rhythm. Anybody who has been to the Savoy Ballroom knows what rhythm in dancing is. But once you get away from there and start watching the art of stage dancing, you find rhythm very rarely. You find many beautiful things—exact control, intelligence, energy, variety, expression; but they aren't quite the same thing as rhythm. Of course rhythm in art dancing is not so simple as in the Savoy "folk" form. But you recognize it wherever you find it. And as anybody can hear that Landowska has rhythm, so anybody can see that Markova has it.

Markova's rhythm is not only due to her remarkable freedom in attacking her steps a hair's breadth before or after the beat, a freedom in which she shows a perfect musical instinct. I think one gets closer to it by noticing her phrasing. And what we speak of as Negro rhythm is perfection of phrasing in a very short dance phrase. What strikes me equally about their two-beat phrases and her very long ones is how clearly each separate phrase is completed. It is perfectly clear when the phrase rises, and when it has spent itself. I feel the impulse has been completed, because I have seen the movement change in speed, and in weight. (In the Lindy the thrust is hard and quick, but the finish—or recovery—of the step is light and seems even retarded; in Markova's incomparable *Sylphides* phrases she prepares during five or six steps with a gentle, uniform downward martellato for one slow expressive and protracted upward movement in her arms.) In musical terms there is a rubato within the phrase, corresponding to the way the balance of the body is first strained, then is restored.

Markova's way of dancing adds a peculiar quality to a ballet by Tudor. Other dancers can make his dramatic intentions clear. They show that each of his gestures carries a meaning: a nuance of emotion, of character, of social standing. They show his precision of timing and placing, so that one appreciates his extraordinary genius for visual rhythms on the stage. They are personally self-effacing, and give a thrilling intensity to the drama he intended. But Tudor's style includes many hampered movements, slow-motion effects, sudden spurts of allegro arrested incomplete, arm tensions straining into space, pelvic displacements and shifts of carriage. They are fascinating effects. On the other hand I notice that in execution the movement looks forced. The dancers have trouble with their balance, they are apt to look laborious and lose their spring. Perhaps Tudor meant the dance to look off balance, but it also looks airless. Now I see that Markova can sense and can show the dance rhythm that underlies his visual phrases. She finds their point of rest. She is easily equal to his dramatic meaning and passion, but she also gives his drama the buoyancy of dancing. As I watch her, Markova—like Duse in Ibsen—seems to be speaking poetry to the company's earnest prose.

Tudor's *Romeo and Juliet* was the world premiere that Ballet Theater presented in its spring season at the Met. It was a great success and fully deserved it. It has a few unconvincing moments, but it has a great many original and very fine ones. (One of the most delicate effects is the special use of toesteps in the part of Juliet; they take on a quality different from any "pointes" I ever saw.) As a whole, I found the piece fascinating.

The plot of *Romeo* is that of Shakespeare's play. Tudor follows the action almost faithfully, but the individual thing about it is that the poetic message is not the same. The ballet's conception of mutual love is far less impetuous, far less straightforward, far less dazzlingly radiant. The difference is clearest in the character of Romeo, who in the ballet is never quite frank; he is like an object of love, rather than a lover. But he is a perfectly real young man. And Hugh Laing—always a dancer full of real character—dances him as one. Tudor's piece strikes me as a personal version of the story, a reverie on the subject, with muted and oppressed images. Shakespeare's openness is its foil. And it is precisely the private deformation Tudor has made which gives to the ballet its core of poetic reality, its odd spell.

That Tudor had no intention of copying Shakespeare is clear enough in his choice of Delius for the music. The various pieces that together form the score have not the theatrical incisiveness of ballet music. But they are used as background music, as sound-track; as such they are of high quality.

But I think the big event and the most telling effect of the *Romeo* production is the extraordinary décor the painter Eugene Berman has given it. I have never shared the complacency with which we New Yorkers accept window-dressing (be it functional or "camp"), as ballet décor. I think ballet sharpens the eyes and opens the heart, and under these circumstances a vulgar set is carrying our cult of lowbrow manners too far. I am shocked to see *Giselle* danced in front of a powder-room wallpaper, or to see the Swans in *Swan Lake* troop out in so many little home-made Dutch outfits, just as if they had rolled up their sleeves for a bout of spring cleaning.

Berman's Italian Renaissance décor is a serious work of art,

like Picasso's *Tricorne* or Berard's *Cotillon;* like the works of
the baroque designers. And I imagine later theater lovers who
look at the record of it will marvel at the refinement of sensibility it presupposes in the audience. As a picture it is shut
in and still it lifts and spreads, it comes forward, and it keeps
its secret. As a stage design it has inventiveness and immense
learning, everything has been made with tenderness and is
useful. The blended perspectives, the contrasted weights of the
materials, the originality of the colors, the animation of the proportions, the energy of the drops, all these show us the many
kinds of visual pleasure the stage has to offer. And in *Romeo*
for once, the scene painting and the execution of costumes are
superlative.

6

Ballet Music and Decoration

A COMPOSER unfamiliar with the theater who is interested in writing ballets should certainly see the big companies as often as possible and watch what happens. I think he should start by watching *Sylphides* or *Carnaval* (now in the Monte Carlo repertory), because both are obvious and successful; the relation of dance steps to music in both ballets is blunt but bold. If he watches the dancers and listens to the music at the same time, he will see how the visual rhythm frequently goes against the acoustic one. He can see how the choreographer runs over the end of a phrase, distributes effects and accents sometimes with, sometimes against the pattern of the music. Look at the group accents in the final measures of most of the *Sylphides* numbers; or at the way in the Schumann the same motive is danced with different steps, or the rhetoric of a piece is broken into by different entrances.

If he looks more closely he will see how a dance phrase rests on several accents or climaxes of movement which other movements have led up to or from which they will follow, as unaccented syllables in speech surround an accented one. He will see that the dance accents frequently do not reproduce the ac-

248

cents of a musical phrase, and that even when they correspond, their time length is rarely identical with musical time units. (A leap for instance that fills two counts may end a shade before, and the next movement begin a shade after the third count.) The variations of energy in dancing around which a dance phrase is built are what make the dance interesting and alive; and they correspond to a muscular sense, not to an auditory one. I think it is the fact that in ballet technique these instants of emphasis are not expected to be identical with the metrical units to which they are set which keeps the ballet rhythmically alive as dancing—just as in Negro dancing the effect of rhythm is derived from the fact that energy does not stick to the metrical values, but increases or decreases in a time value of its own. (The beat and off-beat as the dancer executes them are differently long.)

Many musicians are bothered by noticing that dancers "can't keep time." I often notice how dancers who are keeping time become dull and unrhythmic. Keeping time at all costs destroys the instinctive variability of emphasis, it destroys the sense of breathing in dancing, the buoyancy and the rhythmic shape of a dance phrase. To be sure, an exaggerated rubato on the other hand looks loose; and it destroys the spring and force and cumulative sweep of the beat. In performances of music, musicians understand very well this problem of adjustment; dancing presents another form of it, made more complicated by the fact that the edge in accentuating a bodily gesture (which underlines its correspondence with the musical beat) is a device that rapidly becomes monotonous to the eye and that tends to dehumanize the look of a dancer on stage. A dancer on stage is not a musical instrument, she is—or he is—a character, a person. The excitement of watching ballet is that two very different things—dancing and music—fit together, not mechanically but in spirit. The audience feels the pleasure of a happy marriage at least for the fifteen minutes the piece lasts.

Ballet music is conceived as music that is marriageable—its inherent animation will not be destroyed by the physical presence of dancing or even by the unavoidable racket that dancing makes on stage, and its continuity will not collapse under the rugged conditions of theater presentation. The more delicately hermetic the composition, the more necessary it becomes to listen with absorption and the more necessary it becomes to play it in just one way. For dancing however the conductor has to see to it that dancers hear their cues and can meet the tempo—and even (as in opera) temperamental variations of tempo are inevitable with good dancers. So a composer is safer if he does not count on orchestral subtlety of emphasis in theater execution, which the poor quality of ballet orchestras, the lack of rehearsal time, the physical necessities of dancing and the plan of the choreographer are each likely to endanger.

No one who watches a good ballet with attention can hear the score as distinctly as he would in concert. Once the curtain is up the music functions in the show as a spiritual atmosphere for the stage action, as giving the general emotional energy of the piece, its honesty, cheerfulness, steadiness or amplitude; with occasional bursts of danciness, of lyricism, of wit or rhetoric, and an effective conclusion which are more consciously heard. A composer cannot count on finding a choreographer as exceptionally musical as Balanchine. But he should count on finding a choreographer, a dance company and an audience who respond to the inherent character of his musical communication. He can count on an audience that appreciates perfectly well the largeness of imagination—if not the technical detail—

of ballet scores like Tchaikovsky's or Stravinsky's, and responds to their imaginative scope with an eagerness rare in concert audiences—*October-November,* 1939.

NEW BALLET SCORES

O NE of the normal activities of a ballet company is the commissioning of new scores. It was Diaghileff who established this function of ballet, and the fact that he commissioned the score of *Petrouchka* is to many people his enduring monument. The general good will Diaghileff won for ballet by his musical policy is still of use to the present companies. For the musical public his continuous production of new scores proved that ballet is a normal part of the intellectual life of its time and place.

Over here, the smaller American ballet companies, the late Caravan especially, have done extremely well in commissioning new music by local composers. But the big companies, Ballet Theater and Monte Carlo, have been far too remiss in this matter. In the case of Ballet Theater, the only independent musical contribution I can recall is Brant's uninteresting score for *The Great American Goof* several seasons back. The Monte Carlo can be praised at least for last winter's one new American score, Aaron Copland's *Rodeo.* But I have not heard of any further commissions for next season.

There is no lack of local ballet composers who have already written successful ballets. All three of Copland's scores have been successful in the theater. Marc Blitzstein, Paul Bowles, Theodore Chanler, Carlos Chavez, Camargo Guarnieri, Walter Piston, Virgil Thomson are all reasonable choices for ballet commissions. And there are others. Not to mention that Milhaud is here now, too.

Such a lack of interest by the big companies in living musicians of some originality is very sad. They seem to have no curiosity about the intellectual life around them. It is perfectly proper for a ballet company to choose old music of contemporary interest for some new ballets. But there is something fossilized about a company that cannot go out and buy itself a brand new score or two every spring.

It is hardly a question of funds. Both companies find funds for handsome new productions set to existing scores. The six hundred dollars or so a commission costs (plus about three hundred for copying parts) is not a prohibitive extra charge. Nor does the public refuse to listen to new music. *Rodeo*, for example, was a phenomenal success all over the country; the Copland score evidently didn't discourage anyone from coming. And to go a little beyond the strict subject of new music, it struck me that during this last winter here in New York the general enthusiasm for anything approaching ballet "experiment" has been astonishing. The more novelty a ballet had in any respect, the more eagerly the public seemed to welcome its appearance. It was true of *Rodeo*, of *Apollo*, of *Romeo*, and even of *The Wanderer*.

This is one side of the argument: The public expects new scores, the composers available are adequate and the financial risk appears to be slight. But, even if the risk were greater, there is a necessity for ballet companies to experiment. They don't owe it to us, they owe it to themselves. The spirit of a com-

pany, the vitality of the dancers, begins to sag without an occasional contact with what is liveliest and boldest in the artistic
activity around. Not that dancers understand intellectual values
more sharply than other people. But they seem to require for
their best efforts an occasional atmosphere of intense outside
interest in the work they are producing. The reckless expendi-
ture of spiritual energy by everyone concerned in it that goes
with the making of a completely new, a so to speak, disinterested work revives them. It is so much fresh air in the ballet
studio. And unless a management now and then considers this
susceptibility on the part of its dancers it will find itself with a
dispirited, demoralized company on its hands, the public will
lose interest and our present active and healthy balletomania
will pine away for lack of loving care—*July* 4, 1943.

SIR THOMAS AT THE BALLET

SIR THOMAS BEECHAM conducted *Romeo and Juliet*
last night at the Metropolitan. He made the Delius selections of which the score consists shimmer and glow, swell out
and sink to a whisper. Ballet Theater's orchestra, unusually
good this season, never played so well; the rather ponderous
music never sounded more sumptuous. Just the same the dancers on stage, even the great Alicia Markova and wonderful Hugh
Laing, did not seem comfortable, and did not seem sure of
support. They have danced *Romeo* better when the music was
played less as a show piece; more as a high-grade soundtrack,

which serves to time their gestures and often to underline their expression and dynamics. *Romeo* is a fine ballet, and there was no harm seeing if anything can be done to make the musical aspect of it fine, too; the experiment failed.

Sir Thomas' pauses between the selections were an improvement though. Last night's *Romeo* was a little longer than the version of last fall. A good deal of new business has been added —or rather new details of rich dance gesture; last night some of these seemed confused, probably due to the surprise of the dancers to find a very familiar score ringing with so different an emphasis. Sir Thomas' legato obliterated the landmarks they were used to.

While Ballet Theater was giving the "Grand Pas de Deux" from *The Nutcracker,* with Rosella Hightower and André Eglevsky, for a second number, I dashed uptown and caught that very number at the City Center, danced by Alexandra Danilova and Igor Youskevitch. They were performing it up there as part of the third scene of the Monte Carlo's three-scene version of *The Nutcracker,* with which that company opened its program last night. Coming in its proper place as the climax of a long ballet, the number is much more affecting than when it is given as an isolated parade piece. The grandeur of its grace, the poetry of its bodily acrobatics were perfectly expressed by these two great stars; and the noble sweetness of their manner, the melody of their movement were extraordinary. They both soften the contours without in the least blurring them; they find the perfect emphasis for the phrase; the suavity of their head positions and arms is especially remarkable—*June* 4, 1944.

BALLET CONDUCTING:
BEECHAM-BERNSTEIN

THE great Sir Thomas Beecham and brilliant young Leonard Bernstein conducting as guests for Ballet Theater this spring—the first, *Romeo and Juliet,* the second, his own *Fancy Free*—not only added to the season's glamor, they also proved how immensely valuable a conductor can be to the dancers. For the conductor, leading a ballet is very different from leading a symphony. As a performer, he has to yield the spotlight to the ballerina; and even as a musician he can't let the music take the spotlight. He has to adjust the score to the rhetoric of the drama on stage—and when a ballet story has been set to music composed for another purpose, the points of emphasis are often quite different ones. The ballet conductor has to take the cue for his dynamic climaxes from the theatrical moment. When the audience has become absorbed by the action, when it has grasped the situation, an increase in loudness may clinch the big effect; but if the audience is not warmed up, if it has not yet caught on to the rhythm of the piece, a big noise will only puzzle, distress or alienate it. Most important of all, the conductor has to adjust to a speed that the dancer can use, according to the sequence she executes, according to her physical temperament; and if that speed is tough on the musical sense, he has to find a way of making it sound slower or faster than it is. The fixed common term between the dancer and conductor, between the rhythm of music and the rhythm of dancing, is the beat or pulse of the music. The more steady and reliable

255

the beat is, the more freedom for inspiration the dancer will have.

In *Fancy Free* Leonard Bernstein's beat was steady and, better still, it was buoyant. His downbeat, delivered against an upward thrust in the torso, has an instantaneous rebound, like that of a tennis ball. He can give the illusion of an increase in speed by increasing his buoyancy and adding a dynamic crescendo; so he doesn't have to quicken the tempo to pep up the show. Such a beat gives a lift to the dancers and it gives them confidence; they feel that he won't hurry them breathlessly in a lively spot, nor die out on them in a nostalgic cadence. And you could see that the dancers, even when they came on tired, responded to Mr. Bernstein like hepcats to Harry James.

Dancers and conductor didn't have so easy a time getting together in *Romeo and Juliet*, but in this ballet there isn't any groove for them to get into. The Delius selections which serve as score don't by nature follow the logic of the action; nor is their beat or even their rhythmic lilt clearly distinguishable in the web of luxurious sonorities. *Romeo* has always been a theater hit, a richly involved and sensitive spectacle in a deliberately luscious neo-Pre-Raphaelite style. But the dancers have been lucky if they heard most of their cues, and they have had a good deal of trouble getting their complicated sequences and shifts of balance to flow with the music. On account of musical trouble, *Romeo,* after a year's run, still hadn't settled when Sir Thomas was invited in to conduct it.

Even he didn't solve the matter at once. But the eighth (and last) time he conducted, the audience saw throughout the most brilliant and the most exact performance the ballet ever had. This time the orchestra was astonishingly transparent. One heard distinctly the variety of impetus the interwoven musical phrases have; their devious and delicate qualities of motion, as they rise to the surface and shift and overlap and get lost again in a sort of harmonic undertow. The dancers not only recognized their cues, they could find in the musical phrase they were cued to the exact impetus which suited their momentary phrase of dancing. Tudor had counted on these correspondences of impetus from the first. But only Sir Thomas understood completely on the stage and in the orchestra what aspect of the score it was that Tudor had counted on, and he made this aspect musically plausible and expressive. The result was a unique performance by the entire company; in fact, the delighted dancers, especially Miss Markova and Mr. Laing, probably inspired Sir Thomas quite as he did them; artists like to reciprocate inspiration.

I wish Sir Thomas or Mr. Bernstein could conduct *Swan Lake* several times next season; it would give the company a clue to how much more they might get out of the music and out of the piece. Meanwhile Ballet Theater is to be thanked particularly for having both of these distinguished guests conduct often enough so that the dancers could really profit by their exceptional musicianship—*June 4, 1944.*

VARIETIES OF DISCOMFORT

WITH the opening of the new season the Fleischmann Monte Carlo Ballet also returned—world premieres, stars, rich refugees and all. Dali's *Labyrinth* is the pudding's plum. It is the height of fashionableness and of bad manners.

Dali hogs the show so completely he won't let you see Massine's part of it, or hear Schubert (whose *Seventh Symphony* is played throughout). He focuses your eye at a spot so high on the drop, that every time you pull it down to look at the dancers below you feel acutely uncomfortable. Besides dwarfing the dancers he dresses them in incredibly bad taste, as if in the rented rags of a burlesque chorus. The colors and materials coalesce like a stew. He jams the dance between a drop hung too far forward and a litter of props; and finally distracts the audience by some idiotic revue tricks, doves, dolphins and roosters, which are all that emerge recognizable from the hectic mess. The dance looks like the milling Times Square subway platform on New Year's Eve. And the music is an irritating noise that keeps on and on. There is no doubt that this is what Dali wanted. The drops, four of them, which alone survive the general rape, are grandiosely frantic and frozen. The effect of it all is absolutely real, as acute as discomfort. And its complete disregard for the audience's comfort is what makes it so terrifically fashionable. The first time I saw it, it put me in an excellent humor. There was nothing second hand, nothing pedantic about it. It was a real world premiere, something made this minute and made for all the world to look at. At the second performance of course there wasn't any novelty left and I was bored. That no doubt condemns the piece as art, but not as a production. I think the Monte Carlo owes us such manifestations among other things; this is the first time it has given us a real one, and I feel very pleased about it.

Oh yes, the subject of *Labyrinth* is the return of art to the classic tradition. If you think art can leave I suppose you think it can return. That's all nonsense to me, so I wasn't bothered by Dali's little blasphemies, either.

A different kind of discomfort was that of the Massine-Weinberger *Saratoga*. The music is as ingratiating as a restaurant waiter. The dance is inept and half unfinished. Franklin to be sure danced brilliantly whenever he could. But still *Saratoga* marks an epoch in our ballet. Way at the back of the stage hangs a drop neighbored by a little kiosk, done by a new designer, Oliver Smith. It is the first time I have seen anything on our own stage that has color, size, and air-quality all completely personal and right. And then you see that the rest of the set helps, too. You see it doesn't fade as time passes, but grows brighter. (And to put white in the sky is quite an achievement.) It is as poetic and as real as anything the Parisians used to make. For this discovery Massine—who up to now has been as unlucky as Broadway in his local designers—deserves cordial thanks. Alvin Colt's costumes—well, never mind—*November-December*, 1941.

ABOUT BALLET DECORATION

BECAUSE ballet dancers keep moving all over the stage and because in looking at them you keep looking at all the scenery all the time, ballet decoration is observed in a livelier way than play or opera decoration. In fact as a ballet unfolds and your interest in watching it grows, you become more susceptible to visual impressions and so more sensitive, too, to the decoration. In plays or operas you forget the scenery for long stretches while the performers stay still and you listen more and more captivated to their voices. The real dramatic power of a play or opera is felt to such an extent by listening that you can be thrilled even when you sit at the radio with no stage to watch at all. But the dramatic power of a ballet is in its visual impact. You feel it by seeing just how the dancers move, seeing their impetus in relation to each other and also their force in relation to the entire stage—how far they choose to go in contrast to how far they might go.

The force with which dancers approach, touch or separate, come forward toward you or retire, take possession of stage center or pause isolated near the wings, these changing intensities are meant to have a cumulative effect. You appreciate this best if you sit far enough back to view the whole stage at a glance, so that its height and width can act as a fixed frame of reference. Ballet scenery and costumes are meant to make the action of the dance distinctly visible at a distance and also to give a clear coherence to its variety, a livelier common term to its action than the mere empty stage area.

For this purpose a décor so busy that it confuses or so stuffy that it clogs the animation of the dances is no use. But it cannot be timid. It must have power enough to remain interesting and alive as the dancing gradually sharpens the visual susceptibility of the audience. One of our finest sets—Pierre Roy's *Coppelia*—does this without attracting any notice to itself at all. The effect of a décor is right when as the ballet gathers momentum the dancers seem to have enough air all around to dance easily; when you see their long dance phrases in clear relation to stage center; when the flats keep the force of the gesture from spilling aimlessly into the wings; then the dancers—no matter how odd they looked at first—can come to look

natural in the fanciful things they do, the natural fauna of the
bright make-believe world they move in.

The present standards for ballet decoration were set by
Picasso, whose *Three-Cornered Hat* is still pictorially alive after
twenty-five years. The reason easel painters are better designers
for ballet than anyone else is that they are the only craftsmen
professionally concerned with what keeps pictures alive for years
on end. When they know their trade they make pictures that
hold people's interest for hundreds of years; so making one that
will be interesting to look at for twenty minutes is compara-
tively easy for them.

A ballet set has to stand up under steady scrutiny almost as
an easel painting does. At first sight it tells a story, it has local
color or period interest or shock value. But then it starts to
change the way a picture in a museum does as you look at it
attentively for five or ten minutes. The shapes and colors, lines
and textures in the set and costumes will act as they would in a
picture, they will seem to push and pull, rise and fall, advance
and retreat with or against their representational weight. The
backdrop may tie up with a costume so that the dancer's figure
seems to belong in it like a native, or it may set him plainly forward where he has a floor to dance on. A good ballet décor, like
a good painting, does different and opposite things decisively;
like a painting, it presents a bold equilibrium of pictorial forces.
And when the bold equilibrium in the décor corresponds in
vitality to that of the dancing and that of the score, then the
ballet as a production is alive and satisfactory.

The decorations by Picasso, Roy, Berman and Chagall in our
current repertory (Berard's and Tchelitcheff's are at the moment
in storage) set a satisfactory standard—the highest in the world.

It is a standard worth keeping because it is clearly a pleasure; worth keeping for the time when other native American easel painters join Oliver Smith in working for ballet, as despite management and union, they obviously should. Painters as they are, they will enjoy furnishing the pictorial power and nobility of presence ballet thrives on; and to see their American invention so openly presented would be a great pleasure to them and to us—*November* 26, 1944.

DALI TO THE HILT

DALI'S *Mad Tristan*, which Ballet International offered at the International Theater Friday night, is a masquerade that only a genius could invent. Dali takes Wagner's music and Massine's choreography and uses them as props for a spectacle, but what a show he puts on.

Fantastic backdrops, costumes, stage effects tumble out over the stage for half an hour in frenzied profusion. It is a theater thrill that Billy Rose might envy; a proliferation of decoration no one in the world but Dali can rival.

Mad Tristan is meant as a hallucination in the mind of Tristan, who "sees himself devoured by Isolde's Chimera," the program says. The piece has two scenes. The first opens with Isolde waving the fatal scarf; proceeds to a horridly confused acrobatic love duet with Spirits of Death like shivering maniacs and Spirits of Love like enormous dandelions in seed milling about. It ends with the revelation of two Isoldes, both equally fascinating and differently horrid; King Mark with two soldiers wondrously armed enters.

The second scene shows Tristan on a version of Boecklin's *Isle of the Dead,* plagued by a sardonic shepherd, plagued by a beautiful bouncing ship, plagued by the Isoldes and the Spirits and other faceless figures. It ends with Tristan dying for love as backstage his own repulsive mummy is lowered into a vault caressed by white wormlike dismembered living arms.

There is, as you can see, a vague connection with Wagner's *Tristan,* with Freudian symbols, with symbols that recur in Dali's work. The ballet has not, on the other hand, any of the exalted hypnotic immobility on stage nor any of the long-drawn climactic surge of *Tristan.* In fact, though excerpts from *Tristan* are played as accompaniment, the visual hysteria of *Mad Tristan* must be revolting to an absorbed Wagnerite; and as the music sounds thin with the small orchestra that plays, it is just as well to take the score not as Wagner, but as an effigy of a masterpiece, a literary reference.

As the score isn't music, so the ballet isn't dancing. Its best effects are properly stage effects, disjointed ideas rather than organized dances, such are the first shivers of the insane Dead, the parallelism of the two Isoldes, the shepherd sticking to Tristan like a leech. Indeed, there aren't quite enough such non-dance effects; they belong to Dali's passion for the inappropriate. One would like to see people reading the newspaper, or brushing their teeth; one would like to see a straight fist fight among the ballet steps.

Mad Tristan is nothing like a classic ballet, it is not something to be seen over and over. It is fascinating as a contradiction of classicism. It is fascinating too for its imaginative abundance, for the largeness of its pictorial presence. And it is wonderful how Dali turns whatever pictorial reference he offers into an immediate insignia of the unconscious world within us. And to put it more simply, as a show and the first time you see *Mad Tristan* there isn't a dull moment in it.

Besides Dali, there was one other hero Friday night, Francisco Moncion, who took the part of Tristan. He carried off the most acrobatically strenuous part ever seen without a flaw, and more than that he projected the character and the story convincingly. He is a very fine dancer indeed, and a quite exceptionally imaginative one. Toni Worth, the real Isolde, is beautiful in a rather Vargas-like way. She and Miss Maslova, her double, who did the dancing of the part, were perfectly acceptable executants. The Fluteplayer, Mr. Armstrong, was excellent.

Mad Tristan murders Wagner, but does it to the hilt; with this novelty International has given us a first-class mental carnival—*December* 16, 1944.

CHAGALL IN WONDERLAND

MARC CHAGALL'S décor for the new version of *Firebird* is as wonderful a gift to the season as a big Christmas present to a child. It is heartwarming and scintillating, it is touching and beautiful, as the eye plays in its fairy-tale depths and fairy-tale coruscations. You can fly in the sky, you can peer into a magic wood and see people living in a dragon. One sits before it in childlike enchantment, watching the drops and costumes while the orchestra plays Stravinsky's elegantly enchanted score rather poorly and while, alas, Markova, Dolin and the Ballet Theater company wander about, hop, lift each other, or merely stand endlessly like an opera chorus waiting for a big effect. Dancing there is none to see.

I saw Markova once being lowered from a lift into Dolin's arms and she looked ravishing for the moment, in her loveliest style; and I saw Miss Adams bend and yield charmingly several times in the Berceuse. But the poverty of the choreography was amazing. Adolph Bolm, the choreographer of this new version, is a justly respected great figure of the ballet world— thirty years ago one of the greatest of character dancers, and since 1916 an indefatigable figure in American ballet. But his *Firebird* is mere nonsense, if you should go expecting a ballet.

The charms of Chagall's décor kept me in so happy a frame of mind, I couldn't be angry at the silly sequences the poor dancers had to execute. But since the décor is so beautiful a work of art, one hopes Ballet Theater will, out of respect for Chagall's genius and Stravinsky's too, get a first-rate choreographer to reset it completely. It could be a glorious ballet— *October 25, 1945.*

7

Ballet in Books, Prints, Photographs & Films

NOTES ON NIJINSKY PHOTOGRAPHS

LOOKING at the photographs of Nijinsky, one is struck by his expressive neck. It is an unusually thick and long neck. But its expressivity lies in its clear lift from the trunk, like a powerful thrust. The shoulders are not square, but slope downward; and so they leave the neck easily free, and the eye follows their silhouette down the arms with the sense of a line extraordinarily extended into space, as in a picture by Cézanne or Raphael. The head therefore, at the other end of this unusual extension, poised up in the air, gains an astonishing distinctness, and the tilt of it, even with no muscular accentuation, becomes of unusual interest. Nijinsky tilts his head lightly from the topmost joint, keeping this joint mobile against the upright thrust of the other vertebrae. He does not bend the neck back as some contemporary ballet dancers do. Seen from the side or the rear, the upward line of his back continues straight into the uprightness of the neck, like the neck of a Maillol statue. But Nijinsky alters his neck to suit

266

a character role. The change is striking in the *Scheherazade* pictures—and Mr. Van Vechten, who saw him dance the part, describes him as a "head-wagging, simian creature." Another variation is that for *Petrouchka,* where the shoulders are raised square to break the continuity of the silhouette; to make the arms dangle as a separate entity, and make the head independently wobbly as a puppet's is, on no neck to speak of. The head here does not sum up or direct the action of the body; it seems to have only a minor, a pathetic function. But it bobs too nonsensically to be humanly pitiful. In the role of the Faun the shoulders are slightly lifted when the Faun becomes dimly aware of his own emotion; but the neck is held up firmly and candidly against the shoulder movement (which would normally press the neck to a forward slant); and so the silhouette is kept self-contained and the figure keeps its dignity. Notice, too, the neck in the reclining position of the Faun. Another poignant duplicity of emotion is expressed by the head, neck, and shoulder line of the *Jeux* photographs— the neck rising against lifted shoulders and also bent sideways against a counter tilt of the head. The hero in *Jeux* seems to meet pathos with human nobility; not as the Faun does, with animal dignity.

Looking in these photographs farther along the figure, at the arms in particular, one is struck by their lightness, by the way in which they seem to be suspended in space. Especially in the pictures from *Pavillon* and from *Spectre,* they are not so much placed correctly, or advantageously or illustratively; rather they seem to flow out unconsciously from the moving trunk, a part of the fullness of its intention. They are pivoted, not lifted, from the shoulder or shoulder blade; their force— like the neck's—comes from the full strength of the back. And

so they lead the eye more strongly back to the trunk than out
beyond their reach into space. Even when they point, one is
conscious of the force pointing quite as much as the object
pointed at. To make a grammatical metaphor, the relation of
subject to object is kept clear. This is not so simple in movement as a layman might think. A similar clarification of subject and object struck me in the bullfighting of Belmonte. His
own body was constantly the subject of his motions, the bull
the object. With other fighters, one often had the impression
that not they personally, but their cloth was the subject that
determined a fight. As a cloth is a dead thing, it can only be
decorative, and the bull edged into the position of the subject;
and the distinctness of the torero's drama was blurred. Nijinsky gives an effect in his arm gesture of himself remaining at
the center of space, a strength of voluntary limitation related,
in a way, to that of Spanish dance gesture.—This is what
makes a dancer's arms look like a man's instead of a boy's.

An actual "object" to a dancer's "subject" is his partner. In
dancing with a partner there is a difference between self-
effacement and courtesy. Nijinsky in his pictures is a model
of courtesy. The firmness of support he gives his partner is
complete. He stands straight enough for two. His expression
toward her is intense—in *Giselle* it expresses a supernatural
relation, in *Pavillon* one of admiration, in *Faune* one of desire,
in *Spectre* one of tenderness—and what a supporting arm that
is in *Spectre,* as long and as strong as two. But he observes as
well an exact personal remoteness, he shows clearly the fact
they are separate bodies. He makes a drama of their nearness
in space. And in his own choreography—in *Faune*—the space
between the figures becomes a firm body of air, a lucid state-

ment of relationship, in the way intervening space does in the modern academy of Cézanne, Seurat, and Picasso.

One is struck by the massiveness of his arms. This quality also leads the eye back to the trunk, as in a Michelangelo figure. But it further gives to their graceful poses an amplitude of strength that keeps them from looking innocuous or decorative. In particular in the Narcissus pose the savage force of the arms and legs makes credible that the hero's narcism was not vanity, but an instinct that killed him, like an act of God. In the case of *Spectre,* the power of the arms makes their tendril-like bendings as natural as curvings are in a powerful world of young desire; while weaker and more charming arms might suggest an effeminate or saccharine coyness. There is indeed nothing effeminate in these gestures; there is far too much force in them.

It is interesting to try one's self to assume the poses on the pictures, beginning with arms, shoulders, neck, and head. The flowing line they have is deceptive. It is an unbelievable strain to hold them. The plastic relationships turn out to be extremely complex. As the painter de Kooning, who knows the photographs well and many of whose ideas I am using in these notes, remarked: Nijinsky does just the opposite of what the body would naturally do. The plastic sense is similar to that of Michelangelo and Raphael. One might say that the grace of them is not derived from avoiding strain, as a layman might think, but from the heightened intelligibility of the plastic relationships. It is an instinct for countermovement so rich and so fully expressed, it is unique; though the plastic theory of countermovement is inherent in ballet technique.

Nijinsky's plastic vitality animates the poses derived from

dances by Petipa or Fokine. It shines out, too, if one compares his pictures with those of other dancers in the same parts. This aspect of his genius appears to me one basis for his choreographic style, which specifies sharply plastic effects in dancing—and which in this sense is related both to Isadora and to the moderns. Unfortunately the dancers who now take the role of the Faun do not have sufficient plastic discipline to make clear the intentions of the dance.

From the photographs one can see that the present dancers of *Faune* have not even learned Nijinsky's stance. Nijinsky not only squares his shoulders far less, but also frequently not at all. He does not pull in his stomach and lift his thorax. Neither in shoulders or chest does he exhibit his figure. His stomach has more expression than his chest. In fact, looking at his trunk, one notices a similar tendency to flat-chestedness (I mean in the stance, not in the anatomy) in all the pictures. It is, I believe, a Petersburg trait, and shared independently by Isadora and Martha Graham. In these photographs, at any rate, the expression does not come from the chest; it comes from below the chest, and flows up through it from below. The thorax, so to speak, passively, is not only pulled at the top up and back; at the bottom and from the side it is also pulled down and back. Its physical function is that of completing the circuit of muscles that hold the pelvis in relation to the spine. And it is this relation that gives the dancer his balance. Balance (or aplomb, in ballet) is the crux of technique. If you want to see how good a dancer is, look at his stomach. If he is sure of himself there, if he is so strong there that he can present himself frankly, he (or she) can begin to dance expressively.—I say stomach because the stomach usually faces the audience; one might say waist, groin, or pelvis region.

In looking at Nijinsky pictures, one is struck by the upright tautness about the hips. His waist is broad and powerful. You can see it clearly in the Harlequin pictures. If he is posing on one leg, there is no sense of shifted weight, and as little if he seems to be bending to the side or forward. The effort this means may be compared to lifting a table by one leg and keeping the top horizontal. The center of gravity in the table, and similarly that of his body, has not been shifted. The delicacy with which he cantilevers the weight actually displaced keeps the firmness from being rigidity. I think it is in looking at his waist that one can see best the technical aspect of his instinct for concentrating the origin of movement so that all of it relates to a clear center which is not altered. He keeps the multiplicity, the diffusion which movement has, intelligible by not allowing any doubt as to where the center is. When he moves he does not blur the center of weight in his body; one feels it as clearly as if he were still standing at rest, one can follow its course clearly as it floats about the stage through the dance. And so the motion he makes looks controlled and voluntary and reliable. I imagine it is this constant sense of balance that gave his dancing the unbroken continuity and flow through all the steps and leaps and rests from beginning to end, that critics marveled at.

Incidentally, their remarks of this kind also point to an extraordinary accuracy in his musical timing. For to make the continuity rhythmic as he did, he must have had an unerring instinct at which moment to attack a movement, so that the entire sequence of it would flow as continuously and transform itself into the next motion as securely as did the accompanying sound. To speak of him as unmusical, with no sense of rhythm, as Stravinsky has, is therefore an impropriety that is due to a confusion of meaning in the word "rhythm." The choreography of *Faune* proves that Nijinsky's natural musical intelligence was of the highest order. For this was the first ballet choreography set clearly, not to the measures and periods, but to the expressive flow of the music, to its musical sense. You need only compare *Faune's* assurance in this respect to the awkwardness musically of Fokine's second scene in *Petrouchka*, the score of which invites the same sort of understanding. But this is not in the photographs.

Nijinsky does not dance from his feet; he dances from his pelvis. The legs do not show off. They have no ornamental pose. Even in his own choreography, though the leg gestures are "composed," they are not treated as pictorial possibilities. They retain their weight. They tell where the body goes and how. But they don't lead it. They are, however, completely expressive in this role; and the thighs in the *Spectre* picture with Karsavina are as full of tenderness as another dancer's face. It is noticeable, too, that Nijinsky's legs are not especially turned out, and a similar moderate *en dehors* seems to be the rule in the Petersburg male dancers of Nijinsky's generation. But the parallel feet in *Narcisse* and *Faune*, and the pigeon toes in *Til* are not a willful contradiction of the academic principle for the sake of something new. They can, it seems to me, be properly understood only by a turned-out dancer, as Nijinsky himself clearly was. For the strain of keeping the pelvis in the position the ballet dancer holds it in for balance is much greater with parallel or turned-in feet (which contradict the outward twist of the thigh); and this strain gives a new plastic dimension to the legs and feet, if it is carried through as forcefully as Nijinsky does.—I am interested, too, to notice that in standing Nijinsky does not press his weight mostly on the ball of the big toe, but grips the floor with the entire surface of the foot.

I have neglected to mention the hands, which are alive and simple, with more expression placed in the wrist than the fingers. They are not at all "Italian"; and are full of variety without an emphasis on sensitivity. The hands in *Spectre* are celebrated, and remind one of the hands in Picassos ten years later. I am also very moved by the uplifted, half-unclenched hands in the *Jeux* picture, as mysterious as breathing in sleep. One can see, too, that in *Petrouchka* the hands are black-mittened, not white-mittened as now; the new costume makes the dance against the black wall in the second scene a foolish hand dance, instead of a dance of a whole figure, as intended.

The manner in which Nijinsky's face changes from role to role is immediately striking. It is enhanced by make-up, but not created by it. In fact, a friend pointed out that the only role in which one recognizes Nijinsky's civilian face is that of Petrouchka where he is most heavily made up. There is no mystery about such transformability. People don't usually realize how much any face changes in the course of a day, and how often it is unrecognizable for an instant or two. Nijinsky seems to have controlled the variability a face has. The same metamorphosis is obvious in his body. The Spectre, for instance, has no age or sex, the Faun is adolescent, the hero of *Jeux* has a body full-grown and experienced. Til can either be boy or man. The Slave in *Scheherazade* is fat, the Spectre is thin. It does not look like the same body. One can say that in this sense there is no exhibitionism in Nijinsky's photographs. He is never showing you himself, or an interpretation of himself. He is never vain of what he is showing you. The audience does not see him as a professional dancer, or as a professional charmer. He disappears completely, and instead there is an imaginary being in his place. Like a classic artist, he remains detached, unseen, unmoved, uninterested. Looking at him, one is in an imaginary world, entire and very clear; and one's emotions are not directed at their material objects, but at their imaginary satisfactions. As he said himself, he danced with love.

To sum up, Nijinsky in his photographs shows us the style of a classic artist. The emotion he projects, the character he projects is not communicated as his own, but as one that exists independently of himself, in the objective world. Similarly his plastic sense suggests neither a private yearning into an infinity of space nor a private shutting out of surrounding relationships; both of them legitimate romantic attitudes. The weight he gives his own body, the center which he gives his plastic motions, strikes a balance with the urge and rapidity of leaps and displacements. It strikes a balance between the role he dances and the roles of his partners. The distinction of place makes the space look real, the distinction of persons makes the drama real. And for the sake of this clarification he characterizes (or mimes, one might say) even such a conventional ornamental show-off, or "pure dance," part as that in *Pavillon*. On the other hand, the awkward heaviness that *Faune, Sacre,* and *Jeux* exhibited, and that was emphasized by their angular precision, was not, I believe, an anti-classic innovation. It was an effort to make the dance more positive, to make clearer still the center of gravity of a movement, so that its extent, its force, its direction, its elevation can be appreciated not incidentally merely, but integrally as drama. He not only extended the plastic range in dancing, but clarified it. And this is the way to give meaning to dancing; not secondhand literary meaning, but direct meaning. Nijinsky's latest intentions of "circular movement," and the improvisational quality *Til* seems to have had are probably a normal development of his sense of motion in relation to a point of repose—a motion that grew more animated and diverse as his instinct became more exercised. (An evolution not wholly dissimilar can be followed in Miss Graham's work, for instance.) And I consider the following remark he made to be indicative of the direction of his instinct: "La grâce, le charme, le joli sont rangés tout autour du point central qu'est le beau. C'est pour le beau que je travaille." I do not see anything in these pictures that would lead one to suppose that Nijinsky's subsequent insanity cast any premonitory shadow on his phenomenally luminous dance intelligence.

In their stillness Nijinsky's pictures have more vitality than the dances they remind us of as we now see them on the stage. They remain to show us what dancing can be; and what the spectator and the dancer each aspire to, and hold to be a fair standard of art. I think they give the discouraged dance lover faith in dancing as a serious human activity. As Mr. Van Vechten wrote after seeing him in 1916: "His dancing has the unbroken quality of music, the balance of great painting, the meaning of fine literature, and the emotion inherent in all these arts"—*March, 1943.*

ABOUT SOVIET BALLET

THE Soviet Ballet is quite a legend in this country. We hear from travelers that the Russian academies continue to produce new dancers as astonishing as Pavlova and Nijinsky; that ballet is phenomenally popular over there, much more so than before the Revolution—as popular, some say, as baseball is here. We hear of excellent companies in every city, even as far off as Siberia and Turkestan; and of excellent ballet schools, too, in wild-sounding places. We know that over there the ballet is a state institution, that their working conditions are better than ours, that exceptional talent has been rewarded officially and handsomely. We know, too, that performances continued during the winter of siege and air raids and privation, and the great ballerina Lepishinskaya has written of dancing for the soldiers at the front on a platform built over an American truck.

But all this doesn't tell us what Soviet ballet really looks like, how their style and expression is different from ours, how sincerely their new ballets would touch us—as Americans—in actual performance. We trust we shall find out when the war is over. And meanwhile some fresh information has turned up. *Dance Index,* the scholarly New York magazine, devotes its current double June-July issue to Soviet choreography. On the cover is an action picture of a fantastically superb leap by Miss Ulanova, the Moscow ballerina. Inside you find twenty-three more photographs, a brief history of the Soviet ballet by Joan Lawson (of London) and a descriptive listing of thirty ballets produced since 1924, including several from provincial theaters. The information is largely technical and objective, and reading carefully one can for the first time get some view of a fascinating subject.

One learns that the Soviet Ballet has scarcely been affected by the innumerable choreographic innovations of the Diaghileff epoch (1910–1930), nor by what has happened in Europe or America since, either in ballet or modern dance. A Soviet ballet is generally in three acts, a full evening's entertainment —not just one act, like ours. Their big companies are four times as big as our Ballet Theater company. The dance style is firmly based on straight nineteenth-century tradition, and the old ballets are still brilliantly danced. In these old pieces such modernizations as have been tried are generally being discarded again. One of the old ballets, *Don Quixote* (dating from 1869), was last winter, as Mr. Hindus told me, one of the two great current hits.

Some of the new works made since the Revolution are directly in the old manner. But a great many others have attempted to find a new dance style. It seems as if Soviet experimentation had been choreographically more timid, or at least far less restless than ours. In the middle '20s the major tendency of the innovators was toward simple "real life" devices. They tried introducing a contemporary Soviet moral in the plot, they tried naturalistic pantomime in the action scenes, even some revue dancing and athletic parades here and there. But after a while it became apparent that these novelties did not add to the dance value of the ballet, they had too little expressivity as dancing to make good theater. Wonderfully performed though these ballets were, few of them are still in the repertoire.

In the '30s the young choreographers decided that the traditional ballet style was really more expressive than the flat devices that were meant to improve on it. At the same time they became fascinated by folk-dance forms—especially Russian ones. This double tendency led on the one hand to the invention of vivid character dances (as folk dances adapted to ballet technique are called); on the other hand, to a new freshness of emotional expression in composing strict classic variations. An example of the new vitality are two ballets by the Tartar Chaboukiani, a magnificent classic dancer himself. One of them, *Laurencia,* is a story told in Spanish dance forms merged with classic forms; the other, *Heart of the Hills,* classicizes Georgian folk dances. Both are highly dramatic without direct pantomime passages. They sound very novel and very fine. *Heart of the Hills,* incidentally, has a score by the brother of the New York choreographer, Balanchine.

In contrast to this new classic-character dance ("in which acting does not exist without dance") is a successful three-act *Romeo and Juliet* by Lavrovsky to a Prokofieff score. It seems to be mostly stylized pantomime, it follows the Shakespeare play quite closely, and it led to animated disputes between a pantomime faction and a dance faction. Judging by photographs in a 1940 Leningrad publication there is no similarity between this *Romeo* and our 1943 Tudor one.

It is of interest too that the twenty-two ballets listed in *Dance Index* as produced by the Leningrad or Moscow companies are credited to eleven choreographers—not counting six collaborators. The Russians seem to give lots of people a chance to try. Another little fact of interest, this one has to do with *Red Poppy*. In the days of this patriotic ballet's greatest success, the shortcomings of its choreography were sharply dis cussed in its own program-libretto. What a pleasant novelty it would be to find an acid note like that in one of our own programs.

I have often thought of an amateur film I saw five or six years ago, showing part of a carmagnole from the Leningrad ballet, *The Flames of Paris*. It struck me as completely fresh in feeling, astonishingly spontaneous as dancing and unfinicky in choreography. I imagine that post-war Russian audiences will be delighted by the originality and subtlety of our best choreography, and we will be amazed at the impetuosity and the simple openness of their ballets and dazzled by the power of their dancing—*August* 22, 1943.

A POET ON PAVLOVA PHOTOGRAPHS

AN ALBUM OF PAVLOVA PHOTOGRAPHS with "accompanying notes" by Marianne Moore is the very astonishing contents of the latest issue of *Dance Index*—price, one quarter; admirers of Pavlova and admirers of Miss Moore will not want to miss so remarkable an item. There are thirty-one photographs of the great ballerina, who holds the rank of greatest in our century, despite Kshessinska and Egorova, Karsavina, Spessiva and Doubrovska, who were her brilliant peers in the days of her glory. And there are six pages of comment by our great poetess—scholarly, subtle and accurate, in an impeccable prose that has the floating balance, the light pauses and the recurrent soaring instants of classic dancing.

The style is an homage to the dancer, precisely delicate and delicately spontaneous.

Miss Moore's article is first of all a collage of quotations from the celebrated appreciators—Svetloff, Levinson, C. W. Beaumont, Olivéroff, Dandré and Stier. They tell very little of Pavlova's craftsmanship, of that technique she worked at so devotedly and which must have been full of discoveries and procedures worth passing on to later dancers and dance lovers. Miss Moore includes what technical hints she has found, but the eye-witnesses describe Pavlova's dancing mostly by the device of spiritual rhapsodies. Miss Moore quotes the most vivid evocation, Levinson's description of the "Dying Swan," and translates it beautifully. From the innumerable other tributes she selects a phrase here, a sentence there and re-assembles them with so keen a sense of style that they give you a clearer picture of dancing than in their original context.

Still the quotations keep their bias—a parlor-like spirituality that is unsatisfactory. Miss Moore does not shatter their decorousness; she vivifies it by adding to it herself physical and moral perceptions of real elegance. Like Gautier she can manage a rapturous moment without losing her balance. "In the photograph of her . . . in the grass . . . the descending line of the propped forearm, of her dress and other hand, of ankle and foot, continues to the grass with the naturalness of a streamer of seaweed—an inevitable and stately serpentine which imparts to the seated figure the ease of a standing one." Or, "We see her in the gavotte advancing with the swirling grace of a flag and the decorum of an impalla deer."

But it is by her private moral perceptions, appearing for an instant and at rare intervals, that Miss Moore gives us the sharpest equivalent for the actual fact of classic dancing. She notes on a picture of twelve-year-old Pavlova: "the erectness of the head, the absolutely horizontal brows, indicating power of self-denial; the eyes, dense with imagination and sombered with solicitude; the hair, severely competent; the dress, dainty more than proud." And after describing a hand pose, "These truthful hands, the most sincere and the least greedy imaginable," she notes Pavlova's use of the passive voice when the dancer wrote: "I was permitted to style myself Premiere Danseuse . . . later I was granted the title of Ballerina." This classic modesty Miss Moore recurs to: "She had power for a most unusual reason—she did not present as valuable the personality from which she could not escape." And later, suggesting the quality of Pavlova's expression, Miss Moore asks, "Why should one so innocent, so natural, so ardent be sad? If self-control is the essential condition of conveying emotion and giving is giving up, we still cannot feel that renunciation had made Pavlova sad; may it have been that for lives that one loves there are things even love cannot do?" And later Miss Moore herself answers, "That which is able to change the heart proves itself."

Morally speaking, this describes correct classic dancing; it is a poet's metaphor of its final grace. A journalist asked the sprightly Danilova what was the most important quality for a ballerina. "Modesty," she answered quickly—*June* 18, 1944.

ROMANTIC BALLET IN LONDON

DANCE INDEX, the valuable monthly sponsored by Private Lincoln Kirstein, has brought out a new issue dated September-December, 1943, under the title, "The Romantic Ballet in London, 1821–1858." It is a well-illustrated monograph on the subject—practically a book on it—by George Chaffee. Like two earlier *Dance Index* numbers by Mr. Chaffee on American ballet prints, this new one is of special interest to ballet print students, containing as it does the fullest and most accurate catalogue of English romantic ballet prints there is.

But the catalogue is only a small part of the text. Mr. Chaffee's general notes on ballet in London during these years are remarkable for their range and good sense. Almost all the information he gives is new. He points out that in addition to the celebrated imported Parisian ballet at the Italian and Royal Italian Opera there were several largely native English companies, dancing at the English opera houses, Covent Garden, Drury Lane, and at smaller theaters. It is their activity, which has been neglected by English writers, that he stresses. Full-length ballets were the fashion then, billed after an opera or a play. Often the same ballet, in English and Parisian choreographies, ran with success at two London theaters simultaneously. These local productions, Mr. Chaffee believes, were quite as good as those of English ballet nowadays.

In establishing the quality of London dancers, he throws new light on some who were popular in America too at the time—Celine Celeste, for instance, who made $200,000 on her second American tour, 1834–37. He throws new light on the fine English comics, comparing them to Dolin and Tudor—and comic ballet is a subject hardly touched by other writers. (On the same bill, right after a tragic ballet, the great star might see herself burlesqued in her prize number by a comic.)

And we learn that the brilliance of those years, both in the resident and the imported ballet, was due to a few ballet-loving managers, particularly Bunn and Lumley, who were constantly in and out of funds. Bunn died in 1852, and Lumley could not recover financially after 1858; and so a dazzling show, the richest ballet of its period, collapsed. Without Lumley and Bunn, neither the dancers nor the London public could keep serious ballet going. Without a National Academy to fall back on, London forgot what first-class ballet was like till a new impresario in the grand style arrived—Diaghileff.

Incidentally, Mr. Chaffee's research corrects some of the dates you find in ballet books—dates such as the earliest record of toesteps, now an 1821 London print of the Paris dancer, Fanny Bias; or the earliest record of a ballet d'action (a story-ballet something like our own), now a 1717 London program of a ballet by John Weaver. These new facts and Mr. Chaffee's notes on them will be a surprise to readers of dance-history books.

To the general reader, of course, the stream of dance history is very dim, indeed. But I think the general reader will like knowing that we have here in town remarkable historians of ballet, meticulous scholars who also know ballet as it is in the flesh and therefore can study it as something real people have been doing for centuries before we were born. Others are Lillian Moore, a dancer herself; Marian Hannah Winter, whose work on early American ballet has appeared in *Dance Index;* and Arthur Michel, who has been contributing to *Dance.* All this too is a natural part of the intellectual life of a big city—*February* 13, 1944.

FIVE CENTURIES OF BALLET

DURING the last two weeks, 100,000 people here in town have been to see a ballet program. A few years ago ballet was said to be moribund, effete, perverse and un-American; now it rivals the circus. I think one reason people like ballet is that nobody on stage says a foolish word all evening and just now that alone is an intense relief. At any rate the Metropolitan and the City Center have been filled every night and the audiences have looked perfectly satisfied when they left. The audience at the Met has been a little the more experienced and discriminating. I doubt if it would have taken to the silly *Red Poppy* or the tawdry *Scheherazade* that were hits at the Center. I hope it wouldn't have. But at both theaters the public is the normal large public. A dancer who shows off and who is crudely energetic gets a big hand; then twenty minutes later the same house will be applauding a poetic moment or a fine work. Even people unaccustomed to ballet seem to sense that though youthful athleticism is fun at the moment you see it, style in dancing is what ballet is really about.

Style in dancing is the quality that makes the fugitive dance

impression keep its brilliance afterward in your memory. This
is what finally counts with the audience. A momentary thrill
isn't worth the trouble and expense of going back to the theater a third and fourth time. But if there is a likelihood that
the flavor of it will last, that is another matter. Ballet has been
trying every day for several centuries to establish solid principles of dance style. It isn't true that ballet style is an imitation of eighteenth-century court manners; on the contrary the
courtiers took lessons from professional dancers. Ballet style is
based on what the human esthetic visual apparatus normally
responds to, and its procedures have been continuously tested
all over the Western world for several centuries.

You don't have to take my word for it. You can go to the
Wildenstein Galleries and look over the exhibit there, "Five
Centuries of Ballet (1575–1944)." The show is very pretty
just to glance at casually. But it is also extremely well selected
to give you an easy survey of ballet history—especially up to
1900. Two-thirds of the material come from Mr. Chaffee's
extraordinary collection, and he has contributed a very remarkable catalogue.

At "Five Centuries of Ballet" you can follow dance style
from a Primaticcio, said to picture a late sixteenth-century
court ballet scene. It looks very much like a group of Duncan
dancers. It illustrates balance of movement without tension.
The seventeenth-century professionals add concentration in
the torso, they are consciously "turned-out." The early eighteenth-century stars keep this self-contained silhouette, but deploy and elongate the lines of the arm and lower the shoulder.
In Noverre's time they accentuate the value of countermovement in the limbs, breaking the line dramatically at the joints.
At the opening of the nineteenth century they add bold exten-

sions at right angles to the trunk. And the Romantic stars who follow keep this open largeness of line but make the plastic accents at the joints more subtle and tantalizing. How these long curves were again broken by Nijinsky, and how he added to dancing the contrast of weight and immobility is not illustrated in the show. But most people know something of modern ballet without knowing the long tradition it assumes the dancer is trained in and without which the "modern" innovations look merely bizarre.

"Five Centuries of Ballet" is illuminating in many other respects, too. The splendor of dance production has always been an essential quality of ballet style. You will see here lavish sets and fantastic costumes that will show you what proper ballet should look like. And you will see the celebrated stars of history, with their long noses and worn faces off stage and their ravishing expressions in action. You will realize that ballet is a collective effort of human ingenuity and sensibility so ample, intense and protracted that there is nothing foolish about taking ballet seriously as an art or in expecting it to satisfy the spirit as an art does—*April* 23, 1944.

TWO NEW ENGLISH BALLET BOOKS

IF YOU are one of those who have come to enjoy ballet and would now like to know some more about it—technically and practically—the best way, of course, is to attend lessons. If you go to any ballet school, introduce yourself to the secretary and say you would like to watch a class at the school's convenience, you will, I am sure, be welcome. The pupils will give you a stare and then forget you are watching. The exercises will puzzle you, but it is likely that in the course of an hour you will see some beautiful moments and you will perhaps feel some of the special atmosphere, so serious and so innocent, that characterizes a good dance lesson. You may begin to see, by comparing the pupils, how the personal physique of a dancer changes the plastic value of a regulation step, and you may even see how the character of the dancer colors and vivifies the correctness of execution. Only, just as the dancer shouldn't strain for an effect, so the observer shouldn't try at any cost to see something significant or lovely. Take dancing as it comes, and when you see something you like, then remember the impression.

But books, too, can help you to exercise your eye. There is a new English one, *The Ballet Lover's Pocket Book: Technique Without Tears for the Ballet Lover,* that is exactly what its title describes. It is written and illustrated by Kay Ambrose, a lady whose action drawings of ballet dancers have appeared in previous books. This one contains clear (and quite charming) drawings of dancers, showing many basic exercises, steps, leaps and poses, giving the French names and diagraming the sequence of motion. It also contains in its sixty small pages an amazing amount of sound information about ballet art and ballet life; for example, useful advice to fans, to beginners and to "ballet mammas." It is a sensible, accurate and cordial book.

There is an older (1939) American book I also recommend highly to ballet lovers who are looking for technical information, Lincoln Kirstein's *Ballet Alphabet*. It gives an immense amount of fundamental theory and history, cleverly compressed into seventy pages, and it has few but very vivid illustrations. The London ballet critic, Arnold Haskell's *Ballet* (1938), is another easy introduction. I read it with interest, but it is written in a rather careless style, and I am not sure that a layman who takes it up can distinguish between what are the facts and what are the author's private opinions.

A new book by Mr. Haskell—his fifteenth—has just arrived here, *The National Ballet, a History and a Manifesto*. Although it is meant for British consumption, as a boost for the London Sadler's Wells ballet company, it also brings much information on productions and personnel, past and present.

It is a pleasure to read about the wartime Ashton and Helpmann choreographies, it is interesting to look at the photographs of dancers and speculate about them. And then one is curious whether that is all there is of value in English ballet, for five other English companies are now dancing over there.

There is however, one aspect of Mr. Haskell's "National" idea that is peculiarly puzzling to us over here: his omission from it of the English dancers we have come to admire. Antony Tudor, for instance, is barely mentioned in passing; Hugh Laing and Frederic Franklin, not at all. Markova, the very paragon of English dancers, although treated with deference, is not invited to join a National British ballet. Well, we are only too glad to keep them all if they care to stay.

But I don't believe Mr. Haskell could have meant to slight the English dancers who so brilliantly exemplify for us the idea of English ballet. And there are things in the book better worth speaking of. Fundamentally, Mr. Haskell pleads for a ballet that will be a part of the normal cultural life of its own country, and this is exactly what we too are after. He points

out that such a ballet needs a permanent home, where it can
rehearse with concentration; it needs a permanent school to
train its dancers; it needs all the local collaborators it can find;
it needs serious artistic guidance. He also makes the excellent points that such a company should not restrict itself to
self-conscious nationalism in theme or dance style, and that it
should preserve the masterpieces of the past as points of comparison with the present.

Unfortunately, we are still far from a national ballet in this
sense. But I believe we need such a stable organization if our
ballet—so glamorous at the moment—is not to deteriorate
sharply in the next five years. There is no substitute in the
arts for artistic integrity. And integrity needs a home where
it is valued. That is a plain fact that any sensible person
knows from experience—*November 7, 1943.*

BALLET PHOTOGRAPHS—1942

AT THE Modern Museum there was a show of dance
photographs by Gjon Mili, many taken by his new stroboscopic and multiflash process, which records successive
phases of a movement at intervals of fractions of a second on
a single plate. All of his pictures are intelligent documentation, and phototechnically they are very handsome indeed;
and often they have a kind of friendly drollery in stopping the
dancer dead just when he was making so very earnest an
effort to rush ahead. Well, as I was looking at them and think-

ing of the many dance photographs I have seen, I wondered why most of them depress me so. Of course I like to look at dance pictures of myself as much as any ex-dancer does. But other people's—documentation aside—generally look pretty foolish to me; the dancers in them look so busy getting nowhere. A shot can show you only one gesture, which is like hearing only one note of a piece of music, or one word of a poem. The more painstaking the photograph, the more pointless the effect. You don't see the change in the movement, so you don't see the rhythm, which makes dancing. The picture represents a dancer; but it doesn't give the emotion that dancing gives as you watch it. A dancer on stage doesn't look strained and she isn't a dry amoeba-shaped blob, a configuration of swirls of cloth and rigid muscles and swollen veins fixed forever in a small square of nothing, like a specimen on a slide. The dancer isolated in the camera field seems to be hanging in a void, in a nowhere.

Dance pictures get livelier, the more sure you are of just where it happened, and the more air there is all around. My favorite photographs of violent motion are the strange series Rudolph Burckhardt took of Orson Welles rehearsing *Horse Eats Hat* among half-built scenery on the stage of the Maxine Elliot. In these pictures the place and purpose of the movement are clear. And so the monstrousness of arrested motion on the photograph and the subhuman shapes make sense. But the movement in this case isn't the special kind that is made by dancers.

Among ballet photographs I should like to mention some thirty-year-old ones I very much like to look at. Curiously enough, many of them were not even taken in action, nor all by the same photographer. They are the photographs of Nijinsky. In nearly all his pictures one feels, besides the documentary interest, an immediate sense of movement, of the impulse to dance. Is it because they so clearly give the sense of expressive energy radiating from the pit of the stomach up out at the top of the chest and the base of the neck, and radiating down through the small of the back and out along the legs? This might be one explanation. But one can also note that the photographer did not so much try for an elegant or a novel two-dimensional outline in the dancer's pose as for a three-dimensional and plastic interest. Since the interest of the pose is a three-dimensional one, you notice the air all around it; and since the ornamental outline of the limbs isn't the main thing in the picture, you see the weight of the body better, and the movement indicated looks more like a voluntary action and less like a freakish explosion. Nijinsky's own powerful dance intelligence illuminates his poses and because in them you see his easy control of action-in-repose expression, you have confidence too in his control of expression in the livelier parts of the dance, that are not photographed. He looks to me as if his body remembered the whole dance, all the phases of it, as he holds the one pose in the picture; he seems to be thinking, I've just done that, and then I do that, and then comes that; so the body looks like a face lighting up at a single name that evokes a whole crowd of remembered friends. As you look at him you see the pose breathe and move and start to glow. Quite apart from the style of movement they represent, some of his pictures should be in the hotel room of every dancer, to remind him of the real radiance of movement, to cheer him up when he wonders what it's all about, anyway. And dance lovers need such reminders and such cheering up from time to time, too—*March-April,* 1942.

A FILM OF PAVLOVA

PAVLOVA enthusiasts will go on a pilgrimage to the Modern Museum this week to see the film of Pavlova dancing, which is being shown there in a program called "The Dance in Film (1909–36)." The Pavlova reel is a record of portions of six dances; it was made privately by Douglas Fairbanks in Hollywood in 1927, and it is probably the best film of Pavlova that exists. It will touch those who can remember her glamor on the stage. But without the help of memory it does not recreate the legendary Pavlova effect. I think you can get a better suggestion of the effect the great dancer produced from some of the still photographs of her, especially the early ones (taken around 1910) from St. Petersburg.

Dance students, however, will be grateful that the film exists and is accessible. In itself it is plain and straight. It records several aspects of Pavlova's technique in motion, and to the student this is of great interest. He sees how firm her attack was for all the delicacy of her manner; he sees her clear control of speed; her ability to pause, her wide, simple arm gesture; her extremely rapid pas de bourrée—which the camera can't keep up with. And the student notes that she was not as strong or correct in the thighs and knees as in the ankles and feet and that she could overdo facial miming—details which her contemporaries criticized and which evidently did not detract from her effect on the stage.

The other items on the Modern Museum program are of varying interest. Incredibly absurd is a film from 1913, show-

292

ing the celebrated Moscow ballerina Gelzer doing a fake Fokine Greek-tunic number. She is supported by a stout, mustachioed premier danseur, who observes her in ecstasies of rapture; what is disconcerting is that he looks like a respectable middle-aged bartender gone mad and doing ballet with a diaper over his tights. Another film shows Rudolph Valentino in a "passionate" Argentine tango, dancing it with an innocent sultriness that is very winning. There is also a Charleston by Joan Crawford, an Astaire trick dance with chorus, and the famous Disney *Skeleton Dance.*

Dance expression and dance recording are two separate functions in the cinema that rarely coincide. The motion picture is the only means of accurately recording dancing, but dance lovers are aware of how rarely it projects anything like the dance quality one knows from the theater. When we watch dancing anywhere, the more distinctly we can see the plastic quality—the three dimensional quality—of the movement, the more clearly we feel the point of the dance. But the camera gives a poor illusion of volume, it makes a distortion of foreshortening and perspective and it is plastic only at short range. A further trouble is the camera's narrow angle of vision. A dance on the stage becomes clearer by the relation of the movement to the architectural space around it, that is, to the permanent stage space and permanent stage frame in which the dance moves back and forth and right and left. Theater choreography is movement suited to a whole, fixed area. But the film cannot show the whole stage and also show the dancer large enough so we can see just what she is doing. When the camera moves up to her the stage frame is lost; when the camera follows her she seems to be flailing about without making any appreciable headway—she bobs around against a swirling, fantastically liquid background. Altogether, when a stage dance has been photographed from various distances and angles and the film assembled, the effect of the dance is about like the effect of playing a symphony for the radio but shifting the microphone arbitrarily from one instrument to another all the time. Listening at home, you can hear the noise all right, but the symphony doesn't make any sense that way.

These are the difficulties of projecting the dance value in dancing in the cinema. They have been overcome occasionally in ways I shall describe next time—*August* 1, 1943.

DANCE IN THE FILMS

WHEN you watch the film version of a ballet intended for the stage, why should good dancers so often look unnatural in a way they don't in the theater? Well, for one thing, you watch a dancer on the cinema screen as you would if she were dancing for you in a living room. You see her close by, at a distance ranging from two to twenty feet. In the theater she makes her big effects across a distance of a hundred or three hundred feet. What looks expressive away on the stage, looks absurdly overemphatic near at hand. The hard thrust with which a stage dancer attacks a movement, the spread-wide openness of gesture which is eloquent in the theater, the violent speed at which a dancer can cover a large stage space— these phases of dancing are effective only at a distance. They are proportioned to a large space and not to a small one; so is

the physical effort involved in doing them, which looks unreasonable and unattractive at close quarters. (Even in the
theater many people are disappointed when they watch a great
dancer from the first row; they are embarrassed to see her work
so hard.) In short, the present manner of filming a dancer
close by puts her into an intimate relation to the audience; she
is, therefore, restricted to intimate effects and cannot use the
full dynamic range of serious theater dancing. She is most successful when she looks not like a dancer at work, but like a
non-dancer who, incidentally, does some winsome steps; and
when in expression she restricts herself to understatement.

A dance style like Astaire's that makes a fine art of understatement is, for this reason, the most immediately effective
style in a film. It looks natural a few feet away. It does so not
merely for the psychological reason that tap dancing is what
we think of as a natural way of dancing in this country, but
much more because tap dancing lends itself technically to an
exquisite salon style. The dynamic range is narrow but sharply
differentiated; the dramatic miming is barely indicated but
perfectly intelligible; the presentation is intimately charming,
and the dance itself rarely needs much room. A complete
dance phrase can generally be photographed close by in a
single camera field, and the continuity to the following phrase
is generally so casual that a shift in the camera between
phrases does not interrupt very much. These are the technical
advantages which allow Astaire—who is certainly a great dancer
—to give a more complete sense of dance expression on the
screen than good dancers in other styles can. But there are in-
dications that dance expression of a less miniature sort may
also be possible in films. In Chaplin's early pictures there were
often dance numbers that were not salon pieces—such as his

own acts on roller skates, as a boxing referee, as a drunk, or "choral movements" like those of the crowds in *The Cop*. The film technique of the day was not so obsessed with intimate nearness, and Chaplin often performed a full dance sequence in a single camera field, giving the complete continuity.

In the present film technique Disney's animals have been more successful than human dancers in giving a wide range of dance expression to movement; and Disney often composed the dance to fit the field—as a choreographer does for the stage. Balanchine (in "the Goldwyn Follies") tried composing serious ballet dancing to fit the successive camera fields (and camera angles). And this procedure is the sensible approach to making dancing in the cinema more than a mere recording or more than an amiable incident; it is an approach that might make film dancing as variously expressive on the screen as theater dancing has become on the stage—*August* 8, 1943.

FORUM ON FUNCTIONS OF DANCE CRITICISM

AGNES DE MILLE speaking on a forum on dance criticism last Wednesday made a point I should like to pass on to other dancers as the wisest advice I know on the relation of the dancer to the critic. She spoke of the alternate confident and uncertain periods through which artists pass and how in his uncertainty the dancer longs for assistance and clarification. He is tempted then to turn to the critic to lead him out of his confusion by an authoritative estimate of his individual creative gifts. But Miss de Mille warned against relying on reviews in such moments of doubt. A good critic will tell the dancer which elements in a work get across and which do not. But that alone does not necessarily indicate the most productive, the most sincere direction for the dancer to take. An artist will find his own real strength not by listening to what is said about his work, but in the creative process itself. And it is safer for him to rely on himself to find his own identity; for it is unlikely that anyone else can find it for him.

The forum at which Miss de Mille spoke so brilliantly was held at the Y. M. H. A. during the storm last Wednesday night in a large comfortable crowded room. The other speakers were Mary Jane Shea, the very gifted choreographer of *Sailor Bar,* B. H. Haggin of the *Nation,* George Beiswanger of *Theatre Arts, Dance Observer* and *Dance News,* and Milton Robertson, a young radio writer; I acted as chairman. The audience took a lively part in the discussion, which turned on the function of the dance critic, what one can expect of him and what he is good for.

Mr. Robertson affirmed that a critic should be a propagandist, that it is his function to create a movement in the right direction, to popularize good art and teach as large an audience as possible what and how to enjoy. But this radio-minded view met with opposition. Not one of the other speakers, and few, it seemed, of the audience could see the critic as a glorified teacher with all a teacher's classroom authority. Most of those present agreed with Mr. Haggin, who stated that the best critic is a man of exceptional perceptiveness who reports as clearly as possible to his reader. His merit does not lie in dictating what is to be right or wrong. It lies in animating the reader's own perceptions, so that he can see the work more distinctly for himself. This much one can expect of a good critic. But to direct new movements, to popularize the appreciation of masterpieces, to encourage artists, these are not the critic's function; he has no power and no authority to affect them.

On the subject of the critic's lack of authority, Mr. Chujoy, the ballet critic, remarked from the audience that for ten years each season every dance critic has condemned *Scheherazade*, but *Scheherazade* continues to be given and is as popular as ever.

For myself, I too quite agree with Mr. Haggin's realistic view of what the critic at best accomplishes. I find the critic looks ridiculous in the role of a dictator of taste and also in that role against which Miss de Mille warned, that of a fortune teller for artists. And yet in practice both roles are constantly being assigned him. With charming good humor, some members of the forum audience, after agreeing that the critic was not a teacher, asked if he couldn't though teach just a little. I guess a critic won't quite avoid being a bit of a pedagogue and a bit of a charlatan. But I'm all for everybody's recognizing that these are not his functions, that his function is as Mr. Haggin said: to notice, to order, to report; or as Virgil Thomson has said: to put down a sort of portrait of what went on—*April* 2, 1944.

8

Modern Dancers

LOOKING HUMAN

WHEN I saw Agnes de Mille's dancers standing in profile making an arm gesture, it looked so natural it looked just like Margie, Amy and Sue lifting their arms. It looked concrete, as though there was nothing else to it but what you saw; as in a morris dance, they were doing what they were doing and they were whoever they were. They looked human. It may sound harmless enough, but it was a pleasant surprise. And then it occurred to me that one of the things that have made me uncomfortable at recitals of modern-dance groups is the way the dancers seem to disappear as human beings and only function as instruments. When you see six of them on the stage, all you can do is count six, you can't tell six what. They don't seem to be girls combining with other girls, they don't seem to have any human relation to one another. They seem artificially depersonalized, and their bodies operated from off stage. I smell a Führer somewhere, and I get uncomfortable. I wish our dance groups would look as if they were free agents. I wish they would look as if they liked being together, at least as much as folk dancers do, or Lindy-hoppers.

Well, another thing that makes me uncomfortable with modern groups is that they don't even look as if they enjoyed dancing. We all know that expression of sobriety they wear not only on their face but on their body, too. It covers a group of them like an unattractive army blanket. From their programs, from their choreographies, they mean to express all sorts of things; but they don't show them. They seem to be thinking of the next movement as though they were afraid they'd forget it, instead of enjoying the one they are doing while they are doing it. When I think of the natural kind of dancing, or folk dancing, I notice it doesn't express anything but the pleasure of being in a dance. The ballet (and vaudeville dancing too) teach in school to express, to project the natural pleasure in just movement. But the modern schools pay little attention to projection even of this simple pleasure. I think that is a serious weakness as far as appearing on the stage goes. When a dancer learns to show his delight, the audience begins to "understand" him. You cannot understand without liking, and how can the audience like unless the dancer shares his liking with them. But our dance groups set themselves problems in expression far beyond this simple one. They skip it and jump in at the second story. They don't care about your liking, they want you not only to understand, but to believe. They want their movement to awaken your imagination, so that it will join the movement you see to others you consciously or unconsciously remember. This would be really sensational dancing.

Real sensationalism is wonderful, but besides emotional control it requires physical ease. Really sensational dancing will pass through violent shifts of balance without breaking down the body's assurance. The balance is real, you can see it shift back and forth and all the while the body continues moving as a whole. This is what our modern groups expect of themselves and often pretend to be doing; but actually a violent step or gesture upsets the relation of one movement to the next, breaking the dance, forcing it to start up in the middle. Natural dancing avoids this difficulty, limits steps and gestures to amusement, so that the body moves consistently as a whole. But our groups, afraid of being too simple, would rather fake sensationalism even if they leave us with a not quite pleasant feeling afterwards.

I am not trying to "invalidate" the modern-dance groups; on the contrary I would like to clear the confused prejudice against them, by pinning down the unfavorable impression they make to specific aspects. We all know they have made discoveries from which the dance world is benefiting. Perhaps the modern-dance group should establish its own technical and emotional academy; but that would mean abandoning the semi-professional status which is one of its virtues. Anyway it is interesting that there may be now a tendency toward a new method, toward a more natural and "concrete" style. Besides finding it in Agnes de Mille's group, I thought I saw it too in Anna Sokolow's *Opening Dance* and—though in a more proper form—in Hanya Holm's *Dance Sonata*. These pieces are easier to do, more danced, less sensationalistic. They haven't much propaganda, but in point of propaganda I think our groups will find a warmer audience and their themes will come across with more meaning, when they give more meaning on the stage to what they themselves are: natural young people who enjoy dancing, recognizable Grade A proletarians—*March-April*, 1939.

FAMOUS AND AUTHENTIC

RUTH ST. DENIS appeared, doing dances that went back to 1905. It is extremely interesting to see how decorative these famous dances are, how boldly and happily unauthentic, and how charmingly lady-like in their tone. As theater there is no foolishness, no fake in them whatever. The power of these dances is not in their composition but in the extraordinary projection Miss St. Denis gives them, the flood of unspecific good intentions and the personal charm by which she makes the whole house feel comfortable and friendly. She would have no trouble at all winning the Broadway audience all over again —*January-February*, 1942.

HIGH-CLASS AND TIMID

ANGNA ENTERS, who is of course a realistic mime and not specifically a dancer, appeared in new and old impersonations. The clarity and unobtrusiveness of her action, the elegance of her accessories, her pointed sense of "genre," and a certain rhythmic instinct in forming a scene, all this is expert and high class. So is the extremely intelligent piano tinkling off stage. The evening is a specialty of understatement and inference. But the emotion is not always distinct and it is mostly small. For me, grateful though I am for so much good taste and so little pretentiousness, I find an entire evening of it gives me an impression of timidity. Of course I know that for a century or more a notable characteristic of the American school in art and in taste has been timidity of expression. But now and then it seems to me an absurd standard for grown up people—*January-February*, 1943.

MARTHA GRAHAM CHRONICLE

IN DECEMBER Miss Graham presented a new heroic dance suite for herself and her group called *Chronicle*. It deals with division, grief, and final adjustment. I wish I had seen it again to clarify my own impression and to be able to point specifically to its more or less successful elements. As it is I can only speak of it in general terms, and confusedly.

Seeing Miss Graham with her group and in solo recital, I was impressed by her courage and integrity. She believes in the biggest possible gesture; so she has trained herself to execute these extraordinary movements as accurately as a ballerina would her own most difficult feats. She believes in unexpectedness of composition, and she succeeds in keeping up an unremitting intellectual tension. There is no slack anywhere, physically or intellectually. She has, besides, an emotional steadiness in projection that binds together her constantly explosive detail, a determination which controls what might otherwise seem unrelated and fragmentary.

These are certainly rare qualities. I think anyone who likes dancing will admire her. But it seems to me her courage could go even further. She seems to watch over her integrity with too jealous an eye. She allows her dance to unfold only on a dictatorially determined level. But a dance unfolds of its own accord on a great many contradictory levels. And I miss the humanity of these contradictions.

To speak more in terms of dance, it seems as though Miss Graham were too neat. Her group is excellently trained. They do each motive given them with accuracy and decision. But from time to time, accidentally it seems, Miss Graham herself has a softening of contour between moments of emphasis where her natural subtlety of body substitutes shading, continuity, and breath for the geometry of constant tension; and it is at these very moments, which seem unintentional, that Miss Graham gets her audience most, gets them to feel something of the drama she is trying to tell about. I have the impression that Miss Graham would like to keep a dance constantly at the tension of a picture. She seems to be, especially in her solo dances, clinging to visual definition. Even her so-called angularity springs partly from a fear that the eye will be confused unless every muscle is given a definite job. The eye would be confused. But our bodily sense would not. Our bodily sense needs the rebound from a gesture, the variation of hard and soft muscle, of exact and general. As I said, Miss Graham herself has an instinct in this direction; but she seems to hesitate to rely on it in composition. I think it is this lack of confidence that she can communicate her tension directly to the body of anyone in the audience that makes her dances so "difficult." Isadora did not have this lack of confidence, and so her dances—though perhaps pictorially undistinguished—were always compelling, and gave the effect of beauty. But I don't want to go off on too theoretical a discussion, though Miss Graham is a controversial figure and important to us.

For musicians Miss Graham's programs are especially interesting because a number of modern American composers write for her, setting her dances to music after the dance has been composed. In general they seem anxious to stick literally to the rhythmic detail of her dance, the way many dancers—inversely —might try to stick to the rhythmic detail of music. It isn't a good method. Especially because Miss Graham's motives are so obvious they need no reiteration in music and they are structural body rhythms rather than ornamental gestures. For the musicians the result of following her is that, instead of making their piece a whole, they divide it up into a series of brief phrases, each stopping on an accent. It seems to me that the rhythmic structure of dance and that of music are parallel but not interchangeable. Time in music is much more nearly a mathematical unit than in dance—in the dance-pulse stress and recovery (the down and up beat of the measure) are often not of equal time-length as music, and stress in music is more regularly recurrent. A good dance goes along with a piece of music with plenty of points of contact but many of duality. A dance needs a certain rhythmic independence—similar in a sense to the rhythmic elasticity the voice is given in our popular songs. But to give this freedom to the dance the music must have a life of its own as music; and the more unassuming this life is, the more definite it should be. In any case it is no fun seeing a dancer dance smack on his Gebrauchsmusik, and he looks as dramatic doing it as a man riding an electric camel—*January-February,* 1937.

LETTER TO THE WORLD,
EL PENITENTE

MARTHA GRAHAM has now presented to New York her two dance works, *El Penitente* and *Letter to the World,* which are full of interest and full of poetry. *El Penitente* looks like a Mystery Play. A young woman and two young men come on the stage carrying a bright banner. Their manner is collected and cheerful. You watch them act out a play which tells that though man's duty to Christ is hard, his pain is relieved by a Divine Grace visiting him in turn as a virgin, a seductress, and a mother. Sometimes they use their banner as a little curtain from which emerge supernatural apparitions; once, they strip off the cloth, and the frame suddenly is a cross. When the play is over, the three performers add a little dance of jubilation in their character as farmers. The style of gesture reminds you of New Mexican primitives—the votive pictures and bultos. It suggests—as they do—a double emotion of unlimited space all around and of solid weight at the center, there where you are. There is an apparent naïveté of timing and placing which is charming in detail and carried through with distinction. All this might be true either of a real Catholic piece or of an exquisite tour de force. But the dance seemed to have a poignancy other than Catholic and a reality beyond that of charm. The gestures are not made so much for their symbolic meaning as for their shape and rhythm as dancing; the dancing does not exploit its own limpidity, invention, and restraint, but moves you by its dynamics as a whole, a personal meaning which makes the form real, which makes the religious style real, too, but in an oblique way. Partly because the scenes between the man and the woman are placed down stage, partly because they are the most expressive, partly because it is Miss Graham who dances in them, it was not the relation of man to the Divine but the relation of a man and a woman that seemed the true subject. On me the effect was that of a tender and subtle love poem, a real love held nearly in suspense by a remote terror. It was as though Miss Graham had used the Spanish-Indian farmers' expression of religious faith as a metaphor for her own faith in the strangeness love can have. It is a sincere and touching and very attractive work, whether you choose to describe it in these terms, or find better ones.

Letter to the World is a longer, richer, and more uneven piece. Much of it is not clear to me after seeing it once. But it contains such astonishing passages one is quite willing to forgive the awkward parts it also has, and remember it as a masterpiece. *Letter to the World* is about Emily Dickinson. There is a legend that Emily Dickinson fell in love with a married minister, whom she saw once or twice and might have run away with. On the stage you see the garden door to a New England house and a garden bench. You see a woman move about as though she were dancing to the rustling in the trees and with the odd swirl of the breeze. She appears and disappears mysteriously, suddenly or delayed, like a leaf, or a mouse, or a word. Other figures, too, appear, sometimes one, sometimes several. You see a tall and dominating woman in black, you see a crowd of stiff boys and girls, you see a solemn and violent man, and a boy who is ironic to the heroine and exuberant alone. The heroine herself appears at one point in a funny dress with trousers under it, and plays games with herself like a school girl, even upsetting the bench and doing happy stunts on it. Much later, the man pays little attention to her, and in the end, according to the program, "out of the tragedy of her loss will be born the poet."

The passages for the other characters, except the "Death" dance for Jane Dudley and the "March" leaping dance for Merce Cunningham, did not seem very interesting; but many of those for Miss Graham are extraordinary for their devious grace, their unpredictable and fascinating current. Often they have a round buoyancy like that of waltzing, with poignant gradations of greater and less airiness. Her funny dance, "The Little Tippler," is a sort of polka of impish pranks, like Thoreau's squirrel—"all of his motions, even in the depths of the forest, imply spectators as much as those of a dancing girl." And altogether wonderful is her sitting on the bench toward the end, half turned from the audience and reflective in a pure, Victorian attitude; with a passionate heroism of repose that has all the amplitude of Isadora Duncan. The continuity of a lyric line, the contrast of dynamics (the sense that a gesture is not always a thrust but often a caress), both of these are a new development in Miss Graham's way of composing; as is also the use of different kinds of projection (the sense that she dances at times more publicly for the audience, at times more privately for herself). From many points of view *Letter to the World*, no matter how uneven it appears at first sight, is a moving and noble work one cannot praise too highly—*March-April*, 1941.

PUNCH AND THE JUDY

PUNCH AND THE JUDY is a comedy taking place in a white-collar apartment; the reiterated "squabble and scuffle," as the program says, between a husband and wife. Most of the audience thought it was very funny, the indicated kicks and slaps, the parodies of tragic gesture, the general air of middle-class self-importance and nervous activity. It happens that continuous stylized pantomime doesn't make me laugh much; so I was following the action. It seemed to me that the protagonists were quite untroubled by their quarrels, untroubled by sex, too, and not much interested in their child. Their infidelities didn't seem to interest them especially, neither did jealousy. And the wife had nice dreams. So I gathered that they were a good-natured conventional young couple, who didn't notice much. Then what is the piece about? Maybe, as in Noel Coward, the theme is the unfeeling couple's incidental charm and liveliness. Occasionally the husband reminded me of the charming Dagwood in the comics. But that didn't offer a clue to the theme. I was confused by the multiplicity of detail in gesture and rhythm, and brusque shifts of spacing, the clutter, the unsympathetic staging and costuming and the clumsy spoken words. I could find no appreciable point of repose from which to see the figure of the movement. I was rather appalled by the stubborn parody in all the expression. Maybe the real theme is something sinister, even malevolent. Or maybe, as so often happens to me at a new Graham piece, I will get a very different impression when I see it again.

It was clear however that Martha Graham and Erick Hawkins in the title parts danced with an admirable fluency, a complete control of the timing, the attack, the extent and the transformation of a gesture; keeping it perfectly placed in style, in character, in quality. They made other modern dancers look wooden and awkward, as you watched—*January-February*, 1942.

(At Second View)

At the first view I was puzzled by the emotional effect of *Punch and the Judy*—what the piece really means. So I am coming back to it again, now I have seen it a second time: I leave you to judge, by comparing your own impressions with mine, whether I got it this time, either.

The program says it is a domestic comedy. The dance opens with some silly words and foolish ornamental overlarge gestures by three unsympathetic ladies, billed as the Three Fates. Then you see a young wife waking up with a headache. Her husband on the other hand wakes up at the top of his form. You get the situation, the joke of the ensuing friendly rough-house. You think it's a comedy. You see too that the characters move in marionette style: they are Punch and The Judy. But you notice that their movement has not merely a puppet style (familiar in dancing, and rather a bore) but it also seems real human movement, with a motor force not outside but within the torso. You admire the subtle adjustment of the two opposite styles. You admire how clearly you can follow the "meaning" of the separate gestures, as in a pantomime; and how at the same time these gestures in cut, contrast, and rhythm form a dance sequence. Nor do the gestures repeat themselves, or mark time, or utilize clichés; they are packed with inventive detail. And a kind of brutal plainness in the stage spacing is very deftly suggested.

As the story continues, you notice that the other characters are less real than the protagonists, they are straight puppets. Their dances amuse you as gags, but they don't have any inner drive of their own. Even the Three Fates, though they dance witty parodies of decorative movement, don't become a dynamic factor. The Power of Dreams, which appears as Pegasus, has a mysterious airiness in dancing, but the influence remains remote and brief and plays an ornamental and not a dramatic part. The two central characters are left with only unreal puppet foils. They themselves, part puppet, part human, never can act toward the others humanly. I had hoped till the end that at least in conflict with each other they would break through their own stylization, become completely human, and that then the emotion would open up, become a real conflict with a real resolution. It did not happen. Their relation to one another is unchanged after they have gone through all their puppet antics. And the futility of the action is expressed in the last spoken words: "Shall we begin again?"

It is then that you realize the action you watched was not as above-board as you at first imagined. Was there a kind of slyness, the way you were lured on to a pointless result? No, you were warned by the unpleasant opening. But now the jokes have a bitter taste, when you find they were not real people who made them. It has been a puppet story, not a drama but a monologue. The gags were the author's wisecracks at life and she didn't give life a chance to answer back. You expected to see the humor of man and wife living together, but what you have seen is the folly of it, the pointless folly. The folly might have found a point if it had had the contrast of sentiment; or if it had had the added force of fury to drive it into the vastness of the unconscious where folly is at home. But the point this work gives folly is a different one; it is the very care of its workmanship and execution. It is a high-class folly.

And so I found the piece easy to watch and hard to take. I found it not pleasant or open; but in its peculiar prejudice serious and interesting—*March-April*, 1942.

DEATHS AND ENTRANCES

IT ISN'T often I've seen the lobby in the intermission so animated in its discussion of a ballet as it was after Martha Graham's new *Deaths and Entrances*. The piece is a harsh one: it has neither a touching story, nor a harmonious development, nor wit and charm to help along. But at both its recent performances it has held the audience spellbound. What fascinates is the movement itself as it takes place on the stage—the rapid succession of curiously expressive and unforeseen bursts of gesture, the urgency they have, and above all the intense vividness of Miss Graham's own dancing.

Her dancing does not look stylized or calculated, it looks spontaneous as movements do in life or as Markova's motion does on the stage. Miss Graham's effect of spontaneity comes from attention to that part of the gesture which is like the following-through in athletics, the part which restores the body to balance after an effort, which relaxes the tension after an outward stress. Most dancers do this mechanically and their dance though accurate looks wooden. Miss Graham, by making the speed of the unemphatic and relaxing movements just a little different from what one would have expected, gives animation and a personal rhythm to the ebbing of energy, too. It makes all her dance look elastic, fresh and ungloomy. Such an unexpectedness of rhythm is what delights us in the playful motions of children and animals; in the calculated clarity of dancing only the great stars can look as free as children.

A spontaneous look has little to do with novelty in the general shape of a gesture. In fact, the more novelty of gesture, the less freedom of movement, is the common rule. Just the same, Miss Graham wants every movement to be a novel one. She finds new varieties of hobbling, kicking backward, sinking in one's steps, going with a bounce; she finds caressing undulations; flights looking downward; reactions to the touch of a hand; spidery dartings of the arms, possessed shoulder-shakes; or a group of deformed graces holding hands. One has the impression of not having seen any of the movements the ten dancers do before, of never having seen bodies take these odd shapes.

Such extreme originality is shocking, and it is suited to the shocking subject of the piece. *Deaths and Entrances* is an homage to Emily Brontë, the stoic young woman who conceived the terrors of *Wuthering Heights*. It is meant in one sense as an image of her heart, and in the dance we see reflected some of the strange wonders that absorbed her—incestuous family love-and-hate, the duplicit need in a woman for both a brutal and a tender contact, "perverted passion and passionate perversity" mounting to real madness and ending heroically sane. Like the actions in Emily Brontë's novel, the movements of the dance look frantic, but not at all indecent.

The current of *Deaths and Entrances* is frenzied, and one is never at one's ease in it. One is never prepared for the next moment. What holds the piece together is the lucid concentration of Miss Graham in the central role, a personage to whom all the actions on the stage are completely real. They are images she contemplates within herself and also sees independently active outside her; and her mobile face lights up at the objective impressions. She is adolescently tender dancing with her two Beloveds at once, she is terrifying and horrible in her mad scene, her final gesture is adult, like tragedy. Very strange, too, is the mysterious elegance which never leaves her.

I hope that Ballet Theater (or the Monte Carlo) when it comes to town will invite Miss Graham and her company to perform *Deaths and Entrances* as a guest production on its programs. As the most extraordinary novelty of the season the general public will be curious to see it and to form its own opinion of it —*January* 16, 1944.

BALLET LOVER'S VIEW OF MARTHA GRAHAM

ANY one of Martha Graham's highly intelligent pieces would gain in theatrical brilliancy if she and her company could present it singly say as an item on a Ballet Theater program. Her particular genius would flash more strikingly right next to the genius of other choreographers and dancers who excel at other aspects of dancing. Some of my friends are shocked by this genius of hers and they tell me she has no style, that she fascinates merely as heretics do, by her contrariness. But I keep being struck in all her work by its intellectual seriousness, its inventiveness and its exact workmanship; and these are qualities I can't think of as heretical or contrary. They offer a moral basis for style. I see no reason why one shouldn't try to place her work in relation to the ballet tradition and see what is special in her dance method.

The special thing about Miss Graham is not that she is a modernist. Almost no one nowadays is anything else. Modernism in dancing is really a conservative tendency. Its first victories through Isadora and Fokine, its boldest ones through Nijinsky and Mary Wigman, its general acceptance in the twenties— these are facts of history. Inside and outside of ballet, modernism has emphasized the interest in bit-by-bit gesture, gesture deformed, interrupted or explosive. It has done everything possible to break up the easy flowing sequence of a dance.

But through all these modernisms well-trained ballet dancers made any gesture, however odd, with reference to their traditional center of motion, and so still gave to a series of disjointed gestures a logical dance continuity. And through all these modernisms, too, ballet retained its traditional formula of the architecture of a piece, with the long dance aria (like the central adagio in *Swan Lake*) as the basic type of an expressive climax. Ballet dancers had sound models for dance coherence and for dance rhythm all around them.

The modern-school dancers, however, had no models for long serious poetic forms: for them the fundamental questions of dance rhythm and dance continuity could not be referred to a traditional type. Miss Graham, for instance, began with the decorative attitudes and the connecting walks of Denishawn "exotica"; her formal point of departure was an actor's loose

gesture sequence, not a dancer's logically sustained dance sequence. But against this enormous handicap she did succeed in
discovering for herself a sound basis on which any sequence of
gesture can keep a strictly logical continuity.

She has done this, I think, by developing an acute sense of the
downward pull of gravity and of balance, and an acute sense,
too, of where the center of pressure of a gesture is. By concentrating motion on these two elements, she can exaggerate or de-
form a gesture as far as she chooses without blurring it, and she
can retract or transform a gesture without breaking the continuity of movement. She is the only one of our modern dancers who has really solved this fundamental problem in all its
aspects.

Ballet began, one might say, on the basis of lightness, elevation and ease; it could add modernism (which was an increased
heaviness and an oddity of gesture) for its value as contrast.
Miss Graham, beginning with modernism, made of heaviness
and oddity a complete system of her own. Brilliancy in heaviness and oddity became her expressive idiom. This is one way of
explaining why much of her style looks like ballet intentionally
done against the grain; or why she has used lightness and ease
not as fundamental elements but for their value as contrast. But
Miss Graham's system keeps expanding, and this season her entire company now and again seemed to be using non-modernist
dance qualities not merely for contrast but directly.

Judged by what I look for in ballet, Miss Graham's gesture
lacks a way of opening up completely, and her use of dance
rhythm seems to me fragmentary. It does not rise in a long, sustained line and come to a conclusion. I find she uses the stage
space the way the realistic theater does, as an accidental seg-
ment of a place; not the way the poetic theater uses the stage—

as a space complete in itself. And I do not feel the advantage to dancing in these qualities of her style. But I am intensely curious to see what her next works will look like, and where the next ten years will lead her. I find watching her not a balm for the spirit, but certainly a very great pleasure for the intelligence—*May* 28, 1944.

ROMANTICISM REINVENTED

MARTHA GRAHAM and her company made their first metropolitan appearance of the season last night, presenting *Salem Shore, Deaths and Entrances* and *Every Soul Is a Circus. Deaths and Entrances* was the most absorbing dance work that opened in New York last season, though it competed with plenty of ballet novelties. If its original shock value no longer operates, both the piece itself and Miss Graham's dancing in it have lost none of their first fascination.

Suggested originally by the life and works of the Brontës and by their atmosphere of passionate intellectual sensuality, heroic in despair, *Deaths and Entrances* in its dance gesture evokes the Romantic stage tragedies of a hundred years ago—the ferocity, tenderness and grandiloquence, the ancestral manor, the duel, the ball, the mad scene, the garland of wildflowers, the goblet and the cushion with an embalmed heart in it.

Our forebears when they saw these tragedies started with horror and wept. They sensed their secret obscenity. Miss Graham brings back the true Romantic impact and effect; it is as immediate now as then, and this is an achievement of genius. If we had expressive tragic actors they would go to *Deaths and Entrances* to learn their trade. For the general theater goer, the ballet is an absorbing experience.

In recapturing Romantic fervor Miss Graham has reinvented the gestures, the poses, the rhythms it needs, and made them startling afresh. Her tumultuous dance sequences are clear and firm. She herself never loses the lady-like elegance, the womanly look that makes formal tragedy communicative. And she does not force her private emotion into the passionate role she impersonates.

Her own role strikes me as the only completely rounded one in the wordless drama. The two men, though handsomely danced last night by Hawkins and Cunningham, are expressive only in their relation to the heroine, they have no independent existence as real characters would. The parts of the three little girls, though small, seem more autonomous than last year. The heroine's two sisters, danced so brilliantly last year by Miss Maslow and Miss Dudley, done now with care by Miss Lang and Miss O'Donell, have become sketchier—*February 7, 1945.*

APPALACHIAN SPRING

APPALACHIAN SPRING is—as usual with Miss Graham's works—different from previous ones in style and like them in the convincing integrity of its differentness. It presents a pioneer celebration in spring around a newly built farm-

house in the Pennsylvania hills in the early part of the last century when the country was still thinly settled. Miss Graham is
the young bride whose house it is to be, Erick Hawkins the
young farmer-husband. The ceremony presents the emotions,
joyful and apprehensive, their new domestic partnership invites. An older pioneer neighbor (May O'Donell) suggests now
and then the rocky confidence of experience. And a revivalist
(Merce Cunningham) with a band of four ecstatic girl followers reminds the new householders at this sacred moment of
the strange and terrible aspects of human fate. At the end the
couple are left quiet and strong in their new house.

All the characters are by turns playful and earnest and Miss
Graham, who has suggested in the course of the piece the community aspects of girl-child, of wife and mother and neighbor,
has near the end a wonderful passage as the individual human
being each person in a community remains.

The dance style of the piece is abrupt and angular and it suggests in this way the rude pioneer artifacts of the place and
time it describes. It suggests farmer vigor and clumsy farmer
mirth. Dance episodes are joined to realistic passages which set
the frame. But the more striking novelty in Miss Graham's
choreographic style in *Appalachian Spring* is that each character dominates the stage equally, each is an individual dramatic
antagonist to the others. So the piece is no passionate mono-
drama of subjective experience but an objective conflict united
in its theme.

Appalachian Spring has a mysterious coolness and freshness,
and it is no glorification by condescending city folk of our rude
and simple past; it is, despite occasional awkwardness, a credible and astonishing evocation of that real time and place. To
show us our country ancestors and our inherited mores as real

is a feat of genius no one else who has touched the pioneer subject in ballet has been able to accomplish.

The company, and quite particularly Mr. Cunningham in a thrilling passage, were excellent. The stage design by Noguchi struck me as too sophisticated, but it served. Mr. Copland's score is a marvel of lyricism, of freshness and strength; and with thirteen instruments he seemed to have a full orchestra playing. The musicians under Louis Horst played admirably.

The opening number on the program was Miss Graham's solo, *Salem Shore*, first presented last year and danced by her last night with a lovely youthfulness. Its picture of the waiting captain's wife, with its strange aqueous motions and seashore play, was once more a triumph of unforced impersonation. There is no American actress more sincere than Miss Graham, no dancer more strikingly, strangely inventive—*May* 15, 1945.

THE CLASSIC VICTIM

H*ERODIADE,* a tragic dance scene for two characters which Martha Graham presented for the first time in New York last night, was first seen like her new *Appalachian Spring* at the Coolidge Festival last fall in Washington, for which both works—their score and choreography—had been commissioned. And here at the National, like *Appalachian Spring* on Monday night, yesterday's *Herodiade* was another complete audience success. But apart from that, the two pieces resemble each other not at all.

The scene of *Herodiade* as the program states is "an antechamber where a woman waits with her attendant. She does not know what she may be required to do or endure. Fragments of dreams rising to the surface of a mirror add to the woman's agony of consciousness. With self-knowledge comes acceptance; as she advances to meet the unknown, the curtain falls."

This is an accurate outline. *Herodiade* is an immolation scene and might take place in the antechamber to the Cretan Labyrinth. It has the tone of a mythological rite and a classic sense of the grandeur of destiny. Miss Graham's motions are passionately and nobly contained, and marvelously natural as she makes them. A few large static gestures of tragic splendor and a few small desperate outbursts in complex hammered rhythms are enough to express the richness and dignity of the protagonist's fate. Her slow entrance; a later passage in "archaic" profile; a few crouching insane and blinded steps in which she approaches and touches the attendant; a twisting walk from the back with her feet parallel to the footlights; another with one hip thrust wildly sideways and held so; two grand poses heroically reminiscent of Isadora at the Parthenon: That is what gives to *Herodiade* its sustained wonder, its amazing human power and sense of human knowledge.

The second role, that of the attendant, is far less interesting. It has a kind of coarseness that contrasts with the leading character's exquisite elegance. And the moment when Miss Graham, who is the victim of the action, turns to console the attendant is like a hint from the *Phaedo*. But one wishes this other woman had more character, either as a rude jailer, or even as a comic foil. But this dramatic weakness in the piece is counterbalanced by the brilliant inventiveness of the chief role and the superbly restrained performance of Miss Graham in it.

The score of *Herodiade* by Paul Hindemith is a beautiful work, full, flowing and somber, and the orchestra played it very well indeed. The title *Herodiade,* incidentally, is the title of the score—Mr. Hindemith chose Mallarmé's celebrated poem of that name for his subject. Though the ballet has very little relation to that poem, Miss Graham, who first had called her work *Mirror Before Me,* now uses Hindemith's title—*May* 16, 1945.

MARTHA GRAHAM NOTES

O N SEEING Martha Graham's new *Appalachian Spring* a second time a quality which touched me particularly was the fresh feeling of hillside woods and fields the piece conveys. It does it partly in the way the still figures look off as if at a horizon of hills. The horizon is not the treetop garden horizon of *Letter to the World* nor the expanse of summer sky and sea of *Salem Shore,* but it is the real open air that is suggested in all three. *Herodiade* and *Deaths and Entrances,* on the other hand, happen in a room of some kind, and in these pieces, when Miss Graham suggests in her gesture a great space about her it is, so to speak, the intellectual horizon of the character she depicts. The precision of such differences in suggestion is one of the fascinations of watching her repertory.

Appalachian Spring describes the landscape not only in terms of its contour, but also in terms of living conditions. The separateness of the still figures one from another, which their poses emphasize, suggests that people who live in these hills are ac-

customed to spending much of their time alone. Their outlines
don't blend like those of townsmen. "In solitude shall I find entertainment" (*"Einsam und allein soll mein Vergnuegen sein"*)
is painted on an early Pennsylvania Dutch bride chest, and the
bride in *Appalachian Spring* might well have read it. It is touching how gently the piece persuades you of the value of domestic
and neighborly ties by giving you a sense of rural isolation.

The Appalachian isolation of the pioneer farmhouse in the
piece is suggested even more imaginatively by a note of wildlife
that keeps cropping up in the dances. A passage of Miss Graham's first solo looked to me as if she were a hillside girl darting after the little beasts her playing flushed from cover. And
the Revivalist's four ecstatic girl followers suggested in their
fluttering and breathless darting the motions of chipmunks and
birds on the ground, as if they were four small wild animals
that were not frightened away by people; the Revivalist, too—
part St. Francis, part Thoreau—seemed to treat them like tame
wildlife rather than like girls. And the way his part merged
evangelism with animism served in the ballet to join domestic
ties to nature magic.

After seeing *Herodiade*, Miss Graham's other new piece, a
second time I think Virgil Thomson's account of it in his article
in today's music section more accurate than mine of last Wednesday. The secret of the piece lies much more in the complex and
completely individualized elegance of the heroine than it does
in the classic allusions of her gesture. Her elegance of motion is
her private integrity. We watch it in conflict with her instincts,
we watch her transform their force and gain in grandeur; and
to watch so desperate a conflict being fought in middle age
makes the drama the more poignant, the more heroic. But what
makes it real in the first place is the real situation—a lady get-

ting dressed by her maid. It is a pity the maid isn't some sort of real woman too; even her obscene gestures toward the floor look merely wooden—*May* 20, 1945.

TIMID SURREALISM

MISS HANYA HOLM and her group presented us with a serious surrealist alchemistic fantasy. First a prologue: dancers in androgynous red tights and beautiful long blonde wigs did some calisthenic weaving and leaping. Then the main part: Several dancers appeared in elaborate costumes, a nest of light-bulbs on the head for instance. The audience recognized these as "surrealist" and tittered. But after the dancers came on, all they did was wiggle a bit, stand around, walk off, come back on, and do it all over. They looked afraid of messing up their pretty, fancy dresses. It was timid and dull; and it could have been dismissed as a minor mistake, if the program had not implied that this was official surrealism. Official surrealism, which kept clear a few years ago of Dali's decorous and cute Monte Carlo ballet, has its own terrific eighteen years of history; its cruel Peeping-Tom thrills—the thrills of a Peeping-Tom who gets to see only the empty part of the horrifying bedroom. I looked up an old Dali ballet libretto, from the pre-House Beautiful period of surrealism, published in George Hugnet's official *Petite anthologie du surréalisme* (1934). At a quiet moment, for instance, a dancer, who had unbandaged his arm, sops a piece of bread a lady has sat on, in a glass of tepid milk, and then—his face expressing a sweet and infinite nostalgia—he presses the wet bread under his armpit. At the end, while a chorus of legless cripples dressed as Japanese are yelling the tango *Renaciamento* (among other things), a woman with opulent breasts and metal shoes is savagely treading a heap of bread, as though seized with a delirium of the feet incident to wine-pressing; when a lot of motorcycles tied to ropes come roaring through the backdrop, and several electric fans and sewing machines fall from the top boxes and are crushed on the stage. The curtain falls slowly.

Miss Holm had another new number in her familiar agreeably fluid style in which the body is kept well in balance and the movement correctly produced from the small of the back. Some people find this agreeably lyric, and others, agreeably innocuous. I think it is all right, but it seems rather more proper than anything I know outside the theater. Miss Holm herself is obviously an excellent dancer, and I would like to see her in a solo—*May-June,* 1941.

MISCELLANY

TWO male modern dancers, Barton Mumaw and Erick Hawkins, have each given complete solo recitals. Mumaw is a very pleasantly proportioned young man with a natural gift, and I regret to say that I see little of interest in the kind of prudish "esthetic" schooling he happens to have received; I like the legs to be livelier. Hawkins, for his part, showed a thorough training in all the complicated exactitudes of the modern school; his dances, too, have interesting themes derived from work movements, from regional habits of gesture, from Amerindian dances, in the best of taste. Unfortunately, he never got going and so what he did felt like a lengthy announcement instead of like a dance. I enjoyed Henry Cowell's music for the Coyote dance on the program, and noticed again how an interesting acoustic accompaniment helps me watch a dance in a friendly and lively spirit.

In the Thirteenth Street studio of Miss Mayo's Repertory Dance Theater is a homebuilt theater which instead of looking dismal (as is the proper style in studio theaters) looks bright and straightforward. The dances looked it too. There was a piece in which the rhythm of ballet steps was brightly superimposed on the flatfooted grace of Bronx adolescents. And there was a "serial-ballet" which was most of it straightforward and part of it moving.

I went to the circus expecting to be shocked by the Bel-Geddes "streamlining," and found he had done more of a pants-pressing, hat-blocking job; the circus is still the mess we all like it to be. For the dance lover, there is a graceful lady elephant who dances the conga with delight; an incredibly beautiful dancing horse called Belmonte; and a happy pack of leaping dogs who play volley ball with a balloon. There is one completely esthetic human act of two Japanese who walk up a tightrope to the gallery and slide down again backward, standing; why it seems so beautiful I don't know. I also liked a camel that went around disguised as a goose.

Some Colorado high-school boys and girls called the Cheyenne Mountain Dancers were to appear up in the Rainbow Room one night at one o'clock. But the dancers I found were Indo-

Chinese, doing what seemed a Portuguese rhumba. The head-waiter told me there had been a last-minute change of schedule, and the cowboys had left. I asked how they were and he said, "Very colorful and neat."

The machine-gun dance in the second scene of *Native Son* gives me a chance to state that among other things Orson Welles is the greatest dance director in our theater. And also that he is the only producer who gives us scenery which is a delight to look at; the only scenery that sets the size of an actor in a dramatic proportion to the frame of the set. I imagine it is the proportion of the actor to the set (as it is in dancing), and not the real detail on the stage, which makes scenery feel real. You can't help but see him in a real relation to the set, instead of as a man wandering about a decorated stage—*May-June*, 1941.

DANCE DRAMA WITH NO STORY

HANYA HOLM, a leader among the older generation of modern dancers, appeared for the only time this season last Saturday. She presented a new long work, for herself, soloists and group, called *Orestes and the Furies*. It looked to me like a graduation event put on by the girls' physical education department; posture work, intermediate and advanced, neatly and seriously performed.

The trouble was Miss Holm's desire to arrange her pedagogic material in the form of a story. It led, as stories will, to groupings on the floor that presented the young ladies from rather awkward angles. (They were being Furies and were in tights.) However, when all these girls galloped friskily across the stage the effect was jolly, and the audience laughed happily, Furies or no Furies. Another time they ran across and each in turn did a leap that looked as if they might land on their faces—none did—and that was an exciting passage.

The program spoke of these Furies as "pitiless" and "relentless." It stated that the piece was a dance drama in two scenes and explained: "*Orestes and the Furies* relates in dance form, as Aeschylus' *Eumenides* did for the Greeks in drama, the mental torment of a man who had killed his mother." Such claims struck me as pretentious and confusing; the real interest was Miss Holm's gymnastic method.

Her method balances the spine on an oscillating pelvis; it moves the limbs as if from the waist and it holds the back straight. This makes for a good carriage in normal life. One can say that as training for a professional dancer it is insufficient; the limbs are not used in clear opposition to the trunk, and so they have the same look a trunk has; they have no vigor and no firmness in articulation, and so no brilliance in rhythm. The method does not touch theatrical expressiveness either; there is no impersonation in it and there is no sex, either adolescent or adult. But for college girls who do not aim to become professional dancers it affords a modicum of body control. And for educators, who have to find some way of teaching "the dance" without offending civic prudery, Miss Holm's method recommends itself too by its Nordic innocence and its smooth look.

Her technique is sufficient also for dances in a sort of out-of-doors barefoot vein, a hygienic pastoral like those evoked by the advertising copy of summer camps. Miss Holm's *Suite of Four Dances,* in this manner, built on mild variations of speed and rearrangements of small groups was thoroughly attractive. It was easy, clean and simple. A duet in it was charmingly danced by Joan Palmer and Paul Sweeney, two dancers with a native instinct for the theater; and after that the rest of the number went off very well indeed. It would please on any program.

This light piece was helped very much by the light music of John Cage, written after the dance was set, which contrived to move delicately in opposition to the dancers, and so did not swamp their mild rhythm. John Coleman's earnest score for *Orestes* was well written, though he had so absurd a task set him.

The evening opened with a long group composition, *Song*, by Mr. Sweeney, to Hindemith music with an epigraph from Whitman. In style it resembled Miss Holm's pastoral manner, though with more emphasis on detail. A solo danced by Mr. Sweeney was a good passage, well performed. His ballet experience gave him energy and definiteness—*January* 30, 1944.

MORE CONTINUOUSLY FLUENT

AT HER studio theater Doris Humphrey presented an all-Bach program. It contained her well-known large composition to the *Passacaglia and Fugue in C Minor*; a new very long solo by José Limon to the *Chaconne* for solo violin (it had interesting references to fencing style and was an honorable failure); and the program also contained two new pieces for small groups by Miss Humphrey, one set to four *Chorale Preludes,* the other to the *Partita in C Major* played on the harpsichord. These new dances, which are often gentle, pleased her faithful audience, but less than the old ones do. I thought them interesting as a further example of the general tendency of the "modern dance" choreographers to compose in a more continuously fluent manner. Five years ago they were chiefly concerned with the emphatic aspect of movement, they socked the active phases of gesture, stamp, jerk, thrust or stop, they gave slow motion a knife edge or contracted with paroxysmal violence. A dance seemed like a series of outcries. The moderns had always cultivated continuity in their intellectual concepts of dancing; but they did not build their dances out of a continuity of expression. Now they are interested in the value of the unemphatic phases as well, in the continuous support on which the continuous dance line rests (as in singing or piano-playing). I think they are interested in the confidence the continuous line can express, and in the melody of a continuous movement.

Modern dancing is not dead, of course not. It has an appreciative public. Its intentions are extremely intelligent. Its execution varies from the student-like to being fresh and real. But it sets itself the highest standards. Musically it has brought us this season several pieces by Cage, a novel music of freshness and delicacy; and *Modern Music* reported in the last issue two new ballets by Harris for Hanya Holm. Even when modern dancing is conventional, we who watch are happy over the disinterested love of serious dancing that motivates it. Any child knows by now that there is no money in it, and little enough glory. But young people do it just the same, with the obstinate generosity that keeps turning up in our species—*January-February,* 1943.

A CASE OF RATIONAL MEANING
IN DANCING

DORIS HUMPHREY'S new *Inquest* is a dance that leaves
no doubt as to its story or its point. The story is clearly
told by a speaker, who reads a newspaper report of an inquest
held in 1865 in a London slum. We hear of a destitute family,
father, mother and son, who lived in a squalid room. The son
began to go blind; finally the father died of starvation. As we
listen to the words we also watch the scenes they tell us of,
they are acted out in quiet pantomime upstage, in a small space
like a room. When in between the pantomime scenes a number of persons pass in files across the darkened stage it is easy
to think of them as neighbors passing along the streets. When
the story has been told and the neighbors begin a rushing
dance sequence to music it is clear that this dance is their emotional reaction to the story.

But the story has made a further specific point. By quoting
sentences spoken by the two survivors at the inquest, the news
account has shown us the devotion of the three central characters to one another and to their home. In the pantomime scenes
Miss Humphrey, Mr. Weidman and Mr. Hamilton, who portray the three, give the sense of the dignity of a united family
very strikingly. They make us realize that the theme of the piece
is the destruction of a home. And so when the movement, which
during the story portion was slow and repressed, then bursts
into rushing violence in the dance sequences, with stamps and
clenched fists, we are quite ready to accept it as expressing our

own anger and grief. And at the end, when it grows calm and sustained, we take it as expressing a firm and valid reproach. The piece has pointed out that poverty destroys humane values we all believe in. We applaud it as a sincere and eloquent sermon on the theme of the freedom from want.

If a dancer feels like preaching he has as good a right to do it as any other citizen, and the theater has always liked a sermon now and then. *Inquest* is a piece that appeals to our moral sensibility, it aims to be clear and its esthetic appeal is secondary. The audience approved of it very much indeed. For my part, I was also interested in something that has often struck me in dances with an excellent propaganda purpose: the difference in speed between getting the ideas and following the dances. One grasps the moral implications quickly and agrees with them. But the full rhetorical exposition of these ideas in dance form takes a good deal longer. The result is that one's response is complete before the dance is finished; and at *Inquest*, too, I was ready for a new idea while, for the sake of emphasis, the dancers were still dwelling on the old one. As the secondary purely esthetic appeal was slight, there was a gap in the interest.

Intellectually speaking, an interesting dance is a continuous discovery. The ideas it presents do not precede it, they are formed after one has perceived the movement. And because an interesting dance creates new ideas it is often not at all easy to understand nor in accord with what one would reasonably expect. This, of course, does not do for propaganda.

Inquest is concerned with reminding us of an idea we all approve and urging us to act on it—and that it does rationally, with complete clarity. It begs the question of how a dance creates its own novel meaning as it goes along—*March* 12, 1944.

A JOKE AND A FEW DUDS

THE season opened with the Jooss Ballet, presenting eight or nine pieces by Jooss, and one brand new one by Agnes de Mille. First, Miss de Mille's *Drums Sound in Hackensack*. It is about New Amsterdam, the fur trade, how the cheated Indians found a Dutch girl in the jungles of Jersey, and what happened then. To show us New Amsterdam, Miss de Mille begins with a folk dance, adds a Puritan hop and a de Mille wiggle, and we all get the joke, and smile easily. When she comes to the serious parts, terrors of the forest and Indian savagery, she invents some gestures as simple as those an earnest child would hit on. Again everybody gets the point and is perfectly satisfied to go on watching until something else happens. So the piece comes out a hit. The stage Indians, either woodenly noble or tomtomish, I liked especially. I like Miss de Mille's work in general. Though her heroines are inveterate wigglers, she has a real sense of how the body dances, she composes properly, and she has a gift of rhythm completely congenial to Americans.

Jooss's works, however, one looks at very seriously. They are on the plane of "masterworks." Jooss has a great reputation too, as a leader in serious theater dancing, and as a systematizer of modern technique. Just the same, watching the stage, what I saw was one dud after another. There is one exception —the famous first scene of his *Green Table*. This is brilliant and curiously different from all the rest, different in rhythm, style, humor, and theatrical punch.

The Jooss dancers are engaging, accurate, lively, and devoted executants, without mannerisms or bad manners, dancers by nature. They were fine for Miss de Mille. But when they dance the Jooss choreography, what do you see them do on the stage? Well, the best thing you see is a controlled, clear, wide movement in the arms. (And they can stop an arm gesture more neatly than most good dancers.) Their hands and necks are plain and good. The breastbone is held high and the chest is open. This upper third of the body is excellent. But below it, the belly is dull, the buttocks heavy, the small of the back sags in. Where is the shining tautness across the groin, a glory of Western dancing? These people might as well be sitting down, as far as the expressiveness of their middles goes. And below, the leg gestures are forced and heavy. The leaps are high and strong, but they have only bounce, they don't soar (except one boy in *Old Vienna*), they don't hang in the air, either. (The low wide leaps are the interesting ones, but get monotonous.) The feet in the air look thick. On the other hand these dancers land better from a leap than most ballet dancers. Does this add up to a satisfactory new norm of technique? It does not. Neither does it exhaust the possibilities of the modern school. Because the Jooss norm of the outward chest and inward middle is fixed, and modern technique demands that any portion can vary at will from outward to inward. It's a terrific demand, but it's the essence of widening the expressive range beyond that of classic ballet.

Or take the Jooss stylization of rhythm. I see an emphatic pound (this is a gesture stopped and held). Then comes an unaccented moment (no gesture, change of position). Then comes another equally emphatic pound (a new gesture, stopped and held). This keeps up all evening. In the pit the music pounds down on the beat at the same moment the dancer pounds out his gesture. The effect is very dispiriting.

What happens is that there is a systematic alternation between emphatic and unemphatic movement, like that between beat and non-beat in a bar. There is also an unusual continuousness about the time quality of the movement. Many people are dissatisfied with a kind of hoppitiness in classic ballet. They point out that there is a fraction of a second between steps, between arm positions, that goes dead; in the way a harpsichord goes dead, but not an orchestra or even a piano. Jooss has stretched a movement to fill the time space completely; he uses a pedal. It was Dalcroze who thirty years ago made us most conscious of this possibility in moving.

When a dancer makes his gesture coincide as closely as possible with the time length and time emphasis of musical rhythm, he is apt to be as pleased as a hen is who has laid an egg. He tells everybody, look how musical I am, and everybody cackles back, isn't he just the most musical thing. Rationally it seems odd to confuse the metrics of music with musicality. And also to assume that the metrics of dancing are identical with those of music. It strikes me that there is in fact an inherent disparity. The proportioning of time, as well as the proportioning of emphasis, between the stress and the follow through of a single metric unit is much more regular in music than it is in movement. Apart from theory, in practice this kind of measured gesture draws attention to itself and away from the body as a whole. In practice, too, the dancer loses a certain surprise of attack, which is one of his characteristic rhythmic possibilities.

Well, in point of musicality, listen to the music Jooss uses. True the dancers obey the metrics of music, but the music in its rhythmic development obeys beat by beat the rhythmic detail of the dance. The piece makes no musical sense. It is merely a cue sheet for the dancers. It sounds as if it kept up a continuous gabble about the mechanics of the steps. It's like a spoken commentary in a documentary film, that names every object we see, while we're looking at it. Music that can't make any decision on its own is functioning on a bare subsistence level, and it is apt to be as glum as that. Poor Frederic Cohen's voluble cue-sheets for Jooss are utterly depressing, they reminded me most of cafeteria soup gone sour. I don't think much of the musicality of a director who makes me listen to such poverty. If this is collaboration, it must be the Berlin-Vichy kind. I detest a dancer who is satisfied with it.

But the issue of dance music has led me away from the subject of Jooss. Besides technique, rhythm, and the use of music, there are many other aspects to choreography. In the Jooss ballets I did not see any I cared for. He has systematized grouping so that diagonals, cubes and spheres cut across each other by the dozen. But they look stupid because they have no relation to the size of the human figure on the stage. He has systematized the representational aspect of movement, with the result that every gesture can be translated so exactly into words the dance might as well be a series of signals for deaf mutes. You imagine it would have the same meaning if performed by non-dancers. The dancers add neatness, but they don't by dancing create the meaning, a meaning which undanced would not exist. Looking at it another way, all the gesture is on the same level of signification. The wonderful shift possible from pantomime to lyric (like a new dimension of spirit); or the shift as in Spanish dancing from standing around to taking the stage; all this with all the rest in dancing that is tender and variable and real only the moment it happens, has been systematized away.

A systematization of modern dancing, like the literary adoption of the heroic couplet, makes a great deal of sense to dancers floundering between the arrogant academicism of the ballet on the one hand and the uncompromising private language of some studio dancers on the other. I remember fourteen years ago in Germany the attempt to establish a new academy, a new order, seemed of the greatest importance, and we all watched Jooss's gradual discoveries (for he was the leader of the movement) with delight. The results shown here this fall are well worth acrimonious theoretical dispute. But what I actually looked at on the stage was a stodgy, self-satisfied and petty solemnity, pretending to be serious and, worse, significantly ethical—*November-December,* 1941.

ON ISADORA'S TECHNIQUE

THE recital of Maria Theresa (one of the original Duncan dancers) who danced several of Isadora's Chopin pieces, was interesting because it brought up again some of the technical procedures of Isadora: The large plain phrases in which a single gesture is carried about the stage; the large, clear contrast between up and down, forward and back; and the way the body seems to yield to the music and still is not passively "carried" by it, but carries itself even while it yields. It seems to me the effect of these dances, technically speaking, comes from the kind of support the gesture has, rather than from the interest of each new gesture. The gesture in itself, in the softness with which it begins, in the shape it takes and its accentual rhythm, is monotonous enough; but the support it has is a kind of invention. The support seems continuously improvised and always active, always a little stronger than the gesture in energy and just ahead of it in time. Such an accurate proportioning of energy, as it decreases from a central impulse in the torso through the joints to the extremities, gives the limbs an especial lightness, the hands, head and feet an attractive, as if careless, bearing. It also gives the observer's eye a definite center from which to appreciate the body movement as a whole; and a feeling of following the dance continuously. It requires a technique on the dancer's part, and no easy one. Just remember how even good dancers confuse your attention by jerking your eye from one detail to another; how often even good dancers give you the sense that their impulse to move operates by fits and starts; how often they seem to be dancing now and then during their number and the rest of the time merely executing according to plan. It struck me that in the Duncan method the dynamics of movement (the flow and current of the impulse) becomes intentionally the most carefully controlled and the most expressive aspect of dancing. In ballet this aspect is not systematically taught, it is left individual and instinctive. The modern-school method, from Mary Wigman on, has tried to analyze dynamic control; but it replaced the Duncan gesture with an infinitely more varied kind, and in consequence the problem of making the dance coherent became far more difficult to resolve, technically. I am speaking here of technique in its gymnastic aspect; the Duncan coherence which derives from the coherence of the music you hear as you watch, and the "modern" coherence derived from the non-dance ideas you are invited to recall while watching—these I am not now considering.

I am less convinced than I was ten years ago that classroom instruction in dynamics is much use to the dancer. A panacea against absurdity as many hoped it would be, it certainly has not proved; and even with Duncan dancers, her own method did not turn out to be foolproof. But I think Isadora's technical approach to dancing (I mean distinct from her unique greatness as a dancer) is an interesting subject to clarify. It seems to me nonsense to imagine that she could have had so sweeping a success with highly perceptive audiences, could have created so disinterested an enthusiasm by numbers that she performed over and over, without (as many affirm) having a technique. The photographs seem to me not to show very much, but on several one notices a neck and shoulder line that is strikingly plastic, strikingly aware of three-dimensional expression. On her last American tour I watched a program from up in the Carnegie Hall gallery from where she looked, all alone on the stage and facing the full blare of a Wagnerian orchestra, very small indeed. But the slow parts of her Venusberg dance and her Siegfried Funeral March remain in memory two of the very greatest effects I have seen; I can still feel their grandeur and their force.

Incidentally, when you observe the early Chopin numbers of Isadora's which Maria Theresa now has revived you get to thinking that Fokine's *Sylphides* (also to Chopin) is hardly at all characteristic of the dancing of Taglioni and Grisi, as often supposed, but instead is full of Duncanisms. I mean, in the "sensitiveness" of its extended phrases; in the stress it gives to contrasts in space—downward, upward, forward, backward; in the yielding quality of many arm gestures and back bends. These last look correct as ports-de-bras and renversés but the timing is unclassical. And maybe too the rose-petal hands, the loosely drooping fingers that Fokine or Nijinsky invented for the *Spectre* were suggested by a gesture of Isadora's. It is of course equally true that the relaxedness of her manner superimposed on the solid leg and hip rigor of ballet created a very different effect from hers; an effect of inherent contradiction, a poignant sense of perversity that has gone to the heart of most civilized people during the last thirty years— *March-April*, 1942.

NOT TIED TO ANY APRON STRING

PEARL PRIMUS and Valerie Bettis, two young modern-dance soloists, gave the most dramatic recital that any young dancers have given this season. Miss Primus, the young Negro star who has been appearing at Café Society Downtown since last April, is vigorous, clear and direct; Miss Bettis is intense, delicate and intellectual. Both are thrilling to watch in motion, and neither has any of the careful academicism that makes many young modern dancers less effective on the stage than in the classroom. They represent a new generation of modern dancers, full of theater vitality.

Miss Primus' subjects were African, Haitian and North American, several of the last quite naturally concerned with race oppression. What she intends her gesture to mean is always completely clear. But her sense of movement is so powerful that beside telling a story, her dance has constantly the direct force of dancing. The spring in her legs, the sweeping undulations of the torso and arms are thrilling. Her bare feet are not just feet without shoes, they can grip, caress and strike the floor as if feeling the ground were natural to them. At several sudden high leaps the audience audibly gasped. But it is not her technique that she intends to display or that you admire, it is the dramatic form and the dramatic point of her dance. In several numbers she attains a fine Negro grandeur, and in a Haitian play dance she has a West Indian charm that is spontaneous and sweet.

In style nothing could be more different from Miss Primus than Miss Bettis is. Her dancing is about civilized frustrations, intense virginal quiverings, hesitations, momentary illusions of rest. Her phenomenally rapid leaping, her drumming delicate feet, her strange pauses that turn into a rapid shaking motion are admirable in their elegance; but they too serve her particular dramatic purpose. One has not the sense of watching a dancer's dance inventions, she looks like a beautiful young woman who is agitated, like a character in a situation. And one number, a dance play, where a number of voices off-stage developed a story in dialogue, and Miss Bettis answered them in dancing or else in speaking, showed that she is an actress of very great talent; not unlike Bette Davis in her effect. To my mind, Miss Bettis has difficulty concentrating on a simple climax and resolution; she hesitates between a lyric and a dramatic form. But she is a dancer of real power and originality.

The recital had musical interest as well: Miss Primus' fine Afro-Haitian drummers, Messrs. Koker and Cimber, whose drumming is fascinating in rhythm and intonation, and two pieces for Miss Bettis by John Cage, that as dance music were sensitive and very civilized—*January* 24, 1944.

ELEGANCE IN ISOLATION

AT THE small Humphrey Weidman Studio in the darkness of Sixteenth Street, Merce Cunningham and John Cage presented a program of solo dances and of percussionist music last night which was of the greatest esthetic elegance. The audience, an intelligent one, enjoyed and applauded.

It was Mr. Cunningham's first solo recital, though he is well known to dance audiences as soloist in Martha Graham's company. His gifts as a lyric dancer are most remarkable. His build resembles that of the juvenile *saltimbanques* of the early Picasso canvases. As a dancer his instep and his knees are extraordinarily elastic and quick; his steps, runs, knee bends and leaps are brilliant in lightness and speed. His torso can turn on its vertical axis with great sensitivity, his shoulders are held lightly free and his head poises intelligently. The arms are light and long, they float, but do not often have an active look. These are all merits particularly suited to lyric expression.

As a dancer and as a choreographer of his own solos, Mr. Cunningham's sense of physical rhythm is subtle and clear. His dances are built on the rhythm of a body in movement, and on its irregular phrase lengths. And the perfection with which he can indicate the rise and fall of an impulse gives one an esthetic pleasure of exceptional delicacy. His compositions too were in no way derivative in their formal aspect, or in their gesture; they looked free and definite at the same time.

The effect of them is one of an excessively elegant sensuality. On the other hand—partly because they are solo dances,

342

partly because they lack the vigorous presence of the body's deportment characteristic of academic ballet style—their effect is one of remoteness and isolation. This tone may well be due to the fact that Mr. Cunningham is still a young dancer, who is only beginning to discover his own dramatic resources. But I have never seen a first recital that combined such taste, such technical finish, such originality of dance material and so sure a manner of presentation.

Mr. Cage accompanied the six dances on "prepared" piano and his compositions for them were perfect as dance accompaniment. He also played six piano solos of his own, accompanied Juanita Hall in two songs (one to a text from *Finnegan's Wake*), and directed his quartet *Amores,* performed at the Modern Museum last year. The new pieces were applauded—as had been those heard last year—for the delicate sensuality of their odd timbres, for their rhythmic subtlety, and their willfully remote tenuousness of construction. His music, like Mr. Cunningham's dancing, has an effect of extreme elegance in isolation—*April* 6, 1944.

THE MODERN DANCE—TWO KINDS

RECENT recitals have presented the Dudley-Maslow-Bales trio (with Frieda Flier taking the place of Miss Maslow) and Merce Cunningham. These are four of the leading soloists who have been trained in the modern-dance technique, and they show in different ways the direction the young mod-

ern dancers are taking. The modern dancers have been shifting their attention from social protest to lively dance action.
They are taking ballet lessons, they are listening to the beat
of dance music, learning a friendly stage manner and quick,
neat footwork. They will leap up lightly whenever they get a
chance. Probably they will soon dress as elegantly on stage as
they already do off it. They go in more for professional finish
and less for creative personality. And many are finding work
in musicals. I think it will all help those among them who
are really serious to find out just how serious they are.

The Dudley-Maslow-Bales trio has for some seasons represented a moderate point of view in this general tendency.
Their recitals have looked capable, varied, unpretentious. They
combined modern-school inventions of gesture with an easier
audience appeal—a flavor of country dance, of jazz, a hint of
de Mille and now of Robbins. Miss Flier, the substitute mem-
ber, is a very well trained dancer, with defter feet and a
quicker balance than the other two and she has a feminine
delicacy that is attractive and that is still unusual in modern
recitals.

But I was disappointed in the general effect of the evening.
As intelligent moderns trying for a friendlier, more open style,
the trio had raised expectations. They seemed to be looking
for a lilt in dance rhythm and for an objective impersonation
of character; and one forgave the clumsy side of their first
attempts in this new direction. But now instead of working
ahead on the line they took, they mostly go on repeating their
old numbers and slick over the mistakes. Watching them
once more, one cannot help noticing how lifelessly the gesture
is clamped to the beat of the music, how wooden the characters are, how fussy and unmusical the setting is for such a

folksong as *On Top of Old Smoky*. Mr. Bales seemed self-conscious as soon as he defined his movements clearly or raised his head. Miss Dudley changed her silhouette at will to practically anything in Picasso, but she had no resilience of rhythm. They may well be tired of the numbers; in any event, I hope next winter they bring us a new program.

If the trio represent the eclectic popularizers in the modern school, Mr. Cunningham reminds you that there are pure dance values in pure modern technique. He is a virtuoso, relaxed, lyrical, elastic like a playing animal. He has an instinct for a form that makes its point by repetition, each repetition being a little different, and the phrasing of each difference exceptionally limpid. He has a variety of drive and speed which phrases his dances; and better still an improvisatory naturalness of emphasis which keeps his gesture from looking stylized or formalized.

The kind of elastic physical rhythm he has strikes me as something peculiarly American, and it is delicately supported by the elastic phrases of John Cage's music. But Cunningham's stage character is still too cautious to carry a solo program. He appears either as a lonesome youth or as a happy hooligan; you would like him to show a franker character, too, or see him in contact with different people. So strong a body should also harden and strike, force one phrase and throw away another; it could risk a firm beat, or an attack open and generous. A serious solo program calls for more risks in expression. Amiable popularizers like the trio don't lead you to expect much of a risk. Cunningham does, by his poetic style, by his brilliant gifts. There is no reason why he shouldn't develop into a great dancer—*January 29, 1945*.

FASTIDIOUS, SUBTLE, WITTY

SYBIL SHEARER, certainly in the first rank of the younger modern dancers, appeared yesterday afternoon in a program fastidious and subtle in invention and exquisite in execution. Miss Shearer's formerly reticent stage presence was far more open this time, and her dances, new and revised, were much freer in their lyric line. The audience, a keenly professional one, applauded her demonstratively and went home with a good many new ideas to try out.

Admirable was Miss Shearer's exactness in the basic carriage of each number and the lightness with which the gestures and steps seemed to arise from the stance and be lifted or carried by the rhythm of the breathing. Her wrist and ankle movements, fantastically quivering or easily pliant, are unique; but her sure hip and torso control, though less obvious, are what allow her so glittering or so casually fluid a detail.

Often, as in the turns of *You Can't Eat Your Cake*, the Duncanisms and arabesques of *Little Faith*, the leaps of *In Thee Is Joy*, Miss Shearer gives to a movement its spontaneous, airy expressiveness—which saves a solo dance from looking oppressively isolated. At other times she seems to stress too repetitiously the frustrated pathos of isolation. Miss Shearer has, however, a brilliantly acid wit, as well, which she illustrated in a *Sarabande*, where a panniered lady had a good deal of intimate trouble with her clothes; the audience was still chuckling long after the dance was over. Miss Shearer's costumes, excellent all through, were conceived as recognizable

346

clothes, and this, too, gave a novel immediacy to the dances.

Her recital in general showed a visual, as well as a gymnastic and rhythmic originality and discipline which should be highly stimulating to other young modern dancers and open new possibilities to them—*March* 12, 1945.

ADULT ADOLESCENCE AND THE
USE OF TRADITION

ANNA SOKOLOW'S modern-dance recital brought back to mind the striking impression she had made a few years ago in intense numbers evoking proletarian adolescence. Her figure with the small head, the solid neck, the small sloping shoulders and elongated limbs was immediately touching. Her hands and wrists were lovely, her arms light. Her dancing had the directness of a child's motions. When she lifted her forearm, when she ran and leaped, you watched the action itself. It was the action in itself that moved you. In composing, the way she derived dance gestures easily from pantomime, her simple formal arrangements—these "naive" qualities suited her adolescent atmosphere. And when she danced her numbers with subjective intensity the confusion between herself and her dance heroine did not bother anyone.

Conscious of Miss Sokolow's originality, I was puzzled to find her recital unsatisfactory. Her figure is still the ideal one for a dancer, her way of moving as graceful and distinct as ever. She worked with intensity; in fact she often forced out an angry little grunt that sounded like an impatient Spanish *"Eh!"*—as if she were whipping herself on. But the atmosphere of her presence had changed; this time her own presence was not that of an adolescent. It was that of a lady, of an adult.

Unfortunately, Miss Sokolow's present adult subjective fervor no longer suits the girlish simplicity of her former compositions; the more intense she becomes the more she hides their real character. And so the old numbers dealing with such themes as slum childhood, juvenile delinquency or Loyalist Madrid—numbers that once seemed natural as adolescent reflections—now, seen in an adult atmosphere, look artificial and false to their terrible themes.

In addition to old numbers, Miss Sokolow also showed a new long work, *Songs of a Semite* (for four dancers, a musician, a singer and a speaker). It presents a Jewess who feels homeless and lost; she remembers—in the form of dance episodes—the courage of several women of the Old Testament, and then she finally joins them in a brave march. The theme is a special one and the audience applauded the piece. But, though I thought it rounder in movement and maturer in tone than the earlier numbers, it seemed confused in its storytelling and repetitious in gesture, and it seemed inadequate as an evocation of legends so heroic, or an emotion so religious. To me Ruth's dance looked only a little tender. Miriam's, only a little exultant and Miss Sokolow, as the meditating figure, seemed to move more like a torch singer than a real person. The truest moments, I thought, were small and sweet ones.

What about the big moments? I believe the trouble is that Miss Sokolow has not developed enough variety of expression in dancing, a wide enough variety in its technical resources, to represent a complex theme from an adult point of view.

Technically, the dancer's trunk is loaded with energy, but the energy remains latent. It is not used in muscular actions that would give the torso plastic variation, not in weight in the arms, not in lightness in the thighs, not in the play of the feet with music. You don't see the impetus increase or decrease, the body soften or harden, the movement float or break, the figure gain expression by its path on the stage. Such qualities are only hinted at. But they are the expressive material of dancing, and it is to make their contrasts clearer to the audience that modern dancers, from Isadora on, have preferred to abandon the tradition of ballet forms.

Whatever the dance form (ballet, modern or as yet uninvented), the actual realization of such expressive effects is what constitutes the dance tradition. A tradition is not a police regulation; nor is it a device for repetition. It is a practical aid to an artist. It is useful for suggesting practical methods, for reminding him of expressive possibilities, for encouraging him by showing him that other persons have been faced with similar difficulties. A tradition is an artist's home base; or, to reapply Wordsworth's remark, it is the "tranquillity" in which the event that is the artist's subject is "remembered." And his tradition also is, as Auden has said, what he can judge himself by.

Miss Sokolow's own *Songs of a Semite* has, at least in intellectual intention, this same point in view, since it draws the moral that a tradition is a good thing for an adult individual—
December 12, 1943.

9

Dancers in Exotic Styles

MOMENTS OF REALITY

O N THE Carmen Amaya question, it was her comic
"Hay que tu" number that convinced me she is an
extraordinary dancer. A gypsy girl sings to her lover, "You
can't make me jealous; you go on pretending to make love to
others, but you always come back to me and say, 'There's only
you, beautiful, there's only you.'" Amaya was wearing the
typical flamenco dress, with its many flounces and a long
train, but she looked like a girl of thirteen, angular as a boy,
in her first evening gown. She fought her train into place like
a wild-animal trainer. Her voice was hoarse and small, her
gesture abrupt and awkward. All this with the defiance of the
song made the dance comic. But the figure of the tough slum
girl Amaya suggested was as real to you as the stranger sitting
next to you in the audience. You felt its private individual
life, its life before and after the glimpse of it you were catch-
ing. And there was nothing pathetic, no appeal for help in it.
So you grinned and laughed, as much at home as with Villon,
"en ce bourdeau où tenons notre estat"; and the fierce adolescence on the stage looked as wonderful as tragedy does.

Realness in comedy is very rare among dancers; and the

350

cruelly comic is of course one of the special gifts of Spain.
Now that I've seen Amaya do it, I have the greatest admiration for her. Before, I had been rather disappointed. Compared
to the other Spanish stars in town, I had not found in her
dancing the limpidity, the exquisite flow and nuance of Argentinita; nor the diamond glitter, the superb force of Martinez,
the greatest of the Spanish dancers here; Fernandez, the
Mexican, had seemed more plastic. And Rosario and Antonio
—somewhat like Amaya in fiery temperament, in exuberant
blurring of detail, in speed and theatricality—have the advantage of being a couple of kids happily matched, a relation which
makes the dance look open and natural.

True, even in disappointing numbers, Amaya has first-rate
personal qualities. She has sometimes for instance a wonderful kind of rippling of her body in movement, more like a
young cat's than a girl's; she has an extraordinary cutting quality in her gesture, too, as if she meant: here only, and never
elsewhere. She has a thrilling speed and attack. But these impressions of real moments were confused by others when she
seemed to be faking: forcing her "temperament," or driving
her dance into the floor, like a pianist who pounds too hard. Or
she would lose control of the continuity of her dance, put all
her fire into a half a minute of it and not know what to do
with the remaining two minutes; so they went flat. Sometimes
she seemed determined to cow her audience, and I had the
feeling I was watching not a dancer, but an ambitious person.
On the other hand, that, in the course of her first recital, she
could adjust herself to the glum expanse of Carnegie Hall and
finally take charge was a proof of her personal stage power.
But Amaya's unevenness does not bother me any more. Instead, I now understand why all the other flamenco dancers

respect and admire her. And the other evening at Broadway
and Forty-sixth, when I looked up at those Wilson's Whiskey
shadow-movies, and recognized Amaya doing a turn up there,
I was as pleased as if I'd unexpectedly caught sight of a friend
—*March-April,* 1942.

(A Year Later)

Several straight flamenco numbers ended Carmen Amaya's
Carnegie Hall program. They were each one much too short
to have their full effect, but in them everybody can see that
she is a great and a very individual dancer. That however
isn't the curious part of the story. Four-fifths of the evening
was reserved for Spanish dancing, recital style, a form made
illustrious by the great Argentina, and of which Argentinita
is now the star (at least here). Amaya as a flamenco dancer in
process of becoming a recitalist, has naturally chosen the best
model she could find and she has worked hard—the improvement in detail over last year is obvious. But actually in the
kind of number Argentinita turns into a marvel of polish,
Amaya right after some real stroke of genius next looks as if
she had lost the thread of her story, she looks plain or out of
place. Well, she carries off the number by the force of her
presence on the stage, and it is wonderful how silly she invariably makes the Granados or Albéniz music sound by the
edge of her attack; but the whole thing is off balance.

Off balance, but highly interesting. Because Amaya is a
completely honest character, and what you watch is the struggle between two opposite dance natures—Argentinita's which
she wants to reproduce and her own which she can't destroy.
Argentinita's nature is that of a sensible artist, she completely
understands the logical line of a recital dance, she dances a

piece through from A to Z without a false stress or a gap. Similarly she is a purist of movement and her transitions from one gesture to the next are a technical delight. She is also a witty and charming lady, who takes the audience into her confidence in a vivacious and cultivated way. (Some lovers of Spanish dancing even find Argentinita too polite to be thrilling.) Amaya on the other hand has none of these qualities. Form for her is not logical, it is a successive burst of inventions; the rhythmic shock is wherever you don't expect it; gesture is expression and attack, it's a gamble and there is no sense in saving and budgeting; and she has no patience with illuminating and delightful anecdotes on Spanish life, she wants to say straight out what she knows is so.

I admire in Amaya the effort of a great natural dance intelligence to master a form so foreign to it; it strikes me as a noble struggle. The first indication of a new form of her own seems to me the very original though not yet completely successful dance she has enthusiastically called a "supercreation," which though it is a recital number, is a wild piece Argentinita wouldn't dream of performing. In Amaya's more imitative dances it is the flashes of genius that break up the form which I am happiest over.

Technically speaking Amaya's dancing was more controlled and more various than last year. She has also checked her former mannerisms: she doesn't repeat her lightning turns again and again, she doesn't shake down her hair every time, nor dance male parts too frequently. Her magnificent rapidity, her power, her fine originality in handling the sex character of Spanish dancing are all singular virtues; and again and again she can dance as if nothing else existed in the world but dancing and death—*January-February,* 1943.

GYPSY KIDS FAR FROM HOME

ROSARIO and Antonio, the very thrilling and handsome young flamenco team from *Sons o' Fun* and the night clubs, known as "Los Chavalillos" or "the Kids from Seville," gave their first Carnegie Hall recital last night, assisted by a Spanish ensemble. The long program included magnificent moments and inept ones. The audience—largely Hispanic—generously applauded throughout.

"The Kids" deserve the immense success they have had in America. Rosario is a good dancer, a good showman, and she has a very attractive stage personality. Antonio is a first-class virtuoso and a very superb dancer indeed. His youthful fire and his force, his speed and his sharpness of attack sweep her too into a real enthusiasm. His Miller's Dance from *The Three-Cornered Hat* was magnificent in its dance impetus. So were their duets together, whenever they did not stray too far from the established folk or gypsy dance forms. But their Spanish "classic," Madrid low-brow, or storytelling numbers—concert numbers that require a sharp, special flavor both in choreography and in the pantomimic invention—these did not come off so well. And *Song Among the Shadows*, a long straggling group number billed as a ballet, bogged down completely in pink and white garlands and silly costume changes with the superb Antonio looking merely complaisantly vain at the end, like a picture-postcard lover.

These lapses in Antonio's style I should blame on his long absence from Spain and on the "concert" school of Spanish dancing, which, at least in America, refines the decorative aspect of Spanish dancing at the expense of far more interesting qualities: violence of rhythm and a kind of compressed fury. Antonio seems to have learned here variety, clarity and poise; but for so great a Spanish dancer his leaps are too airy, his silhouette not sufficiently held in, his love scenes tend too often to be cute. In the final number, however, he danced once more with that vehement seriousness that Spaniards alone seem to have. I trust he will find his way back to a nobler and severer style, the more chance he has to try it out on the public; he certainly has it in him.

In the supporting company, Antonia Cobos was much applauded for a neat and bouncing solo bolero, and Miss Acuña also performed a solo with success. In the first number I was delighted to see the famous Soledad—once celebrated as a dancer and as a bullfighter—dancing for a moment with an admirable and purely Spanish grotesque flavor; and in another number to hear her singing offstage a *saeta* with no voice but with a marvelous purity of gypsy style. She showed, where Rosario and Antonio's real home still is, and where their inspiration should come from—*April* 10, 1944.

LIMPID VIRTUOSO

THE Spanish salon style—witty, well-informed, lucid and amiable—is Argentinita's great specialty both as a dancer and as a choreographer; and at last night's recital in Carnegie Hall her little company, which consists of Pilar Lopez, José

Greco and Manolo Vargas, was in perfect form to assist her. When the four of them are as lightly exact and as spontaneously responsive to each other as last night, Argentinita and her familiar style take on a new freshness.

It was the little ensemble's evening rather than the star's as it sometimes has been in the past, though Argentinita herself remained the subtlest and the most imaginative of the four. But Pilar Lopez, particularly in a new Bolero of her own, showed an unsuspected delicacy as a dancer and an agreeable originality as a choreographer. She stopped the show in her solo gypsy-style Alegrias, and added a superb little coda as an encore.

José Greco, elegant and suave, has become a limpid virtuoso. To my mind he is still too consistently easy in the torso, and too consistently light on his feet; but the continuity of his dancing and the exactness of his gesture and his steps were very fine indeed. Manolo Vargas, harder, more sudden and with gypsy-like stops is learning variety of nuance. He stopped the show, too, with a solo.

It is admirable how Argentinita has perfected and enlarged the dancing of these two gifted young men in a few years' time. She now can use their individualities together with her own and her sister's to give a little spontaneous drama and humor to her duets, trios and foursomes without breaking the unity of the style. *In Old Madrid,* the 1900 Madrid zarzuela quartet, is delightful in its ingenuity at interplay. So is a new number, *On the Route to Seville,* where the city slicker (Greco) outwits and outsteals the three gypsies. Argentinita's tough arm gestures are very pretty in this; and Vargas incidentally did some remarkable pirouettes here, too.

If Argentinita's wit and storytelling gift are what immediately appeal to a foreign audience, her delicate differentiation between steps, her ingenious sequences, her excellent use of variety in the profile the dancer presents to the public, and the pretty rhythmic effects she achieves are what make them unique in their field. The lady-like tone she gives to them appeals more to some tastes than to others, who perhaps look for a greater forcefulness in Spanish dancing. But she knows what she wants and does it to perfection—*February* 19, 1945.

TO ARGENTINITA

THE death of Argentinita brings to many Americans who loved to see her dance a grief like that of a personal loss. Only the greatest dancers can awaken so personal a response by as restrained an art as hers was. Her spell as a star was that of a special Latin bearing, discreetly sensible and delightfully polite; she seemed a lady vivaciously entertaining her guests, and one could imagine that her expertness as host was only the reflection of the pleasure she felt in seeing her friends. Her dances had the effect of captivating anecdotes about Spanish life, and, more than any other dancer, she made the Spanish style easy for us North Americans to appreciate and enjoy. By her amiable gaiety of spirit, her wit, her tact in sentiment, her perfect grace and perfect courtesy, she established a sure contact, so that in her case the classic reserve of Spanish dance forms seemed even to sentimentalists like ourselves neither remote nor haughty. Argentinita was in this sense a triumphant popularizer of the Spanish style among us; and through her easy and charming approach she opened the eyes of thousands of Americans to the nature of the Spanish tradition she worked in, to its vitality of rhythm, its subtlety of expression and its high sense of personal dignity.

Argentinita's knowledge of the Spanish dance tradition was prodigious. An accurate scholar, she knew it in all its historical, regional and racial diversity, folk forms and theater forms, the special techniques as well as the special deportments. She knew it from living with gypsies, from traveling in the mountains, from talking to poets. But she did not try to reproduce this material literally. Like the circle of poet-scholars and musicians she belonged to in Madrid, from Benavente and Martinez Sierra to Falla and, greatest of them all, Garcia Lorca, her aim was to keep the full savor and amplitude of local traditions in freely invented and consciously shaped personal works of art. Argentinita's personal nature as a dancer was, by witty edge and lyric grace, essentially Andalusian, and she was too honest an artist to falsify it. And so if her Peruvian Indian dance, for instance, or her music hall studies or even her flamenco became her own graceful versions of these dance forms, they were none the less each completely different from the others, each composed in its own specific dance idiom and danced with its characteristic rhythmic impulse and its own dance attitude. And you would scarcely have imagined, watching her in recital, on how strict a discipline in characterization her charming little numbers had been built.

Argentinita's dances as you saw them had a charmingly lady-like air, with no athletics and no heroics. Sometimes the steps and patterns seemed naively plain and the best ones were never very elaborate, but her group numbers were always completely transparent and their comedy points rarely failed to register. Argentinita chose a small range of force as a choreographer, but she was a master in economy of detail, in proportion of emphasis, in sustaining interest and flow. Her gift for continuity and coherence (of impulse and of silhouette) made of slight variations distinct contrasts. Her own manner of dancing was suited to such delicate devices, for it was completely graceful, completely defined and her rhythm was infallible. Her special glory as a dancer were her little slippered feet, in their tiny, airy dartings and in their pretty positions on the floor. Argentinita's dancing naturally included more spectacular elements, but it was in the clarity of small details that one appreciated best the classic craft of her dance technique.

A classic cameo artist she was in technique, in choreography, in characterization. But she was a born star in the quick grace of her movement and a born star in the vivacity of her theater personality. Though she knew for years she needed rest and care, she could not bear to stop dancing. And though her tours overtaxed her, though she was handicapped by halls too vast for her special quality, and sometimes perhaps by the illness she heroically ignored, her hold on the public increased with each appearance. Last spring she seemed more scintillating and more amusing than ever, and her last production, *Café de Chinitas* at the Metropolitan, was her happiest work in a larger form. From the peak of her success she has now slipped away into silence.

At Argentinita's funeral were many who had known her only across the footlights but who loved her. And many more, all over this country, will keep their memories of how delightfully she danced, surrounded by her charming company, by her high-spirited and witty sister Pilar Lopez, and by Greco and Vargas, the young men she had trained so brilliantly— *September* 30, 1945.

COFFEE CONCERTS

LOUISE CRANE'S Coffee Concerts at the Modern Museum have included a good deal of interesting dancing and are well worth going to just for this aspect of them. The finest, no doubt, was the dancing of Martinez in last year's Spanish program. He remains shining in your memory as only the great performers do, and he seems to me the greatest Spanish dancer in America. This season I liked especially Luisita, an eight-year-old flamenco dancer, a very exact little girl, who danced with all the joyousness of a child who is playing her best game. I liked too, Belle Rosette from Trinidad, an intelligent, really gifted and personally modest artist. There was Baby Lawrence, a man who did a tap dance as purely acoustic as a drum solo; it was interesting how he ignored the "elegant" style in shoulders and hips, sacrificing this Broadway convention to the sound he made. But best of all I liked the Yemenite, Israel Tabi, from Miss Leaf's South Arabian Jewish group. Dressed in what looked like a flannel nightgown, this young man danced in a jerky style of thrusts and syncopations, with a decisiveness of rhythm, a sweetness of expression, and a violence of energy that showed him a born first-class dancer. He showed too in his technique a whole unsuspected dance tradition quite different from any I had ever seen—*January-February,* 1942.

***

THE VARIETY IN AFRICAN DANCING

***

AT THE Academy of Swing, a title I did not think particularly auspicious, I saw a lecture recital by Asadata Dafora, the author of the two very interesting African dance dramas of some years ago. I found the performance exceptionally fine. Dafora's subject was the variety of mood and the variety of movement in African Negro dancing. His dances, alone and with two excellent partners, Clementine Blunt and Bessie Nowell, illustrated his point convincingly. They were mostly dances from Sierra Leone. I thought I recognized as the basis of the style the dance-carriage that we know from our own Negro dancing; the lightness of the arms in clear contrast with the solidity of the trunk, the slight forward bend in the hips, the open chest, the calm shoulders and the neck that holds the head free of the dancing body. But Dafora's dancing showed that the West African tradition has developed all sorts of variations in the expression of this carriage; and highly diversified gestures, especially in the arms and hands. Whatever the historical process, Dafora's dancing presented a homogeneous style. It is a theatrical rather than a communal or folk form. As he said, not every African can dance, some just like to look and clap their hands. And he did a very attractive number with a stick, explaining that it had been invented by a great dancer of the past as a gesture of thanks for the gift of a very handsome stick.

All this was interesting, but the joy of the performance was the way Dafora danced. He has of course the verve that makes Negro dancing such a pleasure. But he has, too, the precision and freedom of rhythm, the differentiation of gesture, the impetus of movement, and a modesty and sweetness of expression that are all of them qualities of a great dancer. There is no showing off about it. He, his partners and his two drummers, Koker and Aubucha, created the kind of atmosphere a dance lover is happy to be in.

Dafora's costumes, made by Mrs. Dafora, were authentic. I especially admired a hand-dyed blue skirt showing dive bombers and a pennant inscribed "Victory"—*March-April,* 1943.

A COMPLETELY CIVILIZED ART

THE African Dance Festival, which Asadata Dafora, the dancer from Sierra Leone, presented at Carnegie Hall last week, gave us another of our rare glimpses of African Negro dancing. The main impression was once again that of a completely civilized art. It was the nonritual forms that were stressed. The theme of the festival was a young man's arrival in a village to court his beautiful bride, and the village celebration which ensues; it showed us village dances, expressing the social good spirits of such an occasion.

Drummers set the rhythm; the country girls danced formal dances, the matrons sang; the young groom exhibited in dancing his buoyancy of spirit and his graceful decorum—qualities which in New York too make for a happy married state. As a New Yorker, however, I was struck by the charming ceremoniousness of these villagers. The young man, for instance, did not rudely go straight to his fiancée, he first danced a few steps with each of the other girls in turn, circling about each as if to pay her a special compliment; an attention which each rewarded by a lovely smile and a graceful undulation in her steps.

And later when he danced a duet *Of Acquaintance* with his bride—a dance which began with a boops-a-daisy and continued with a figure where she swayed her bright-colored bustle a little on the left or a little on the right, and his arms drew long caressing curves in the air just out of reach behind her—the elegance of their play and the lightness of their rhythm reminded me in its spirit of an eighteenth-century pastoral. The emotion was natural, but the manners were perfect. The amenities were being observed for the pleasure they really give. And though I had not expected social graces in African village life, they seemed at once completely authentic characteristics; perhaps because among our own citizens Negroes, in particular, value the ceremonial of gentle manners, and perform it with the greatest grace.

The dances of the village girls looked at first quite simple with an odd hieratic stiffness about them. As the chorus moved forward, generally in single file, the feet kept reiterating sharply a syncopated rhythm of steps and sole-taps. The tap was made from the ankle, without moving the knee. Meanwhile the arms performed the dance variations, creating a secondary rhythm. The shoulders were as flexible as the ankles and they often moved in an independent rhythm. Occasionally there were accented motions (like "bumps") in the upper spine. And when the torso turned or bent it seemed to move from the hips. The head was generally kept horizontal, as if unconcerned.

Such a bearing looked stiff; a further sense of stiffness came from the simplicity of the floor patterns as well as from the trait of repeating a small detail of movement over and over; then taking up a new detail and repeating that. And after several dances the insistent foot rhythms tended to sound and to look all alike.

On the other hand, the lucidity of the style was remarkable —the way the body kept clear to one's eye, the feet distinct from the legs, the legs from the trunk, the shoulders, the arms, the head, each separately defined. The definiteness gave to slight variations their maximum effect. And in the end one noticed that the exactness of the posture, the firmness of the rhythm gave to the dance both dignity and force; that the peculiarities of the style could not be "savage" or accidental, but were the outcome of a consistent and highly cultivated dance tradition. The odd grace it had was distinctly elegant and certainly difficult to achieve.

The solo dancers, Miss Premice (the bride), Miss Sutton and in particular Mr. Dafora (the groom), showed the further technical subtleties of the style. In his dancing Dafora only now and then called attention to his percussive foot-beats. Though they were continuous, you watched the upper part of his body, the brilliantly rapid, darting or sinuous arms, the strangely mobile shoulders, the slight shift of the torso as it leaned forward or straightened, the turn of the head, the ani-

mated face. The way he phrased the rhythmic patterns in
these movements and so heightened the meaning of the dance
resembled the way a blues singer phrases her song and heightens its meaning against the steady beat of the orchestra. Dafora's free dance rhythms seemed to soar over the strict drum
rhythms of the accompaniment and over his own steady foot-
beats. His musical instinct was extremely subtle, his dance
intelligence striking.

The displacements in space, the motions of legs or torso, the
dramatic accents were not large. His numbers were modest
ones, as suited their subject, and they looked effortless. He
did not exaggerate to attract attention nor try to be impressive.
But there was never an empty moment or a lax one.

I think the qualities I have mentioned show him to be a
remarkable choreographer as well as a fine dancer. The proportions and the sequence of the dances were excellent. But
beyond this, the dancers he has trained are, after all, American girls, to whom life in an African village would be as foreign as life in a Russian one would be to the Russian-dancing
Americans in our Ballets Russes. Yet this village festival (like
Dafora's previous *Kykunkor* and *Zunguru*) had in performance a definite local atmosphere. It was not mere decorative
exoticism. It brought with it across the ocean the sense of a
real landscape and a real way of life. I wish it were possible
for so sincere and intelligent a choreographer as Mr. Dafora
to bring over across the ocean a small company of real West
African dancers to add to his well-trained American pupils,
and then show us more of the extraordinary wonders West
African dancing holds.

For it is apparently extremely wide in its range. I wish I
had space here for some of the vivid descriptions in Geoffrey

Gorer's brilliant *Africa Dances* (A. A. Knopf, 1935). When you read the book you can see the towns and the countryside, the people, their government, their diverse customs, their beliefs, their extraordinary magic, and as a part of all this daily life, their dancing. There are ritual dances and play dances, hair-raising acrobatic dances and communal frenzies. In many primitive communities there are professional dancers, but the community dances too, when it chooses. Gorer seems to have seen dances everywhere and almost daily—an infinite variety of costumes, of intention, of expression. West Africans "dance with a precision, a verve, an ingenuity that no other race can show, the smallest group has its own ballet, distinct in costume, in movement, in tempo from any other. . . . Africans have only one art [Gorer claims their sculpture is largely connected with dances] but to what a pitch they have brought it!" Gorer was watching them in 1934. Nearly six hundred years before, the Arabian traveler Ibn Batuta was watching African mask dances, so old is this dance tradition—*December* 19, 1943.

MISS DUNHAM IN REVIEW

KATHERINE DUNHAM'S tropical dance revue is a box-office hit, its run has been extended to six weeks, and that establishes it already as a unique success for an entire evening of dance entertainment. In addition Miss Dunham expects to add new numbers during the run, including one to a piece by Aaron Copland, written expressly for her;

and a second edition is promised for the spring with musical additions by Duke Ellington and Ernesto Lecuona. But here I want to talk about the present show as though it were a dance recital, which, of course, strictly speaking, it isn't. Considering the evening as a recital, or as a revue, the central interest remains the same: Miss Dunham herself in her prize numbers—*Bahiana, Shore Excursion* and *Barrelhouse*—which give us her impressions of three "hot" styles, the languid Brazilian, the tough, fast Cuban and the strident Jungletown. She has observed these fashions of tropical entertainment intelligently, she knows what they are each after. Better still, she knows there is nothing arch about a hot style, that its expression is serious and sometimes even angry.

In composing these three numbers she tries to recreate an atmosphere, she does not try for choreographic or virtuoso values, or for abandon. Her dancing is representational, she acts her dance, so to speak. One admires her projection, her stage presence. She does not force herself on your attention, she allows herself to be seen. Her gestures are provocative and yet discreet and she can even keep a private modesty of her own. As a dance entertainer, she is a serious artist.

But she is also on view as choreographer of the evening. The Brazilian, plantation, and Jazz numbers for her group are in the main lively and easy; and her company, which is strikingly spirited, handsome and graceful, is very pretty to watch in them. She has, happily, avoided giving them arm and leg tensions which would be out of key with their pelvic litheness, but she has found a good deal of variety in her dance-hall material and she has made sequences which flow naturally. She has not been as fortunate in her own part in these groups, her passages are often too fast and too scattered for her to shine in them, and in duets she does not make the man's part strong enough for her to play up to. In general, however, the group numbers are effective when they are a playful representation of some actual dance. But when the subject is the abstract idea of a dance, and the gesture becomes stylized and strict, the piece is likely to wander off into pleasant decorative effects.

Miss Dunham's instinct for the decorative values of abstract dancing is good. Her handling of the dramatic values of abstract form is uncertain. This uncertainty shows most clearly in her most serious numbers, the stylized rituals of fertility, male puberty and death, which fall very short of their dramatic intention. Their failure is also complicated by a confusion of technical procedures. The movement is based on African dance elements but the choreographic plan is that of the American modern school. The latter (like any Western art dancing) gets major effects from many kinds of displacement within the stage area, and out of sharply varied gesture. In African dancing, on the contrary, displacement values are of minor importance, individual variations are permissible and gesture gets its value by plain reiteration. To reconcile two such different expressive methods is a big problem. It is a problem that faces all those racially conscious artists who insist on reconstructing a style whose creative impulse is foreign to their daily life.

Not that ritual emotion is in itself a theme foreign to a civilized person. The force of primitive ritual was successfully expressed in terms of ballet dancing, for instance, by Nijinska's *Noces*. But Miss Dunham does not set out to make the complete abstract contrasts between lightness and heaviness, between rest and motion, between movement closed in and movement wide open, by which she could give dramatic meaning to nonrepresentational dancing. For in any technique of art the transport of faith can be represented by the distinctness of contrasts and their surprising reconciliation; as indeed ritual forces are represented in West African sculpture, which is the prime example in human art of the abstract intensity of volume contrasts—*September* 26, 1943.

DUNHAM IN FULL BLOOM

KATHERINE DUNHAM brought back her *Tropical Revue* last night. The show has been very well revised during its year of touring; it is lighter, quicker, more colorful, and the costuming is superlative. The company is as pretty, as lively and graceful as ever, and Miss Dunham, in the full bloom of her successful beauty and showmanship, is a stunning entertainer.

She does less straight dancing and more impersonation than last year, and the numbers have fewer ritual effects and more gaily playful ones; both changes are in line with her especial gifts and with the friendly and witty atmosphere that the show, for all its "tropical" idiom, is distinguished by. Miss Dunham's "bumps" last night were infinitely discreet; she can be as hot as she chooses without them, and her tight slow *Barrelhouse* as well as her lusciously easy *Bahiana* are better than ever.

Miss Dunham's tantalizing quality is not unlike the heat

effects of Mae West, a quality which a critic has recently described as impersonating a female impersonator. It is brilliant showmanship, brilliant timing, and any audience loves it. Sophisticated as Miss Dunham is in her personal performance, so she also proves herself as choreographer in the charming theater use of various Negro dance material from all over the world.

Of her new numbers, *L'Ag'ya,* in three scenes, evokes in terms of highly intelligent entertainment various dances of Martinique, a witty quadrille, a "beguine," a scene of black magic and a very brilliant wrestling and kicking dance, the "ag'ya." Vanoye Aikens, the hero, and Claude Marchant, the villain, were superb in this and the murder was a thrilling one. Particularly notable among the many fine costumes was that of the Zombie King, and Mr. Sebree's front curtain was a very fine one indeed.

Mr. Ohardieno, the Zombie King, and Tommy Gomez have become even better dancers than they were last year; and Miss Ellis, Miss Williams, Miss Fort, Miss Ingraham were all exceptionally fine throughout the evening. The Dowdy Quartet, too, deserves particular mention and the lighting all evening was much the best dance lighting of the season.

Though the first act finale is rather a weak one, it is on the whole an elegant and a graceful revue and Miss Dunham's wit and charm and complete knowingness are the key—
December 27, 1944.

SIMPLE ARRANGEMENTS

LA MERI and her Natya Dancers are presenting ethnological recitals: dances from Spain (both regional and gypsy), dances from North Africa, North and South India, Ceylon, Burma, Java, the Philippines, China, the West Indies, the Argentine, and maybe I've left out a few. The recitals themselves are informative and very pleasant. Informative, because La Meri knows the authentic steps, gestures and poses, and reproduces them clearly; they are in fact easier to identify when she does them than when the exotics do, themselves. She arranges them in simple and straightforward dances, set to native music (recorded) and in authentic costumes. She shows you the technical detail, she gives you the flavor of the style, and she adds—not without a private smile—a dash of the appropriate theater manner.

Everybody knows that the various dance techniques are in their highest forms mutually exclusive. Even in our own tradition no star is personally expressive in both ballet and modern. It seems as if a lifelong concentration in one type of carriage gives a great artist her freedom of dance rhythm, the spontaneity of movement that dances over the music; or looking at it in another way the complete plastic expressivity of the body in motion. La Meri knows this as well as anyone. She does not pretend to dance with the concentration of carriage that such specialists have. She indicates rather than actually expresses the plastic relation of trunk and limb. She indicates, she sug-

371

gests the initial phase of a movement in the trunk, and executes its final phase, especially in arm or hand gesture. By
decreasing, so to speak, the pressure behind a gesture, by
being completely clear about its final shape, she presents the
latter with extraordinary distinctness. And gets the full value
of her marvelous wrist. I had the impression that in her Indian
dancing specifically, she presents the hand pose (the *mudra*)
as the point of emphasis of a gesture; rather than as a confus-
ingly complex ornament that flowers from an impulse in the
torso, sometimes emphatic, sometimes not. Similarly, that she
arranges her Indian dancing in a prevalent 4-4 time, rather
than in the polyrhythmic variety that is interesting but also
confusing to an occidental eye. By not forcing herself beyond
what is possible, she remains an easy and graceful dancer. You
see exactly what she means, and you are grateful that there is
no faking of great art about the presentation.

La Meri does not compete as an artist with the austerity of
elegance that the greatest Eastern dancers alone in the world
attain to; or the uncompromisingly taut carriage of which only
the great Spaniards are capable; the abruptness of a Gaucho;
the brilliant exuberance of a Polynesian. But she evokes the
images of them, and that was her intention. And it is a great
pleasure, far away from the exotic dancers as we are here. I
was particularly happy to watch her Hawaiian numbers; for
the Polynesian dance style is one of the purest delights in the
world, and the natives we see in night-clubs look as miserable
when they dance as if they were caged in a zoo.

La Meri presents herself as the American she is, and now
and then she perhaps turns on the American charm a little.
But her modesty toward the question of art, her vast informa-

tion, her ease and good sense are worth remarking on. I noticed with pleasure too that the girls she has taught are natural on the stage, and easy. They are different one from another, and they express more pleasure in dancing than groups generally do: a credit to La Meri as a teacher—*March-April*, 1943.

SWAN LAKE IN EAST INDIAN

AT THE Ethnologic Theater Saturday afternoon La Meri presented a press preview of her new *Swan Lake* in East Indian dance idiom, and scored a distinct success.

The idea of this version of the famous ballet classic is the following: What would an East Indian, familiar with Indian but not with occidental dancing, imagine *Swan Lake* to be like, were he to hear the score on records and be told the general action? That is what La Meri and her company show you. The story is there, and the music, and the choreographic outline—action scene, dance by the Swan chorus, grand pas de deux, ballabile, and finale scene; all of them are done however in Indian steps and pantomime gestures. La Meri has added a prologue showing how the heroine was first enchanted; an oriental-style combat at the climax between the Enchanter and the Prince; and a last glimpse of the Swans that is effective.

To ballet goers this version offers a running comparison between ballet and Hindu dancing that is very interesting and sometimes—as in the Cygnet Quartet—very witty. La Meri with her usual fine tact does not press the parallel too solemnly; her little joke is a tender and a touching one. She looked lovely as Hamsa Rani (The Swan Queen) and Aldo Cadena was a convincing young prince.

The program opened with La Meri's East Indian pantomime comedy, *Gauba's Journey to Paradise* and with *Seven Classical Indian Dances,* which familiarize the audience both with the meaning of the Hindu pantomime gestures and with the technical resources of Hindu dance steps. La Meri and her Natya dancers present this ancient heritage in a delightful and completely unaffected manner—*February 20, 1944.*

EXACT CONTROL

ONE very good kind of dance music is that of Uday Shan-Kar. I do not mean to criticize it as music, much less as Hindu music. But to a lay ear it sounds pleasant, it sounds as though it made sense without being emphatic, it repeats itself without insistence. The oriental music I have heard always has this independent friendliness toward the dancers. It may have something to do with the fact that the music is made in sight of the audience, and that the musician exists not only as an instrument but also as a person. To me it is theatrically much pleasanter to see the people who make the music for dancing. It puts the dancer into a human perspective, it takes the bombast out of his stylization, and instead shows its real reference to the more usual look of a body. Human beings don't look any better for being alone, on the contrary their beauty is a relative thing; and even their solitude is more lonely when it is imaginary.

Uday Shan-Kar is a fine dancer. What struck me most about him was that though he is a star, though he projects as vigorously as any Broadwayite, he still gives a sense of personal modesty. Many gifted dancers seem to say on the stage, "I am the dance." He says, "Hindu dancing is a beautiful thing and I like to do it as well as I can." We see him and admire him. His exact control of every gradation of dancing—fluidity or accent, lyricism or characterization, space movement or stationary gesture, virtuoso precision or vigorous generality, is marvelous. His intention is always clear and his surprises never offend. Within the limits of what may seem to us supercivilized and adolescent suavity, without either our classic foot work or our modern back work, he finds it easy to run the whole gamut of dancing. Another style of dancing might have a different range, so to speak, but none can have a more complete expressiveness. Although he shows us all this in his own person as a dancer, we do not feel that he is showing us himself, he is showing us something that is beautiful quite apart from his own connection with it. He is a friend of ours who thinks we will enjoy too what he would enjoy so much if he were a spectator. As a result he is glad to show us his company—the coquetry and wit of Simkie, the juvenile eagerness and delight in his own gifts of Madhavan, he shows us even the least expert of his dancers as they are—not subtle of course but agreeable. All these shades of dance personality are allowed to flower according to their nature, and add up to the sense of harmonious and natural completeness. I believe that this use in a troupe of whatever gifts are present, like the sense in a star that he is not the only person, in fact only a detail in the whole of dancing—is the only thing that makes the theater real. Considerations of accuracy, of form for the group, of personal projection or style for the star are not secondary, they are an integral part of the artist's life. But they belong at home in the routine of preparation, they are his private life. In the studio the artist is more important than the whole world put together. On the stage he is one human being no bigger than any other single human being, even one in the audience. The big thing, the effect, is then at an equal distance from them both—*January-February*, 1937.

10

Dancing in Shows

CONCERT DANCERS IN
NIGHT-CLUBS

CHARLES WEIDMAN, Florence Lessing and Peter Hamilton, appearing as the featured trio at the Versailles, do unserious dancing, and do it intelligently. They dance with a rush, but a rush that is accurately modulated. The movement has an air of elegance that comes from serious training. The arrangements (choreography is too solemn a word) are clear and proper, the performers look like intelligent people dancing, and the jokes they make are mild and come natural. For instance, their Hindu number (Singhalese, to be exact) is so lively it slips into a jitterbug step and out again without losing its oriental deadpan expression. Mr. Weidman paces about beating intently on two finger drums tied to his belt, like a frenzied Fifth Avenue bus conductor. Peter Hamilton leaps high, and Miss Lessing smirks complacently—Hindu style—through this New York hullabaloo. The number makes no pretensions, but it has the grace of freshness (and that in a genre—the travesty Hindu—that has become the standard bore of night-club programs). Altogether, the night-club work of these three serious dancers has the charm of personal good

377

manners, a quality one is particularly grateful for in a café atmosphere.

Another concert dancer, a discovery of last season, Miss Pearl Primus, is appearing at Café Society Downtown. She does serious dances—including some Josh White "blues" accompanied by Josh White in person; but her serious style is not inappropriate to this slightly earnest club. She is an unusual dancer and deserves her quick celebrity. All her movement has a native Negro quality—an unction and a spring—that is a great pleasure to watch. In schooling she is a straight "modern"; but the personal simplicity of her dances and her clear sense of drama and climax make her numbers easy for any audience to follow. For her best effect she needs a good deal more room than she has on the floor of Café Society, but at least she couldn't find a more attentive night-club public.

A complete disappointment to this department are the Horton Dancers, a modern group from Los Angeles, three couples of which dance at the Folies Bergères. From the numbers they show it is impossible to guess what their reputation is based on. The floor show has, however, an interesting Chinese contortionist (or control dancer), Miss Lowe. She does her dreadful feats not only with charm, but also with a certain intellectual distinction. She phrases her numbers coherently, like a dancer, beginning each new sequence with a clear-cut dynamic impulse, which she sustains through her contortions till she lets it subside at the close of the phrase.

Rosario and Antonio, the Spanish gypsy team who are in *Sons o' Fun,* are now appearing in the Havana-Madrid too. They are young, attractive, full of magnificent fire, the darlings of the audience. Together, as a flamenco pair, they are unapproached in this country. The program I saw was not straight flamenco, however. It consisted of concert versions of gypsy and Andalusian dances (one of them adapted from Massine's duet in *Capriccio Espagnol*). Antonio's tough gypsy flamboyance has a roughness of finish that is not in proper concert style. On the other hand, these two young people throw themselves into any step they do with a sincere and passionate abandon that is extraordinary, that looks like the actual lifeblood of dancing.

At the Havana-Madrid you also see some expert, elaborately shuffled rumbas done by the customers, in particular by a sailor the night I was there. And the little showgirls have a gaily irreverent way of doing their foolish little drills—in contrast to the pious Ziegfeldian ritualism that is de rigueur for the longer girls who decorate the establishments with higher ceilings—*August* 29, 1943.

SKATING AS A FORM OF BALLET

WATCHING Sonja Henie's new ice revue from the point of view of ballet, as I naturally did, I found Freddie Trenkler's superb comic skating far more interesting than Miss Henie's celebrated sweet kind. And I imagine if skating is to become a form of real ballet, ice ballet is more likely to develop from the comic style than from the graceful one. For it is the comics who use most inventively and most dramatically the peculiar resources of motion on the ice. In the middle of a mad rush they stand quiet. They caper, spin, stop, rush off, fall and scoot headlong. They leap correctly and oddly, they skate clumsily and delicately and you see the point of the difference. They set the smallest movements against the biggest ones; they change the accent of a step, they change their direction, their skating impetus for the precise value the change has, and they don't let the change break the continuity of their number. It is out of the extremes of rhythm that skating alone can have that they build their dramatic effects.

And their dramatic intention, even more than their technical range, is what makes the comedians the real models for a serious ice dancer. Like serious dancers in the theater, the ice comedians don't show off their own person, or even their own proficiency; they show you a number, a dance. They focus your attention on a drama of character or on a drama of contrasted movement. In any form of theater dance it is the dramatic focus that makes the difference between "legitimate" and "cheese cake."

Among the non-comic skaters I have seen, there was one who seemed pre-eminently to have this dramatic approach to a part—Skippy Baxter, who is now in the Army. Technically, too, he could be compared to the best comedians. Watching him made me hope a bold choreographer would make a serious group number, utilizing the full technical resources of skating for a legitimate dramatic purpose. Such a piece would lift the audience out of their seats by the incredible rapidity, the sweep and shock of its movement.

Miss Henie's special style, as far as I can see, does not tend in this direction. Admirable is the bland surfacing she gives her routines; she blends her steps, she joins the longer phrases, and she delivers the routine as a coherent whole to perfection.

But both from the point of view of contrasted movement and from the point of view of dramatic interest her skating does not suggest anything like real ballet. In movement she avoids wherever possible extremes of force and tautness, she stays in the middle of the dynamic range where everything is nice and charming. It is Hollywood's device of crooning-in-movement. Taken out of the tiny camera-field and viewed on a large stage, you see it is just a salon style of motion.

Even if it isn't ballet, there is nothing wrong with a salon style if it has objective dramatic interest—as for example the impeccable dancing of Astaire has. When he dances, he is showing you a dance, he gives it a dramatic focus. But Miss Henie seems not to be showing a dance, she seems to be exhibiting her proficiency and her own cute person. Her amazingly powerful personality rivets one's attention firmly on her personal attractions. I looked at them attentively for four numbers. Very nice, but no drama—*January 23, 1944.*

MISS DE MILLE'S TOUCH IN TOUCH OF VENUS

MISS DE MILLE'S dances for *One Touch of Venus* shine by their good sense. Among our choreographers she has always had in particular that touch of nature that the title of the piece suggests. It is a striking virtue in musical comedy where nature is the last thing you expect. Miss de Mille has not this time the chance for human warmth she had in *Oklahoma,* but she certainly makes the most of what opportunity she has; and in *Venus* she again succeeds in touching the heart of the average audience through the dance numbers in a way no other musical comedy dance director can. The specialized dance lover, on the other hand, who naturally has special standards in the originality and the emotional interest he expects from dancing, will readily recognize in the course of these dances the intelligence of a fine choreographer.

Most interesting of the four numbers is the "Venus in Ozone Heights" ballet in the second act, which depicts what goes on in Venus' mind when she faces the possibility of becoming a suburban housewife. It begins lightly with children playing, they gradually get to be a nuisance, they grow up and start leading their own lives. The goddess remembers more and more distinctly the nymphs and fauns who do not change with time; and finally, with a last salute to human romance, she reassumes her divine majesty. Here at the end, when Mary Martin enters up stage, tall and remote, when she tosses with a quick, high gesture a handful of spangles as a blessing to the Aviator and his Girl, and then paces unperturbed across the luminous stage with a retinue of flying immortals, the dance reaches a clear statement of why a goddess is simply undomesticable—a statement that is vital to the plain story of *Venus,* and which is Miss de Mille's (and Miss Martin's) contribution.

The effect is a true one, and the change of mood from comic and intimate to remote and grand is convincing. It is achieved not so much by novel dance detail as by a change in the rhythm and a change in the bearing of the dancers. It is made possible by the fact that the entire dance is serious in the sense that the dancers represent an action; they do not—as musical comedy dancers generally do—exhibit their personal charm. They have a clear story to tell, and they tell it. And this successful change of mood gives (in *Venus* as in *Oklahoma*) a direct dramatic life to Miss de Mille's ballet.

Among the other dance numbers "Forty Minutes for Lunch" is a new version of the city traffic theme that modern-dance groups used to like. But the topical introduction of the French sailor, the simple intelligibility of the action, and the absence of an over-earnest straining make it a pleasant number, if not a novelty.

The prodigious success of Sono Osato as the star of the dance company is good news to her many admirers who know her in her former ballet roles, but it doesn't come as a surprise to them. In the first act she dances with a precise sharpness in every limb and a rhythmic punch that startles; she is a galvanic comedienne. In the second act, she then transforms herself into a glamorously alluring comic Nymph, who at the end is quite serious and beautiful.

The jitterbug number in the first act, arranged, I believe, by Lou Wills, Jr. for Miss Bond and himself, is a particularly original and happy one. The way they dance it, it stops the show too.

There is no doubt that the public loves any show Miss de Mille touches. And, personally, I look forward to the humanization of musical comedy, which her successes are bringing about, with the greatest enthusiasm—*October* 24, 1943.

POPULAR THOUGH SUPER-SPECIAL

PAUL DRAPER, the tap dancer in the Paul Draper style, and Larry Adler, the harmonica player in the Larry Adler style, are, as everyone knows, specialists as well as excellent showmen; they always get their audience, and they do it with ease and a deceptive reticence. And in their self-made specialties they are unrivaled.

I have never seen an audience that didn't go for both of them in a big way; for myself, I find them charming performers, but not interesting all evening long. The harmonica, even with all the extraordinary sounds Adler makes on it, has for my ears a tinny sound that doesn't carry the musical content of the serious pieces—Mozart, Bach or Debussy—that Adler plays. *Blues in the Night,* however, or *Begin the Beguine,* are great fun.

Paul Draper combines ballet steps and gestures, as well as suggestions of Spanish and "modern" with tap dancing; the result is of course a mixture, but there is no harm in that. I do not find, as many people do, the mixture interesting in itself. I only wish it worked better. I find the "art-dance" arm movement not free enough—the arms look put into position, accurately but not naturally. Tap technique requires relaxed knees and so it blunts many of the lines that ballet technique tries to keep taut. The movement in Draper's dances does not seem large, because the extensions are so often modified and broken. But the effect is a delicate and a very pleasing one. There is lightness and a touching sense of innocence in it. And these

384

qualities—and they are qualities of refinement—are clear to the audience and they delight it.

I wish Draper had more freedom in his neck and shoulders. And I wish he had more rhythmic freedom in his tap rhythms. To my ear he seems to be embroidering the musical rhythm rather than to be creating an independently interesting parallel rhythm. But as after a few numbers I find the sound itself of the tapping a little insistent—expertly modulated though it is—I am not the best judge of this matter. I admire it most in his dance without music—*January* 1, 1944.

THE ROCKETTES AND RHYTHM IN BALLET

THE Rockettes at the Music Hall are an American institution and a very charming one. Their cheerfulness is sweet as that of a church social. Their dancing is fresh and modest, their rhythm accurate and light and everyone can see that they accomplish what they set out to do to perfection. At the end of their routine when the line of them comes forward in a precision climax, the house takes all thirty-six of them collectively to its family heart. It is a very pleasant moment of contentment all around.

The Music Hall has a charming chorus of classic-ballet girls, too, who, like the tap-dancing Rockettes, are perfectly accurate in their timing and exact in their motions. They too dance without affectation in a graceful and modest manner.

Just as the Rockettes avoid what is "hot" and disturbing in taps, so the toe dancers avoid what is intensely expressive in ballet; instead they are phenomenally neat, they never blur anything they do, and everyone can see they fully deserve their applause.

The ballet doesn't, to be sure, establish a family feeling in the house as the Rockettes do, but then you rarely see toe dancing in the living room and you often see tap dancing there. Ballet is meant to be seen at a distance, it isn't relaxed or familiar in its bearing. But there is a further reason why the ballet is less effective at the Music Hall than the tap routine. In both of them the dramatic punch of the number lies in the unique (and apparently effortless) synchronization of all the dancers and of the entire dance with the music. While this feat heightens very much the sense of rhythm you get from the Rockettes, it doesn't somehow heighten the sense of rhythm you get from the ballet; though it's just as difficult a feat for the latter, it doesn't carry so in ballet.

The fact is that tap and ballet rhythm are different to start with, in the way they connect with the music. The tap dancer plays with the beat, he plays around it and he never leaves it alone. Whatever else he does in the way of elegant ornament, it's the beat that interests him, and each beat does. You see his relation to it in his motion and you hear it in his taps and his relation to it is the excitement in the dance. The "hotter" he is the more intimate and dramatic his relation to it becomes; but he can hold your interest just by showing a cool and a sure relation. And a tap-dancing chorus can by complete synchronization fix with a kind of finality the relation of the dance to the music and so reach a satisfying expression. You know what to follow and at the end you know where you are.

But you don't follow a ballet beat by beat. Ballet dancing probably once had a good deal of this percussive quality—so eighteenth-century dance music suggests. In 1880 ballet you can see a percussive dance number in the Cygnet Quartet in *Swan Lake*. Contemporary American ballet tends to use this device more sharply—you see it in parts of *Rodeo* and particularly in *Concerto Barocco*. Here the sound of the dancers' toesteps is part of the effect. But these passages are details. More generally the rhythmic interest in ballet dancing isn't fixed on the beat or on the dancers' relation to it; the interest is in their relation to the musical phrase, to the melody, to the musical period. At such times their rhythm is a "free" one, more like that of a singer in its variety of emphasis than like that of a tap dancer.

Like the blues singer the ballet dancer takes a freer emphasis for the sake of more intense dramatic (or lyric) expression, so he can change his speed against the steady music, so he can make more kinds of effects with his body and travel more freely about the stage. The spring that is the life and rhythm of taps is not tied to the beat in ballet; it has been extended so to speak into a lift in the expression of the dance; you follow the rhythm not by separate steps, but by the rise and fall of extended phrases.

In taps you see and hear two different rhythms, both of them in the same strict musical meter. In ballet you often look at a free meter and listen to a strict one. Complete synchronization of ballet and music is a special effect that works by contrast to other rhythmic possibilities and it satisfies only when used for such a contrast. People accustomed to strict acoustic rhythm often take a while to get used to ballet rhythm so they can follow it, but there are many too who can't follow a tap dancer, who lose track of any dance rhythm unless it pounds the down beat. Well, that's why there are several kinds of dance rhythm to suit different types of the human receiving set—*February* 20, 1944.

SCENES DE BALLET AT BILLY ROSE'S

EVERYBODY goes to *Seven Lively Arts* for Miss Lillie, it is her show and she is more wonderful than ever. Warmed happily by her crooked little smile, the public accepts the evening's main dance attraction as nice enough, if rather vague. The fact that *Scènes de Ballet,* as the feature is called, presents Markova in a new Stravinsky doesn't bowl over the Broadway audience. But it is evidently fond of Miss Markova personally; and so the ballet passes off.

Vague the number looks to a dance lover too, who comes hoping for something remarkable as dancing, whether suitable to a show or not. There is no doubt that the number makes serious pretensions. Dolin, who set it, means to evoke the sentiment of old-time ballet by traditional dance forms—pas de deux and so forth—done to Stravinsky's shifting beat. Markova has a big entrance (she manages to conceal its barrenness), the chorus troops on and off again, and much of the time Markova and Dolin are doing choice bits from *Giselle,* anywhere on the stage.

Honest ballet choreography is not based on choice bits or wow moments, as ballet faked for vaudeville is. It is based on coherent sequences, on a positive rhythm. The sustaining rhythm sets off one phrase against another, leads to various climaxes, and finally gives the sense of a rhythmic beginning and ending, of a dramatic progress which conveys a human sentiment. Dolin's dance arrangement has no positive rhythm, the phrases start up and peter out; the dancing never gets going. He tries to interest by occasional technical feats. But without a coherent rhythm there is no impetus to lead up to them, no timing when they happen, no contrast to show them off. There is not even an effective placement on stage. In *Scènes de Ballet* even Markova, the great showman at holding your attention by phrasing and so making the climax count, can't make her part coherent or her virtuosity carry. Sadly I recalled how wittily she had once danced to Stravinsky rhythm in *Poker Game*.

Lovely she is this time in the arms, as always. And her simple straight manner throughout shows the great artist she is. I hoped that her part would at least include one of her wonderfully slow and high leg-extensions to the side, which she hasn't done since her illness; but it didn't. Dolin, in his part, can't resist gazing impressively at one of his hands in what is meant as a tragic pose. His tights, however, are the finest ever seen, and all the costumes for *Seven Lively Arts* are tailored with a perfection I had thought only Hollywood achieved (Paul Dupont has the credit for supervising). As for the setting, by Bel-Geddes, it is vast and pointless and what Hollywood considers refined.

The Stravinsky, on the other hand, has nothing foolish about it. The dancing "interprets" it as if it were formless mood-music, a sort of Wagnerian yearning, and blurs its shape; and the musical show orchestra, though accurate, overemphasizes the brass. But Mr. Abravanel, the conductor, is a really first-class musician, and thanks to him you can get a truer idea of it than you would expect. *Scènes de Ballet*—the score has that title too—is a dance suite more theatrical in approach, warmer and more romantic in tone, less playful in texture than *Danses Concertantes*. It has a good deal of nineteenth-century expressivity and buildup and reaches a sonorous, beautifully tragic climax.

But the notion of playing a serious Stravinsky in a show or of asking Markova to dance seriously in one is a mistake anyway. Their tragic talents need a more intense concentration, a more sincere curiosity than a show audience cares to give. Markova, however, is also an expert parodist of Romantic ballet, the very best one in the world. It is a pity that Dolin (who in *Seven Lively Arts* shows his engaging comic gift in a spoken scene) did not try to make a parody *Giselle*, set to music like that of Donizetti's comic operas. It would have been an honest job, it would have been just as tony, and everybody would have been much happier—*December* 24, 1944.

DANCING IN SHOWS

JEROME ROBBINS' dances for *On the Town* are fresh, neat, direct and sincere, and that is how they are danced. The spirit they are danced with is where you see his originality much more than in the steps. You can tell what an exceptional gift he has as a director by how clearly the dancers know what to stress and by how spontaneously they do it. All of them, chorus as well as principals, give you the sense of a happy cooperation with the piece and with each other, a cordial glow that they share, newcomers and experienced dancers alike. Looking at them, one wishes some such vivifying warmth had brought together the dancers of Ballet International too and given them a freshness on the stage they might easily have had. International couldn't cooperate in this way because it often didn't get the point of what it was doing in terms of ensemble ballet rhythm. In *On the Town* the company knows how their movements work in terms of ensemble pacing; so they know what they are after, and they can all look intelligent when they dance, unself-conscious and lively.

There are lots and all sizes of dances; they generally tell a little pantomime story, but you don't think of them as distinct from the rest of the show. They generally emerge from the stage action and melt into it again so as to give value to a scene rather than a hand to the dance. Often they express a sentiment, too, much as Miss de Mille's musical comedy dances do. In *On the Town,* the sentiments suit the farce plot especially well, and, besides, Robbins' sentiments are naturally intelligent and attractive ones anyway—serious or funny without affectation.

Just now his dance ideas do not develop in space easily, but he doesn't try to cover up by complicated patterns or ornamental gestures; he concentrates instead on clarity of impulse and variety of pacing. In detail, though, I admired particularly the end of the "Lonely Town" number and the way the singer's one nod completes a dance; the equally simple ending of Miss Osato's "Turnstiles" number; the brief strange rush of the Times Square finale, and the monkeyshines of the principals in "You Got Me," which was for me the most striking moment of all. Less successful, I thought, the Dream number, but Oliver Smith's wonderful scenic effects here are more than enough to carry it.

Miss Osato danced in the dream and everywhere else with brilliant rhythm and a brilliant sense of shades of character (and of hardness and softness). She is an impish and a warm-hearted comedienne, completely natural in the general New York home-town atmosphere. And the fun of the whole evening is the grace of feeling at home here where we are.

Sing Out, Sweet Land, wants to make you feel at home, not here and now, but in our historic customs. Doris Humphrey and Charles Weidman have furnished historical steps (from "squares" to Charleston), and Peter Hamilton's Charleston is a brilliant dance moment. But as for the rest, if you begin to compare the heavy accents and strained postures of the dancing with the limpid, relaxed and delicately elastic rhythm with which Burl Ives, the balladist, sings his songs, you notice how "unauthentic" the dance effects are. You will notice it, if you enjoy our country folklore straight and appreciate its inherent modesty and unassertive spaciousness. But it takes a unique artist like Ives to put across such mild and sweet effects.

Song of Norway when it opened in August, had nothing less than the Monte Carlo, headed by Danilova and Franklin, as its dance company. The stars have since been replaced by Olga Suarez, a highly promising newcomer, and by Dorothie Littlefield, Messrs. Guerard and Starbuck, artists familiar to ballet goers. Revisiting the show last week, I found the numbers fresh, cool and clear as ever. In one sense they are the boldest on Broadway, for they rely on the most civilized of dance virtues—a striking simplicity of line and purity of classic style. Unobtrusive as these Balanchine numbers are, anyone can see that they are pretty and the final ballet offers you, without insistence, modestly and touchingly a sentiment not at all commonplace. *Song of Norway* does not falsify ballet as most musicals do on the ground that adulteration is the first principle of showmanship. Balanchine's numbers are simplified ballet, but of the purest water—*January* 21, 1945.

11

Addenda

A BRIEFING IN AMERICAN BALLET

TOWARD the end of the war, during several seasons, ballet in the United States had a bright moment of eagerness and glory. A number of strikingly original choreographies appeared; and with them, a burst of dance talent, new stars, a new atmosphere on stage and a lovely freshness in classic dancing. The choreographic innovations were ballets by George Balanchine in a dazzling new classicism; absorbing dance-pantomime-dramas of protracted anguish by Antony Tudor; and lively American local-color comedies by Agnes de Mille and Jerome Robbins. The two touring companies of the period, Ballet Theater and the Ballet Russe de Monte Carlo, were largely composed of Americans, young, exact, strong, and charming. It was their new dance impetus that triumphed. They won their first decisive victory in 1942 in Tudor's *Pillar of Fire* at Ballet Theater. Two years later, the Monte Carlo, its style suddenly transformed by Balanchine, presented his *Danses Concertantes*. From then on all over the country the vitality of both companies delighted a great new ballet audience night after night.

The difference between the two companies added to the

pleasure. Ballet Theater's esthetics, under its English choreographer Tudor, tended to dramatic pantomime; the Monte Carlo's under Balanchine toward a classic dance grace. They had different repertories, though both included nineteenth-century classics, Diaghileff, and pre-war pieces. Ballet Theater was the larger, stronger but somewhat heavier and harder company. Both companies had a few remarkable foreign-born principals. And each had a very great artist as its star ballerina. The Monte Carlo's was the witty warm-hearted Alexandra Danilova. Delighted by the fresh stimulus around her she reached in 1944–45 a new magnificence in strict classicism. Ballet Theater's ballerina, on the other hand, was the frail English classicist, Alicia Markova; but Ballet Theater's tendency toward pantomime developed her latent genius as an actress. For several seasons she showed us a shyly dazzling spirituality of expression, the secret force of which captivated alike warworkers, housewives, and intellectuals. Her *Giselle* became New York's big ballet night.

Wartime, here as abroad, made everyone more eager for the civilized and peaceful excitement of ballet. More people could also afford tickets. And in wartime the fact that no word was spoken on the stage was in itself a relief. Suddenly the theaters all over the country were packed whenever the two companies appeared. They sold 1,500,000 tickets a year. The new public fell in love with the stars, with the dancers, and with ballet in general. It liked everything. It applauded a glaring variety effect and twenty minutes later applauded as eagerly a quiet poetic one. When the critics praised a piece, the public rushed to the theater and loved it; when they damned a piece, it rushed to the theater and loved it too. It was not so much a failure of taste as an abundance of stimulation. Thanks to the unconsciously American air the ensembles had in everything they danced, the new public found an unexpected contact with the brilliant strangeness of what they saw. As they watched any ballet, an indefinable something in the atmosphere, in the quality of movement and youthful manners, was unconsciously familiar and immediately touching.

The older ballet-goers, familiar with pre-war performances, had expected nothing like what they now saw. What they expected of ballet was the pre-war Ballet Russe. When the war began in Europe, both of the pre-war Ballet Russe companies, the de Basil Original, and the Massine Monte Carlo, managed to reach New York intact. With the composers and painters of the School of Paris who were here, these extraordinary ensembles intended to continue a brilliant Ballet-Russe-in-exile in peace and comfort. But nothing of the sort happened. Within a few years hardly a trace of Paris-Russian atmosphere or dance style or choreographic fashions remained. Instead ballet had adapted itself to the American dance climate, as it had a few years before in England to the English, and more than a century earlier to the Russian.

The acclimatization of ballet in the United States had begun a decade earlier. It began with local semi-student companies in New York, Chicago, Philadelphia, San Francisco. (Europeans saw Miss Littlefield's Philadelphians tour in '37.) All these groups commissioned local choreographers, composers, and painters. The most interesting of them was Lincoln Kirstein's American Ballet in New York of which George Balanchine was artistic director. About half of our current best talent seems once to have been in this group. On its first program in '34 it produced Balanchine's *Serenade,* which when he presented it in '47 at the Paris Opera astonished the audience by the abundance of its invention and the novelty of its style. But none of these groups was strong enough to compete with the Ballet Russe in scale, stars or repertory. Finally in 1940 Lucia Chase's Ballet Theater opened in New York, with the intention of becoming an American repertory company of as high a quality as the Paris-Russian ones.

Ballet Theater, however, compromised on its chauvinism. It sought assistance from Fokine; Baronova joined it; it soon came under the guidance of its British artists, Tudor, Dolin and Markova. For a season it enlisted Nijinska, and it achieved the celebrity it aimed for as Massine and other Ballet Russe stars joined it. And it was Massine who awakened in Ballet Theater's Americans the dance verve and drive that characterized the company ever after. During these same years, however, the Monte Carlo, as anxious to remain Paris-Russian as Ballet Theater was to remain American, found itself forced to compromise too. Its ensemble atmosphere became more and more diluted. Its American contingent had grown too large to be assimilated. In '42 it even presented the first well-made ballet that had a real American tone and flavor, Agnes de Mille's *Rodeo;* and the "Russians" danced it convincingly. This double direction of ballet in the United States made the situation confusing as late as '42.

But until '42 for the public the prestige of the pre-war Ballet Russe still concealed the changes that were taking place. What firstnighters still expected was the pre-war fashion, its odd elegance and its nervous glamor. There was to be sure a sort of malaise in the air. One group—the Original—had disappeared. Some pre-war stars had vanished, others grown lax, the ensemble style was no longer so vivid and the novelties had less and less point. No doubt the glorious Ballet Russe was a little out of order but the spell of its pre-war prestige covered everything.

The spell was broken by the overwhelming triumph of Ballet Theater at the premiere of Tudor's *Pillar of Fire*. Neither in its style nor in its cast of dancers did it show any traces of Paris-Russianism. And by contrast it suddenly made apparent to everyone how devitalized the pre-war formula had become. Now Tudor's earlier works already in the repertory became popular. Even the most effective of the pre-war-style ballets created here during the war, Massine's *Aleko,* done by Ballet Theater a few months later, could not change the current; though it had far more dance verve than Tudor, its melodrama could not compete with his real anguish. Now that the prestige of pre-war ballet had collapsed, the old Monte Carlo was doomed; poor and desperate, it lost its pre-war stars, all but Danilova and Franklin. Youskevitch joined the Navy. But when in the fall of '44 Balanchine took over the crumbling company and at a stroke rejuvenated it, the triumph of the American-style company, the new Monte Carlo, proved to have ended any interest in the resurrection of a Paris-Russian atmosphere. Indeed no one danced that way convincingly any more; the old stars who remained had now assimilated themselves to the new style. Twice however an exhumation of the past was attempted—by Ballet International in '44 (the single season of which is said to have cost the Marquis de Cuevas $600,000), and by the de Basil Original brought back from South America in '46; both attempts failed.

The decay of the Paris-Russian ballet style in the United States was due to the isolation of the Ballet Russe from its natural sources of vitality in Paris. It affected the pre-war Ballet Russe choreographers disastrously. Massine, for instance, created a dozen or so pieces in this country (including three with grandiose décor by Dali). But of Massine's work only

Aleko—magnificently decorated by Marc Chagall—was at all comparable to his European work. Large in scale, hollow in sentiment, it had an ingenuity, a sweep and a hectic activity reminiscent of his "symphonic" style. None of his other pieces were remarkable and some were appallingly shoddy. Fokine produced two ballets of no interest. Lichine created three or four, some pretending to great spiritual conflicts, but only one fine scene among them—one of exuberant South Russian folk dances. His 1940 *Graduation Ball*, a harmless comedy to Johann Strauss music, remained his best work. Nijinska created several ballets but none as attractive as her pre-war *Chopin Concerto*. The new ones of the '40s were highly ingenious, false in sentiment, willfully odd in musicality, and crabbed in their arbitrary construction of the dancer's actions; she retained however a greater force of style than any of the other choreographers of this group. It was sad to see how inexpres-sive they all became in the dance climate in which they found themselves.

These celebrities did not respond to the human medium which the more and more American ensembles offered to choreographers. A few of the stars sometimes developed inter-estingly in the choreographies in exile, but the effect failed be-cause even then there was no resonance between star and en-semble, no coherent dance atmosphere to create a coherent poetic illusion. The fact was that several fine qualities the Paris-Russians had had by temperament and tradition, qual-ities their choreographers presupposed in a company, were foreign to the American dancers. Correct and clear the new dancers were, stricter in these matters than the Europeans; but the Americans, most of them too young ever to have lived abroad, did not understand those overtones of European local color, both geographical and historical, which the pre-war Ballet Russe often suggested so imaginatively. Ballets presupposing such overtones (from *Petrouchka* to *Gaîté Parisienne*) lost in consequence most of their savor and point. The Americans were unimaginative too in suggesting nuances of social differentiation, or of sexual experience. The foreign choreographers for their part, even after living here, found no inspiration in local manners. But the American dancers had neither an instinct for imaginative characterization through liberties of rhythm and accent in classic variations, nor an ensemble instinct for the kind of rhythmic liberty the Ballet Russe had used for a sweeping collective climax. A European who sees ballet only in such terms may wonder if anything is left without these effects; if all that is left is not merely a machine, hard and monotonous.

The excitement and freshness of our ballet toward the end of the war, after the Ballet Russe impetus had disintegrated, proves the contrary. The American steadiness and exactitude of rhythm, its reticence of phrasing, have not the same but a different clarity and sweep. They do not underline the pathos of a scene by taking sides, but its tragedy by not taking any. They can show largeness of scope and power and they avoid greasiness of detail. The bold decision, the easy calm, and the large openness which Americans derive from the tradition of sports that permeates the country, can give their dancing in complex dance figurations a noble clarity. Their sober friendliness of manner can have, as Balanchine once wrote, an expression such as one imagines angels would have, who can take part in tragic events without becoming themselves miserable. When one watches attractive young Americans in a ballroom or in a dance hall, one notes instinctive traits of dance style not unlike these I have mentioned; their dancing looks different from that of Europeans—it has a different style and expression—but style and expression it clearly has.

Of all the foreign-born choreographers who have worked in the United States, Balanchine has responded most to the stimulus of this country's natural dance gifts. Since he came here in 1933 he has worked successfully in all our forms of ballet, in musical comedy, in opera, in the films (where he was the first to compose dance phrases directly to suit the camera field and camera angle), in student performances (down to the age of six) and with both ballet companies. He can use Americanisms of rhythm or nuance in classic ballets without a trace of self-consciousness. Long before the war he lost interest in the Ballet Russe style of the period; and ever since he has been here he has worked by preference with American dancers. He is more than anyone else the real founder of the American classic style. He has shown our dancers how to be natural in classicism, and he has shown them how to become unaffectedly brilliant in their own natural terms. He has shown the public how effective they are with their charming long-limbed figures, their simple carriage, strong legs, their dazzling speed and their clean grace of line; how animated in the variety of their impetus, in their technical exactness and the exactness of their musicality; how touching in their unself-conscious delight in dancing, their cooperativeness, in the sobriety of their appeal, in the strength of their grace. And when he has come across a dramatic gift, he has placed it where it made its full effect without straining for emotional miming or for a verbal meaning.

Balanchine's choreography, whether during the Diaghileff period or the present one, has always suited the unconscious atmosphere of his ensembles and the innate gifts of grace of his principals. They have always looked both free and brilliant. His recent style differs from his European one in that it no longer shows his former lovely erotic interruptions. Since 1940 it has become strictly classical; the dancer's figure is a clear unit, the dance impetus is unbroken, sustained, and clear. Balanchine has inherited the empire of Petipa and Ivanoff. You recognize their purity of idiom, their harmony of motion, and their power of rhythm. But the effervescence of invention, the exquisite musicality, the variety of momentum, the complexity of structure are new. The startling details are often, technically speaking, novelties in the timing, the size, the transposition or the reversal of classic dance elements or of the phases of a step. Since they remain logical according to the classic technique of balance and impulse, the dancer in them keeps her free impetus. The expression she gives these inventions is merely her graceful freedom, her sovereign assurance; the drama of their happy surprise, of their startling development, of the poignant relations between dancing figures they suggest is resolved by the dazzle and sweep of the ballet's dance rhythm. Balanchine's classicism and his musicality give the dancers the spring in dancing that modern ballets don't have when they try for "meaning." And yet each piece of his touches the imagination with a mysterious expressive message.

The animating subject matter of these new classic ballets is no more explicit than that of *Swan Lake*. Their announced subject is occasionally a plot as unreal as that; more often it is merely the musical structure of the score. But each of Balanchine's ballets has a quality of motion in its development of impetus that is different and specific. One senses that at the core of this dazzling, joyous grace there is, as its source of energy, a specific human gesture, a real image, a slip of fate. Isolated in the imaginary rise and fall of musical time it offers its transfigured drama in silence. It has become a game for dancers. And as one watches their rapid figures, happy in their animation, caught in their buoyant rhythm, the plastic emphasis of a dance gesture, defining for an instant the impetus, looks poignantly beautiful. Beautiful in its proportion, in its freshness. Beautiful in the innocent dignity of the dancer as she darts past. The echoes the instant awakens are worthy of her. The secret of the movement, its human characteristic, reverberates in memory as it does fantastically in the brilliant surprises of the dancing one is watching and of the music one hears. Neither the dancers nor the audience are required to justify the apparition of these evanescent dance images. They strike as lightly as the sound of a heartbreaking word. And the frightful truth of them remains suspended in an innocent and harmonious world of fantasy.

Of Balanchine's eight creations here since 1940 the most astonishing are three dance ballets of the purest classicism whose subjects are their scores: *Concerto Barocco* (1941) to Bach's *Concerto for Two Violins; Danses Concertantes* (1944) to Stravinsky's score of that name—a ballet brilliantly decorated by Eugene Berman; and *The Four Temperaments* (1946) to Hindemith's composition, danced in a décor by Kurt Seligmann. *The Four Temperaments,* formally a set of themes and elegant variations, is a long fantasy of incredible violence and amplitude, savage speed and packed weight. *Danses Concertantes,* formally a comedy-style pas de deux with playful entrees by the chorus, is glittering in sharpness, in jets of power and tenuous resilient articulations, in witty grace, in the mystery of a menace withheld all one's life. *Concerto Barocco,* a long supported adagio framed by allegro chorus entrees, has the effect of an ample grace and a cheerful freshness accompanying like a landscape the savage wound of an individual, its untouched force persisting before and after the private event. At times the sweetness of its plastic harmonies is heavenly. It is a pity it is given in the most meager of décors. The Monte Carlo has had seven ballets of Balanchine in recent repertory, Ballet Theater two, and Ballet Society, a new organization that presents four evenings a year in New York, also has two. For Ballet Society, Balanchine is now preparing Stravinsky's as yet unplayed *Orpheus,* a Rieti ballet, one to Haieff's score and one to Mozart; for Ballet Theater, Tchaikovsky's *Theme and Variation.*

In a completely different esthetic as well as choreographic style is the work of Antony Tudor, artistic director and a principal mime of Ballet Theater, who is the other ballet choreographer of genius working in the United States. Tudor's three major creations have all been very long pieces. *Pillar of Fire* (set to Schoenberg's *Verklaerte Nacht*), half dream, half reality, tells the story of a love-starved English girl tortured by the fear that the young man who frequently comes to call loves not her but her younger sister; it turns out that she has no reason to, and at the end she becomes engaged. Full of self-humiliation, of gnawing envy, sex-frenzied orgiastic images, striking shifts of dance style, fragments of middle-class gesture, full of dance impulses suddenly released and suddenly frozen, it overwhelmed the audience at its first performance. It also established the young American Nora Kaye as a real dramatic ballerina, and the young English dancer Hugh Laing as an intensely imaginative dramatic star. Kaye has since won herself recognition as a classic ballerina as well and had a real success in London a summer ago, when Ballet Theater danced there. A second major work of Tudor's was *Romeo and Juliet* (to several Delius pieces). Its effect is that of a revery on Shakespeare's text that transmutes his fire into a Tennysonian pathos. It is a revery luxuriously embroidered with quattrocento pictorial devices, as carefully cut as an Eistenstein film, and its rhythmic weight steeps the story deeper and deeper in a protracted and absorbing High Church gloom. *Romeo and Juliet* opened with a décor by Eugene Berman, which in its opulence, its wealth of invention and complex grace is itself an event of ballet annals. And Alicia Markova, slight, intensely still, intensely musical was the most luminous of Juliets. Unfortunately the present state of the production is abominable. The third (1945) and least successful of Tudor's major long works was *Undertow* (to a score by William Schuman). It tells the case history of a sex murder, beginning with the hero's birth (breach presentation) and his infantile frustrations; later grown into a repressed and gentle adolescent in the slums—which are full of sex—he strangles the girl who seduces him, and suffers remorse; there are dull stretches and a long evasively symbolic ending; but there are also brilliant passages, notably the rape of a horrid little girl by four little boys.

Tudor's ballets have obvious weaknesses. Their shock value, thrilling at first, does not last; their shaping force is discontinuous; they have a weak and fragmentary dance impetus; they peter out at the end. They can find no repose and no spring because balance is no element of structure in them. Their sentiment, acutely envious, acutely humiliated, weakens into self-pity. But they also have exceptional virtues. They are perfectly serious. Their sentiment is real till toward the end; they are full of passion, of originality, of dramatic strokes, of observation, of brilliant pantomime ideas, and fastidiously polished detail. Tudor discovers dramatic gifts in his dancers and shows them off to striking advantage. There is no vulgarity in his obscene images. His ballets are not primarily dance conceptions; but their sustained expressive intensity is clearly large-scale.

On a much smaller scale than Tudor, derived from pantomime and novel character-dance elements, is the American local-color ballet. Its first great success was Miss de Mille's *Rodeo* in which she dance-mimed the star role. It has an excellent scene suggesting cowboys rodeo-riding and another of Saturday night ranch house dances. The dance steps are lively and the rhythmic sequences well contrasted. Its emotion is humorous-sentimental. It has a lively score by Aaron Copland, who had already written another "western" ballet score, a beautiful and tragic one, for an interesting but now vanished pre-war American piece, *Billy the Kid* (choreography by Eugene Loring). *Fancy Free* by Jerome Robbins (score by Leonard Bernstein, décor by Oliver Smith), is about three sailors in town for an evening, and by far the best of the Americana to date. Its local color is sharply observed, its wry pathos is honest and its jokes sound. The flow of movement, the rhythmic tautness, the concise storytelling are admirable and it proved as successful in London as in New York. It is still a fresh piece to see after many repetitions. Robbins, a remarkable dramatic dancer himself, has since made two small ballets that show a great advance in construction but a sentiment more confused. Though his experience in classicism is not large, formally his choreographic genius is of the highest order. He understands by instinct the formal unity of a ballet in stage space and musical time, a unity created and filled by a coherent dance impetus. He also conceives every dance action in terms of a drama of real characters. In point of expression he has difficulty as yet in the complete transformation of specific pantomime images into the larger and sweeping rhythm and images of direct dancing. But there is no doubt that he is the most gifted of American-born ballet choreographers. At the moment unfortunately he is about to direct plays and films.

A remarkable choreographic talent appeared in the spring of '47 when Ballet Society presented *The Seasons,* the first ballet by Merce Cunningham (score by John Cage, décor by Isamu Noguchi). Cunningham, a pupil of Martha Graham and a prodigiously gifted dancer, is not a ballet dancer but a modern-dance or expressionist one. His piece, though not in classic idiom, was danced cleanly by dancers classically trained. Its subject was phases of weather and subjective states induced thereby, a subject in the tradition of Thoreau. The phrases were brief but clear, the plastic instinct forceful and imaginative. Though the emotion was tremulous and delicate, the piece showed strength as a dance structure. Cunningham may prove to be a choreographer as soundly gifted as Robbins though in a style as hermetic as Robbins is plain spoken.

Though my subject is ballet and not modern dancing, I cannot omit mentioning Martha Graham, the greatest dance celebrity in the United States. Now past fifty, an actress of magnificent power, a dancer of astonishing skill, her choreographies abound in extraordinary plastic images of great originality. They are expressionist in rhetoric, violent, distorted, oppressive and obscure; there is rarely a perceptible rhythmic unit or any dance architecture. But the ardor of her imagination, the scope of her conceptions, the intensity of her presence make her a dance artist of the first rank.

I have tried to give an impression of the character and of the resources of our new ballet. Among its greatest resources are the young American ballerinas now developing. The most interesting now are Alicia Alonso, Nora Kaye, Mary Ellen Moylan, Maria Tallchief; and Ruthanna Boris, Rosella Hightower and Nana Gollner are in the same category. Kaye I have already mentioned; Alonso, Ballet Theater's Cuban-born classic ballerina, with greater natural gifts than Kaye for a rapid and delicate grace, lacks Kaye's large-scale dramatic force. Moylan, with all the facility of a lovely virtuoso and its greatest gift of plasticity in motion, has a verve that suggests a genius for lively characterization; Tallchief has a tragic beauty and a distinction that set her apart. Among the students, Tanaquil LeClercq looks like a ballerina to come and a great one. (Brilliant Tamara Toumanova, Ballet Russe ballerina, appears less and less.) Men of similar quality are rarer—John Kriza and, as a dramatic dancer, Francisco Moncion are the most remarkable; Leon Danielian has great gifts too; the most promising among developing dancers is Dick Beard. Our best male stars during the period have been Eglevsky, Franklin, Laing, and Youskevitch—all European trained.

Though the resources exist, though the public is still eager for ballet, since the war the two companies have not kept the high standards they had reached. Managerial disputes and rising costs have reduced both of them to less than forty dancers apiece; and a number of their best dancers have left them. Ballet Theater's greatest loss was that of Markova some seasons back; unfortunately Markova herself, now touring with

Dolin and their small group, has weakened noticeably as an artist. The Monte Carlo's greatest loss was that of Balanchine. It now has no master choreographer to inspire it and it is doubtful if it can long survive without one. Last season however the artistic energy which the big companies lacked was shown by Ballet Society, organized by Kirstein and Balanchine. In its first experimental season, together with its eight new ballets, it presented four one-act operas; and also gave us a glimpse of the lovely Javanese dancing of Ratna Mohini. After a remarkable second season—notable for the Stravinsky-Balanchine-Noguchi *Orpheus*—Ballet Society has now become the resident ballet company of New York's City Center.

I have suggested the elements of strength in American ballet style. Its chief weakness seems to be in the art of imaginative characterization. The Tudor ballets, with their many personages, give our dancers experience in the field. But his stylized gesture does not pose the question quite distinctly either. A dance character cannot be explained or justified; and he must remain himself in repose, where there is no distortion of mimicry possible. This is a problem of amplitude in style. Another problem of our style is that of differentiation from musical comedy. Our choreographers and many ballet dancers work in musical comedy and this tends to confuse and banalize their approach to ballet. These are not problems to be solved by verbal argument. They are questions the imagination of our dancers can answer only by dancing in ballets of imaginative force. American ballet is well paid, but its working conditions are the most exhausting in the world. The only thing that can refresh its spirit and enrich its style is the sense of artistic integrity, of imaginative abundance that the managements must supply by encouraging our best choreographers to create for them. This is the main problem ahead of our ballet. Contact with the work of artists from other countries with different resources of style will be stimulating too—*Autumn, 1947.*

THE CRITIC

WHEN people who like dancing say a critic is right they mean he is right enough and that his imaginative descriptions are generally illuminating. He can hardly be illuminating or right enough unless he has a fund of knowledge about his subject. In theory he needs to know the techniques and the historical achievements of dancing, the various ways people have looked at it and written about it, and finally he needs a workable hypothesis of what makes a dance hang together and communicate its images so they are remembered. In practice he has to piece together what he needs to learn unsatisfactorily; experience as a dancer and choreographer is an invaluable help to him.

The best organized and by far the most useful chunk of knowledge a critic has access to is that about the technique and history of classic ballet—in particular, ballet as dancers learn it. Its gymnastic and rhythmic technique is coherent enough to suggest principles of dance logic—as expressive human movement in musical time and architectural space. But so far the best-informed of specialized ballet critics have not formulated these clearly. And even French ballet criticism as a whole, though it has had for several centuries nearly all the best ballet dancing in the world to look at, though it has had since as far back as 1760 (since Noverre's *Letters*) a brilliant lesson in how to write about dancing, hasn't yet been able to bring order and clarity to the subject. Though they have been writing steadily for two centuries and more—and often writing pleasantly—the Paris critics have left us as reporters no accurate ballet history, as critics no workable theory of dance emphasis, of dance form, or of dance meaning.

The handicap to method in dance criticism has always been that its subject-matter—dancing that can fascinate as an art does—is so elusive. Other arts have accumulated numerous wonderfully fascinating examples in many successive styles. Dancing produces few masterpieces and those few are ephemeral. They can't be stored away; they depend on virtuoso execution, sometimes even on unique interpreters. They exist only in conjunction with music, stage architecture and decoration, in transitory highly expensive performances. It is difficult to see the great dance effects as they happen, to see them accurately, catch them so to speak in flight and hold them fast in memory. It is even more difficult to verbalize them for critical discussion. The particular essence of a performance, its human sweep of articulate rhythm in space and in time, has no specific terminology to describe it by. Unlike criticism of other arts, that of dancing cannot casually refer the student to a rich variety of well-known great effects and it cannot quote passages as illustrations.

This lack of precision, of data, and of method is not without advantages. It saves everyone a lot of pedantry and academicism, and it invites the lively critic to invent most of the language and logic of his subject. Its disadvantages, however, are that it makes the standards of quality vague, the range of achieved effects uncertain, and the classification of their component parts clumsy. Dance esthetics, in English especially, is in a pioneering stage; a pioneer may manage to plant a rose bush in his wilderness but he's not going to win any prizes in the flower show back in Boston.

The esthetics of dancing—that is, a sort of algebra by which the impression a performance makes can be readily itemized, estimated, and communicated to a reader—is vague and clumsy. The dance critic's wits have to be all the sharper; he has to use esthetic household wrinkles and esthetic common sense to help out. And he has to pull his objectivity out of his hat. The poverty of his dance-critical heritage makes it hard for him to get a good view of his personal blind spots. A critic in the other arts learns to recognize his blind spots and develop his special gifts by finding out how he personally reacts to a wide range of much discussed masterpieces. If he is annoyed by Mozart or Vermeer or even by Picasso and Stravinsky, he can read intelligent opinions different from his own. That way he learns who he is, what he knows and doesn't know.

Gaps and crudities of critical technique are of concern to a professional critic; they are questions of his craft. The earnest craftsman must hope that once a dance script has become established, once the various hints toward a critical method (including those by modern-dance theoreticians or of exotic traditions) have been collected, sifted, and codified, dance critics will seem brighter than they do now.

At present a critic has to risk hypotheses. He can try, for instance, to distinguish in the complex total effect of a performance, the relationships between dance effect and story effect, between expressive individualized rhythm and neutral structural rhythm, dance impetus or pantomime shock, dance illusion or dance fun, sex appeal or impersonation, gesture which relates to the whole architectural space of the stage and has an effect like singing, or gesture which relates to the dancer's own body and so has the effect of a spoken tone. And there are of course many possible relationships of the dancing to the structure or momentum of the music which by creating in the visual rhythm illusions of lightness and weight, impediment or support (for instance), affect the meaning of a passage. Dance criticism would be clearer if it found a way to describe these and other relationships in theater effect; and to describe just what the dancers' bodies do, the trunk, legs, arms, head, hands, and feet in relation to one another. The expression of a reviewer's personal reaction, no matter how violent or singular, becomes no immodesty when he manages to make distinct to the reader the visible objective action on stage he is reacting to.

But to begin with, a critic doesn't screen a dance performance according to such distinctions. What he actually does is to work backwards, so to speak, from the dance image that after the event is over strikes him as a peculiarly fascinating one. He tries to deduce from it a coherent principle in what he saw—among uncertainly remembered, partly intense, partly vague, partly contradictory images. It takes boldness to simplify his impressions so they add up clearly to a forthright opinion; and it sometimes takes a malicious sense of fun too, to trust to his instinct where he knows he is risking his neck. But the intelligent reader need not be at all sorry that dance criticism is in a rudimentary or pioneering stage. It makes it more inviting to poets than to schoolteachers; and though its problems and possible discoveries are not colossal ones, still—

if it succeeds in attracting poets—it should be for a century or so to come fun to write and to read.

An intelligent reader expects the critic—in his role of schoolteacher—to distinguish between good and bad dance technique, to distinguish between good and bad choreographic craftsmanship, to specify technical inventions and specify also the gifts that make a choreographer or a dancer remarkable despite defects in craftsmanship. Here the writer shows his fairness. But what one enjoys most in reading is the illusion of being present at a performance, of watching it with an unusually active interest and seeing unexpected possibilities take place. Reading a good critic's descriptions of qualities I have seen, I seem to see them more clearly. If I don't know them, I try looking for them in performances I remember or try to find them next time I go to the theater. And when you look for qualities a reviewer has mentioned, you may find something else equally surprising. For your sharper eye and limberer imagination are still a part of your own identity—not of his— and lead you to discoveries of your own. The fun in reading dance criticism is the discovery of an unexpected aspect of one's own sensibility.

In reading the great ballet critics of the past one is not impressed by their fairness but by their liveliness. In reading Noverre or Gautier or Levinson, I find accounts that strike me as so unlikely I interpret them—by analogy to contemporaries—as blindspots, or propaganda and rhetoric; even if some of these accounts are accepted as facts of dance history. But it is not the partisan spirit with which they can blindly propagandize their own esthetic views that differentiates them from lesser critics, it is the vividness of their descriptions that is unique. Gautier, who of the three gives a reader the most immediate sense of the sensuous fluidity and physical presence of ballet, expresses theory in terms of chitchat and ignores choreographic structure and technical talk. He seems to report wholly from the point of view of a civilized entertainment seeker, the other two from the backstage point of view of the craftsman as well.

Noverre and Levinson advance theories of dance expression which are diametrically opposite. The force with which they are formulated gives their writing an elevation Gautier avoids, but makes them both far easier than he to misunderstand. Here in a nutshell is the dance critic's problem: The sharper he formulates a theory of the technique of expression, of how dance communicates what it does, the further he gets from the human vivacity of dancing without which it communicates nothing at all. And yet it is difficult to consider the central question of dancing—I mean, the transport and sweep that dance continuity can achieve, the imaginative radiance some moments of dancing are able to keep for years in people's memory, the central question Balanchine in his illuminating *Notes on Choreography* brings up in speaking of "basic movements"—unless the critic finds some way to generalize and to speak vividly of general as well as of particular dance experience.

I trust that intelligent critics of the future will be well-informed enough to discuss such generalized principles of dance expression clearly. They could begin by clarifying the elements of our ballet tradition. The living force of this tradition remains—in one sense—its faith that stage dancing can be a form of poetic theater; in another sense, its vitality lies in the practicable "classic" dance technique it has evolved and around which its many possibilities of expression are grouped.

The tradition has been called classic since ballet adopted the term as a slogan during the eighteenth century, when classicism in the theater referred to the most deeply expressive of current stage styles. But our ballet tradition is older than that period and it has boldly developed since; its long list of achievements, which gain a certain coherence from the two central forces, spiritual and technical, I have mentioned, illuminate the practice of theater dancing as an art. It seems to me that the full range of this tradition, if it were vividly appreciated, is wide enough to include in one set of critical values both what we call the modern dance and what we call our classic ballet—though at the moment the two are far apart in their gymnastic, rhythmic, and expressive structure and in their theater practicability as well. It seems to me that a vivid sense of such an inclusive creative tradition would set the merits of a dancer or of a choreographer in a larger perspective and offer a sounder measure in describing his scope as craftsman or artist. It seems to me it would suggest, too, a number of connections between dancing and our general intellectual tradition—connections sufficient to establish the honorable place of theater dancing among our most civilized habits.

So I should like to read a critic who could make me appreciate in dancing the magic communal beat of rhythm and the civilized tradition of a personal and measured communication. I expect him to sharpen my perception sometimes to an overall effect, sometimes to a specific detail. I should not be surprised to find in some of his descriptions general ideas stimulating in themselves, even apart from his immediate subject, nor to find in other descriptions technical terms of dancing, of music, of painting or theater craft. I should like him to

place a choreography or a dancer with their individual deriva-
tions and innovations in the perspective of the tradition of
theater dancing. I am far more interested, though, if a writer
is able in describing dancing in its own terms to suggest how
the flavor or the spell of it is related to aspects of the fantasy
world we live in, to our daily experience of culture and of
custom; if he can give my imagination a hint about the scope
of the meaning it communicates. But as I read I want to see
too the sensual brilliance of young girls and boys, of young
men and women dancing together and in alternation on stage,
the quickness and suavity of their particular bodies, their
grace of response, their fervor of imagination, the boldness
and innocence of their flying limbs.

A writer is interesting if he can tell what the dancers did,
what they communicated and how remarkable that was. But
to give in words the illusion of watching dancers as they create
a ballet in action requires a literary gift. An abstruse sentence
by Mallarmé, the rhythmic subtlety of a paragraph by Marianne Moore, a witty page-long *collage* of technical terms by
Edm. de Goncourt can give the reader a sharper sense of
what dancing is about than a book by an untalented writer
no matter how much better acquainted with his subject he is.
Such examples lead to fallacious conclusions, but I am drawing no conclusions, I am stating a fact. A dance critic's education includes dance experience, musical and pictorial experience, a sense of what art in general is about and what people
are really like. But all these advantages are not enough unless
they meet with an unusual literary gift and discipline.

Now and then in reading dance criticism one comes across
a phrase or a sentence that suggests such an ideal possibility.
It is to emphasize these passages to people who wonder what

good dance criticism is that I am writing. The fact that dance criticism isn't perfect doesn't invalidate its good moments. Granted it is brilliant far less often than the dancing it commemorates; still the fact that it is after all occasionally brilliant is what makes it as a form of intellectual activity in a modest way worth while—*Winter,* 1947.

INDEX